HATE CRIME

IMPACT, CAUSES & RESPONSES

SECOND EDITION

NEIL CHAKRABORTI & JON GARLAND

SAGE

Los Angeles | London | New Delhi
Singapore | Washington DC

Los Angeles | London | New Delhi
Singapore | Washington DC

SAGE Publications Ltd
1 Oliver's Yard
55 City Road
London EC1Y 1SP

SAGE Publications Inc.
2455 Teller Road
Thousand Oaks, California 91320

SAGE Publications India Pvt Ltd
B 1/I 1 Mohan Cooperative Industrial Area
Mathura Road
New Delhi 110 044

SAGE Publications Asia-Pacific Pte Ltd
3 Church Street
#10-04 Samsung Hub
Singapore 049483

Editor: Natalie Aguilera
Editorial assistant: James Piper
Production editor: Sarah Cooke
Copyeditor: Elaine Leek
Proofreader: Audrey Scriven
Indexer: Martin Hargreaves
Marketing manager: Sally Ransom
Cover design: Francis Kenney
Typeset by: C&M Digitals (P) Ltd, Chennai, India
Printed in Great Britain by Henry Ling Limited at
The Dorset Press, Dorchester, DT1 1HD

MIX
Paper from
responsible sources
FSC
www.fsc.org   FSC™ C013985

© Neil Chakraborti and Jon Garland 2015

This edition published 2015
First edition published 2009

Library of Congress Control Number: 2014948710

British Library Cataloguing in Publication data

A catalogue record for this book is available from
the British Library

ISBN 978-1-44627-250-3
ISBN 978-1-44627-251-0 (pbk)

At SAGE we take sustainability seriously. Most of our products are printed in the UK using FSC papers and boards.
When we print overseas we ensure sustainable papers are used as measured by the Egmont grading system.
We undertake an annual audit to monitor our sustainability.

HATE CRIME

SAGE was founded in 1965 by Sara Miller McCune to support the dissemination of usable knowledge by publishing innovative and high-quality research and teaching content. Today, we publish more than 750 journals, including those of more than 300 learned societies, more than 800 new books per year, and a growing range of library products including archives, data, case studies, reports, conference highlights, and video. SAGE remains majority-owned by our founder, and after Sara's lifetime will become owned by a charitable trust that secures our continued independence.

Los Angeles | London | Washington DC | New Delhi | Singapore

Neil and Jon would like to dedicate this book to the hundreds of thousands of families across the world who are victims of hate crimes every single day

CONTENTS

LIST OF TABLES AND CASE STUDIES

Chapter 8

Chapter 9

Chapter 10

Chapter 11

LIST OF STATUTES

Anti-Terrorism, Crime and Security Act 2001
Care Act 2014
Chemical Weapons Act 1996
Civil Partnerships Act 2004
Commonwealth Immigrants Act 1962
Commonwealth Immigrants Act 1968
Crime and Disorder Act 1998
Criminal Justice Act 2003
Criminal Justice and Immigration Act 2008
Criminal Libel Act 1819
Disability Discrimination Act 1995
Disability Discrimination Act 2005
Disability Rights Commission Act 1999
Equality Act 2010
Gender Recognition Act 2004
Immigration Act 1971
Legal Aid, Sentencing and Punishment of Offenders Act 2012
Marriage (Same Sex Couples) Act 2013
Public Order Act 1986
Race Relations Act 1965
Race Relations Act 1976
Racial and Religious Hatred Act 2006
Sentencing of Offences Aggravated by Prejudice (Scotland) Act 2009
Sexual Offences Act 1956
Sexual Offences Act 1967
Sexual Offences Act 2003
Special Educational Needs and Disability Act 2001

ACKNOWLEDGEMENTS

It has been six years since we wrote the first edition of this book but it feels much longer than that. So much has happened in the world of hate crime scholarship and policy since then and the subject is continuing to evolve all the time. We were reminded of this during the final weeks of writing, which saw some frantic re-drafting following the release of important publications from the College of Policing and the Law Commission: this left us with furrowed brows but a sense of relief too at being able to factor in these developments. We have tried to be as current as possible in our coverage, but invariably new and relevant things will happen between now and the time you read this. We'll talk about those things in the third edition.

We owe thanks to a lot of people, not least Natalie Aguilera at Sage for commissioning this new edition and, along with James Piper, for being such a pleasure to work with. We are also extremely grateful to all the hate crime theorists, researchers, policy-makers, practitioners, advocates and campaigners whom we have been lucky enough to work with in recent years. There are too many of you to mention by name but you have all shaped our thinking. So too have the many hundreds of victims who took part in the Leicester Hate Crime Project. Learning about their ongoing experiences of violence, harassment and marginalisation whilst writing this book reinforced why all of this matters so much.

Neil would like to thank the University of Leicester for granting him a period of study leave; colleagues at the Department of Criminology for being such good people to be around; Stevie and Liz for doing a brilliant job on the Leicester Hate Crime Project; his mother for her limitless compassion and kindness; Tara for her love and support; and DCFC for providing welcome distraction.

Jon would like to thank his new colleagues at the Department of Sociology at Surrey for being so welcoming and his old colleagues at Leicester for providing so many great memories; Stevie and Liz for making the Leicester Hate Crime Project such a success; Paul Hodkinson, Sarah Neal, James Treadwell, Darrick Jolliffe, Cate White, Andrea Warner, Isobel McEwen, Keris and Cathy Howard; Gary Numan; the Meadvale and Kingsmead crews; the Sociology Lads' Club; his colleagues in the Southern Hate Circuit (Drinking Division); his mum; Karen for her love, support and patience; Norwich City for the seemingly endless highs and lows (long may they continue); and last but by no means least, the co-author of this book for being a great bloke and a bit of an inspiration.

And a now customary final mention to 'Death Incarnate' whose 'fan-mail' has dried up a bit in recent years but remains an enduring source of inspiration. If you were upset enough to wish us a 'slow and painful death' after we published *Rural Racism*, Lord only knows what you think of us now …

1

UNDERSTANDING HATE CRIME

Chapter summary

Hate crime encompasses numerous themes that have formed a central feature of contemporary social scientific enquiry, including marginalisation, victimisation and 'difference'. Attempts by British scholars to examine these themes through the conceptual lens of hate had been in fairly short supply as the 'mainstreaming' of hate crime discourse within the domains of academia and policy has occurred only relatively recently within the UK. However, the term 'hate crime' is now used with regularity by policy-makers, activists, practitioners and scholars, although there is often a sense of inconsistency when it comes to its application.

This chapter seeks to develop a clear conceptual understanding of hate crime by examining a variety of definitions used within the academic and policy domains in recent years. It also outlines the legal framework that underpins hate crime and identifies some of the core characteristics associated with hate crime perpetration and victimisation. Through the course of this discussion we shall see that the task of understanding hate crime is far from straightforward due to the complexity and ambiguity associated with the concept.

Introduction

Hate crime is a term that has assumed increasing salience within academic, political and social discourse in the UK in recent times. As a number of scholars have noted (Hall, 2013; McLaughlin, 2002; Ray and Smith, 2002), popular usage of the term in the UK appears to have gained currency in the wake of much-publicised events that took place towards the end of the last and the start of the current century. In particular, the racist murder of black teenager Stephen Lawrence in 1993 – and the ensuing publication of the Macpherson Report in 1999 – drew widespread attention to the problems posed by crimes committed against members of minority groups, as did the racist and homophobic nail bomb attacks of 1999 instigated by the neo-Nazi David Copeland in the diverse London communities of Brixton, Brick Lane and Soho. Similarly, the terrorist attacks in the United States of September 11 2001 and the July 7 bombings in London of 2005 prompted a well-documented backlash against some minority groups on the basis of their faith, which has since intensified following the rise of Islamophobic sentiment popularized by groups such as the English Defence League (Treadwell and Garland, 2011). Correspondingly, much greater recognition is now given to religiously, and not just racially motivated, offending. Although the rationale for choosing the word 'hate' to describe these varied types of offences is somewhat contested, the coining of 'hate crime' as a collective descriptor has seen the various types of victimisation associated with this label become recognised as significant social problems, and prioritised within research and policy agendas to a much greater extent than ever before.

Given the comparatively recent adoption of the concept of hate crime in this country, it is unsurprising that the majority of relevant literature had tended to come from outside of the UK. That is not to say that areas commonly associated with the hate crime label have not been researched and debated extensively within this country. Issues of 'race' and racism in particular have been explored at length, as have relationships between the police and minority ethnic communities. Likewise, an ever-growing body of sociological and criminological literature has provided important insights into issues surrounding sexual and religious identity. Equally, we can turn to a substantial set of texts on victimology and victimisation in order to develop our understanding of the experiences, expectations and needs of victims of targeted violence. Hate crime cuts through numerous themes central to social scientific enquiry, and the empirical and theoretical contributions from writers on these themes will naturally be relevant to our understanding of hate crime. Until recently, relatively few attempts had been made to examine these themes through the conceptual lens of hate, but over the past ten years or so a growing number of British scholars have begun to critically assess the application of the hate crime label to the UK context (see, for instance, Hall, 2005, 2013; Iganski, 2008; Walters, 2014a). Their work, allied with rising levels of activism, research and policy-building around issues of hate crime, has helped to make this a focal point of academic enquiry within the UK.

In the first edition of this book we suggested that the term 'hate crime' had been widely adopted into research and policy domains without there being any firm consensus on its meaning, application and legitimacy. This is still the case today. As we shall see, 'hate' is an emotive and conceptually ambiguous label that can mean different things to different people. This has important implications for the way in which we conceive of the offences that fall under its umbrella framework and of the actors involved in a hate crime, whether these be victims, perpetrators or criminal justice and other organisations. Moreover, hate crime is a contentious concept that has the capacity to evoke passionate responses from those who have supported or opposed the introduction of legislative intervention. These points will be explored in due course, but it is important first to be clear on how hate crime has come to be defined and enshrined within policy.

Definitions of hate crime

Academic definitions

Establishing clear-cut, universal definitions of any form of crime is an inherently difficult task. Hate crime is no exception to this rule; indeed, it could be argued that defining this particular category of crime is especially problematic due to the subjectivity associated with the notion of hate. Attempts to clarify the meaning of hate crime have not surprisingly been more forthcoming outside of the UK, and the suggestions of north American scholars in particular have strongly influenced our domestic frameworks.

If asked to define hate crime, our immediate response might be to suggest that the term refers to crimes motivated by hatred. Curiously though, this is not actually the case: hate crimes are not crimes in which the offender simply *hates* the victim, and in reality crimes do not need to be motivated by hatred at all in order to be classified as a hate crime (Gerstenfeld, 2013: 11). Rather, for Gerstenfeld the pivotal characteristic of a hate crime is the group affiliation of the victim, and not the presence of hate on the part of the perpetrator. She is, though, quick to acknowledge that this simple definition lacks precision in a number of respects, not least in terms of deciding which types of group affiliations should be included under the hate crime umbrella. Petrosino (2003: 10) offers a slightly more expansive definition that gives some indication of the groups that could come into consideration when conceiving of hate crime victims. She suggests that:

(a) most victims are members of distinct racial or ethnic (cultural) minority groups ... (b) most victims are decidedly less powerful politically and economically than the majority ... and last, (c) victims represent to the perpetrator a threat to their quality of life (i.e. economic stability and/or physical safety) ... These common factors suggest the following base definition of hate crime: the victimisation of minorities due to their racial or ethnic identity by members of the majority.

Petrosino's interpretation gives substance to the imbalance of power between the perpetrator and the victim who most commonly, though not always, will belong to the majority and minority groups respectively within a given society. Using a framework of power relations to describe this kind of victimisation allows us to recognise hate crimes not as an extraordinary category of offences *per se* but rather as an extension of the types of prejudice, marginalisation and oppression experienced by minority groups within the structure of everyday society. However, Petrosino's take on hate crime is constrained by two important limitations. At one level, it explicitly acknowledges the victimisation of ethnic minorities but does not recognise any other minority groups who conceivably could be vulnerable to the imbalance of power to which she refers. Secondly, her definition neglects to show how hate crime itself contributes to the subordination of the less powerful. In some respects Sheffield's (1995: 438) definition offers a more advanced account of hate crime:

> Hate violence is motivated by social and political factors and is bolstered by belief systems which [attempt to] legitimate such violence ... it reveals that the personal is political; that such violence is not a series of isolated incidents but rather the consequence of a political culture which allocates rights, privileges and prestige according to biological or social characteristics.

This explanation is helpful in the way it addresses both the political and social context through which hate crime develops and the significance of entrenched hierarchies of identity that underpin hate crime. In a similar vein to Petrosino, Sheffield points to the hierarchical structure of power relations within society and suggests that hate crime is an expression of power against those without the rights, privileges and prestige referred to above. Unlike Petrosino though, Sheffield does not limit her conceptualisation of hate crime victimisation to just minority *ethnic* group membership but instead extends this to include a potentially much broader range of groups marginalised on the basis of their 'biological or social characteristics'. Nevertheless, Perry (2001) argues that Sheffield's definition still fails to account for the impact of hate crime upon the actors involved in the process, namely the victim, perpetrator and their respective communities. This oversight is addressed within Perry's more comprehensive framework (2001: 10):

> Hate crime ... involves acts of violence and intimidation, usually directed towards already stigmatised and marginalised groups. As such, it is a mechanism of power and oppression, intended to reaffirm the precarious hierarchies that characterise a given social order. It attempts to re-create simultaneously the threatened (real or imagined) hegemony of the perpetrator's group and the 'appropriate' subordinate identity of the victim's group. It is a means of marking both the Self and the Other in such a way as to re-establish their 'proper' relative positions, as given and reproduced by broader ideologies and patterns of social and political inequality.

In common with other definitions, this framework gives primacy to the notion of violent and intimidatory behaviour being somehow different when it involves an act motivated by bigotry and manifested as discrimination towards marginalised populations (see also Jenness, 2002). Moreover, like Sheffield, Perry's understanding of such groups extends not only to minority ethnic people but also to 'all members of stigmatised and marginalised communities' (2001: 1). However, Perry's framework offers several distinct advantages over other definitions. Crucially, it recognises that hate crime is not a static problem but one that needs to be seen as a dynamic social process involving context, structure and agency. In this regard, Perry takes her lead from the pioneering work of Bowling (1993; 1999), whose thoughts on racist violence are acknowledged by Perry as being directly relevant to the way in which we should conceive of hate crime victimisation. For Bowling (1993: 238), racist victimisation should be understood not as an event but as a process that captures 'the continuity across physical violence, threat, intimidation ... the dynamic of repeated or systematic victimisation ... [and] historical context'.

If we extend these ideas to hate crime more generally, we can see that the experience of hate crime does not simply stop and end with the commission of the offence, nor does it occur in a cultural or social vacuum. Therefore, by recognising the various features of the process referred to by Bowling above, and by incorporating this within the framework of power, hierarchy and oppression outlined in her own definition, Perry highlights the inescapable complexity associated with hate crime and the need to think of it 'in such a way as to give the term "life" and meaning' (2001: 9).

Another key factor within Perry's framework is her emphasis on the group, and not individual, identity of the victim. She sees the specific victims as interchangeable; hate crimes, for Perry, are acts of violence and intimidation directed not only towards the victim but also towards the wider community to whom he or she belongs, and thereby these crimes are designed to convey a message to this community that they are somehow 'different' and 'don't belong'. As 'message' crimes, acts of hate reach 'into the community to create fear, hostility and suspicion' and in so doing reaffirm 'the hegemony of the perpetrator's and the "appropriate" subordinate identity of the victim's group' (Perry, 2001: 10). Moreover, and perhaps not surprisingly in view of the symbolic status of hate crime within Perry's conceptual framework, she regards these offences as most commonly perpetrated against strangers with whom the offender has had little or no personal contact, with the victim simply representing the 'other' in generic terms through their membership of the demonised group (2001: 29).

Perry's conceptual framework has left an indelible imprint upon contemporary hate crime scholarship. However, hate crime is a more expansive notion than even this framework allows, and those of us theorising, working and researching in the field of hate crime should not be discouraged from stepping outside of its confines when seeking to shape criminological responses. For instance, we have used a simpler, and in some ways broader definition in our own research, which sees hate crimes as acts of violence, hostility and intimidation directed towards people because of their identity or perceived 'difference' (Chakraborti et al., 2014a).

The rationale for framing hate crime in these broad terms will become clear in the chapters that follow. At this stage though, it is worth noting that a definition like this covers forms of targeted hostility and anti-social behaviour that might not be criminal acts in themselves but which can have just as significant an impact upon the victim, their family and wider communities. Equally, whilst this definition is deliberately concise, it acknowledges that some victims can be subjected to hate not exclusively because of their membership of a particular identity group but also because they are seen as vulnerable or somehow 'different' in the eyes of the perpetrator. Moreover – and this is a point that practitioners are often quick to share with us – the more long-winded definitions that we academics are inclined to use sometimes feel rather too complex, too ethereal and too detached from the everyday realities confronting those who deal with hate crime cases in the 'real world' (Chakraborti, 2014). The commonalities and differences between academic interpretations and those used within the policy domain of hate crime can be seen in the following section.

'Official' definitions

It is evident from this initial inspection of academic definitions that hate crime has proved to be, if not elusive, then certainly a somewhat slippery notion and one that is difficult to fully conceptualise. Its ambiguity is such that definitions of hate crime can vary from academic to academic and this can be counter-productive in practical and policy terms, as Hall (2013: 4) wryly observes:

> A policy-maker working in the British government ... lamented that even if you could lock academics in a room for six months with the task of producing a single definition of hate crime, they would most likely emerge with more definitions than they had when they went in, which makes for interesting scholarly debate, but is utterly useless for those tasked with actually responding to the problem of hate crime 'in the real world'.

While hate crime scholars have sought to grapple with what they see as the complexity associated with the term, 'official' classifications have tended to be significantly less intricate in their interpretations of hate crime. Until recently, the key source of domestic policy guidance on hate crime came from the Association of Chief Police Officers (ACPO), whose operational definition was enshrined within their guidelines for police forces in England, Wales and Northern Ireland (ACPO, 2000, 2005). Their 2005 guidelines gave primacy to the perception of the victim or any other person as being the defining factor in determining a hate incident, and described a hate incident and a hate crime in the following terms (2005: 9):

> A hate incident is defined as:
>
> Any incident, which may or may not constitute a criminal offence, which is perceived by the victim or any other person, as being motivated by prejudice or hate.

A hate crime is defined as:

Any hate incident, which constitutes a criminal offence, perceived by the victim or any other person, as being motivated by prejudice or hate.

By distinguishing between incidents and crimes in such a manner, the ACPO guidelines highlighted an important difference between the two: while all hate crimes are hate incidents, some hate incidents may not constitute a criminal offence in themselves and therefore will not be recorded as a crime, but simply as incidents. Chapter 9 considers the policing implications of this distinction, but for the purposes of the present discussion it is important to note that all hate incidents should be recorded by the police even if they lack the requisite elements to be classified as a notifiable offence later in the criminal justice process. At the recording stage, any hate incident, whether a *prima facie* 'crime' or not, is to be recorded if it meets the threshold originally laid down by the Macpherson definition of a racist incident – namely, if it is perceived by the victim or any other person (such as a witness, a family member or a carer) as being motivated by prejudice or hate. Clearly then, if we consider hate 'occurrences' as opposed to just crimes *per se*, the scale of the problem, at least in terms of sheer numbers, becomes much more sizeable than we may initially have imagined.

The ACPO hate crime manual has recently been updated by operational guidance issued in May 2014 by the College of Policing, which is discussed more extensively within Chapters 9 and 11 although some important points should be noted at this stage. First, the College of Policing guidance makes a similar distinction between hate incidents and crimes, and offers almost identical definitions to those outlined in the ACPO manual, although it is 'hostility or prejudice', and not 'prejudice or hate', which are seen as motivating factors in the new guidance (2014: 3). In both cases, these sets of operational guidelines follow the line pursued in some of the academic interpretations described previously by suggesting that the presence of hate is not necessarily central to the commission of a hate crime. In essence then, hate would appear to be an unhelpful term in many respects. Leading practitioner and academic definitions are consistent in drawing our focus towards behaviour motivated by certain forms of prejudice or hostility, which are more expansive notions than hate covering many varieties of human emotion, of which hate may be only a small and extreme part (Hall, 2005). Again, we shall return to this point in due course, but this inspection of definitions reminds us of the need to consider broader notions than just hate alone if we are to fully understand the problem of hate crime.

Secondly, the College of Policing guidance is consistent with the 2005 ACPO guidance in outlining five monitored strands of hate crime. This suggests that it is not just any form of prejudice or hostility which can form the basis of a hate crime, but rather prejudice or hostility against *particular* groups of people or based upon *particular* grounds. This was reinforced in the 2012 Coalition government's Action Plan on hate crime, which made explicit reference to the five monitored strands of 'disability, gender-identity, race, religion/faith and sexual orientation' (HM Government, 2012a: 6). On the one hand, placing official restrictions on the types of 'unacceptable' prejudice that can constitute a hate crime is critical to the viability of the concept because otherwise its scope could become too broad. However, limiting the application of hate crime to certain groups and not others is inherently problematic as this requires difficult decisions to be made with regard to who should be deserving of 'special protection'.

Again, we shall return to this contentious issue in the chapters that follow. The potential for hate crime policy to create a hierarchy of victims, whereby some groups may be seen as being more important or deserving than others, is a dilemma that has been central to debates over the conceptual basis of hate crime. However, this point has been acknowledged within the 2012 Action Plan which gave local areas licence to include other strands in addition to the monitored five when developing their responses to hate crime (HM Government, 2012a: 6). Similarly, the College of Policing guidance observes that the five monitored strands 'are the minimum categories that police officers and staff are expected to record' and makes it clear that forces are free to record other hostilities and prejudices as hate crime in addition to those monitored strands (2014: 7). As we shall see, this wider framework has been developed as a result of tragic cases and an emerging body of research highlighting the targeting of 'other' identities and groups who have not routinely been considered as hate crime victims.

Another notable effort to develop a common understanding that can generate workable responses to hate crime has come from the Office for Democratic Institutions and Human Rights (ODIHR). Their guidance on framing hate crime laws was developed as a practical tool to help statutory and non-governmental organisations in all 57 member states of the Organization for Security and Cooperation in Europe (OSCE) acknowledge and respond to the problem of hate crime. Within that guidance, hate crimes are defined as 'criminal acts committed with a bias motive' (2009a: 16). For ODIHR, this bias does not have to manifest itself as hate for the offence to be thought of as a hate crime, nor does hate have to be the primary motive. Rather, it refers to acts where the victim is targeted deliberately because of a particular 'protected characteristic … shared by a group, such as "race", language, religion, ethnicity, nationality, or any other similar common factor' (2009a: 16).

Again, we can see reference not to the term 'hate' within this framework, but to bias which, like prejudice, is a much more expansive notion than hate. Importantly, ODIHR's guidance does not seek to specify which protected characteristics should form the basis of a member state's hate crime policy, aside from making reference to aspects of identity that are 'fundamental to a person's sense of self' and to the relevance of 'current social problems as well as potential historical oppression and discrimination' (2009a: 38). The reasons behind (and implications of) adopting this broad interpretation are discussed in Chapter 10.

The legal framework

When mapping the contours of hate crime it is important to be familiar with the laws that exist to regulate its status. A number of laws have been introduced which adhere to the principle that crimes motivated by hatred or prejudice towards particular features of the victim's identity should be treated differently from 'ordinary' crimes. This legislation will be examined in greater depth during later chapters, as will the framing of hate crime laws in other countries outside of the UK. However, for the purposes of clarity, at this stage we shall briefly examine the domestic legal framework.

A significant piece of legislation within this context is the Crime and Disorder Act 1998. Under this Act if someone commits one of a list of offences (see Table 1.1), and in doing so demonstrates, or was motivated by, hostility on the grounds of race, then that offence becomes a separate 'aggravated' offence punishable by a higher sentence (Law Commission, 2013). In effect, racially aggravated offences are the aggravated versions of certain basic offences that are set out in sections 29 to 32 of the Crime and Disorder Act 1998. The aggravated forms of these offences carry a higher prison sentence than the basic version, as illustrated in Table 1.1.

Table 1.1 Differences between the maximum sentences for basic and aggravated offences

Basic offence	Maximum penalty	Aggravated offence	Maximum penalty
Common assault	6 months	Aggravated common assault	2 years
Actual bodily harm	5 years	Aggravated actual bodily harm	7 years
Malicious wounding/ GBH	5 years	Aggravated malicious wounding/GBH	7 years
Criminal damage	10 years	Aggravated criminal damage	14 years
Fear or provocation of violence	6 months	Aggravated fear or provocation of violence	2 years
Harassment, alarm or distress	Fine of up to £1,000	Aggravated harassment, alarm or distress	Fine of up to £2,500

(Continued)

Table 1.1 (Continued)

Basic offence	Maximum penalty	Aggravated offence	Maximum penalty
Causing intentional harassment, alarm or distress	6 months	Aggravated causing intentional harassment, alarm or distress	2 years
Offence of harassment	6 months	Aggravated offence of harassment	2 years
Putting people in fear of violence	5 years	Aggravated putting people in fear of violence	7 years

Source: Law Commission, 2014: 5-6

The principle that higher sentences can be imposed in instances where there is evidence of targeted hostility was also extended to include religiously aggravated offences through the Anti-Terrorism, Crime and Security Act 2001. This amendment to the original Crime and Disorder Act makes comparable provision for offences that are considered to be religiously aggravated, and as such under section 39 of the 2001 Act evidence of religious aggravation is regarded as a factor that increases the seriousness of particular offences for the purposes of sentencing. The aggravated offences cover race and religion only, although a Law Commission consultation during 2013/14 considered the rationale for extending this approach to cases where hostility is based on sexual orientation, disability or transgender identity. At present, those latter forms of targeted hostility are currently covered by what are referred to as enhanced sentencing provisions. Section 146 of the Criminal Justice Act 2003 empowers courts to impose enhanced sentences for offences involving hostility directed towards the victim's sexual orientation, disability or transgender identity. Although this Act stops short of creating specific offences for these strands in the same way that the Crime and Disorder Act 1998 does for offences relating to race and religion, it does ensure that the expression of prejudice on the grounds of sexual orientation, disability and transgender identity is recognised as part of the package of legal protection against hate crime.

There are important differences between aggravated offences and those covered by enhanced sentencing provisions. For example, while racially and religiously aggravated offences have their own set of maximum sentences which are higher than the corresponding maximum sentences for the basic offence versions, the maximum sentences for section 146 offences (i.e. offences involving hostility based on sexual orientation, disability or gender identity) remain the same as those for the basic offence (Law Commission, 2013: 6). Equally, while aggravated offences require proof of hostility during a trial, section 146 applies after the trial when the offender has been found guilty of the basic offence and the sentencing judge is deciding upon the appropriate sentence (Law Commission, 2013: 8). The nuances of these legal provisions will be examined more fully in the chapters to follow.

The Law Commission consultation referred to above acknowledged that 'it is undesirable for the aggravated offences not to apply equally to hostility based on race, religion, transgender identity, sexual orientation and disability' because the unequal provision 'sends the wrong message about the impact of such offending and the seriousness with which it is taken' (2014: 14–15). However, rather than recommending an extension of the existing aggravated offences, the Law Commission instead called for a more extensive review of the hate crime legal framework in order to give government and criminal justice agencies a full opportunity to assess the capacity of the current system to meet the needs of hate crime victims. The rationale for this decision is outlined in the Law Commission's 2014 report, and at the time of writing it is not known whether the Coalition government will support the Commission's call for an in-depth review. If (but only if) a wider review is not pursued, the Law Commission's alternative recommendation is for the aggravated provisions to be extended across all five of the statutorily recognised hate crime characteristics.

The concept of hate crime is also recognised through various strands of incitement legislation. Protection against the incitement of racial hatred, originally enshrined within provisions of the Race Relations Acts of 1965 and 1976, can be found in its most recent guise within the Public Order Act 1986. Section 18 of this Act prohibits the use of words, whether oral or written, or behaviour that is deemed 'threatening, abusive or insulting', and puts in place both a subjective standard of guilt where there is intention to stir up hatred and also an alternative objective threshold where 'having regard to all the circumstances racial hatred is likely to be stirred up thereby'. More recently, the Racial and Religious Hatred Act 2006 offers protection against the stirring up of religious hatred by amending the Public Order Act to outlaw the use of threatening words or behaviour intended to incite hatred against people on the basis of their faith. Although similar in many respects to the incitement of racial hatred laws, the more recent offence of inciting hatred towards religious beliefs has a higher legal threshold in that it applies only to threatening (and not abusive or insulting) words or behaviour *and* it requires the prosecution to prove that the perpetrator intended to stir up religious hatred.

Since then, the Criminal Justice and Immigration Act 2008 has created fresh offences of inciting hatred on the grounds of sexual orientation under a similar threshold to that specified in the Racial and Religious Hatred Act. At present there are no equivalent provisions governing the stirring up of hatred against those with disabilities or transgender people, although this is another area that was considered as part of the Law Commission consultation on hate crime legislation (referred to above). In recommending against the extension of the stirring up offences, the Law Commission (2014: 21–2) acknowledged a justification in principle for extending the law to cover all monitored strands, but based their decision on two factors: first, what they perceived as the absence of a practical need for additional laws, and second, the likelihood of there being very few successful prosecutions.

There are numerous ambiguities and concerns surrounding aspects of the various pieces of legislation referred to above. As we shall see in due course, the effectiveness, legitimacy, scope and interpretation of these laws have all been called into question, and these areas of debate are central to our understanding of the hate crime label. For the time being though, it is important to acknowledge the existence of these laws as this itself illustrates a crucial point: namely, that a number of laws have been enacted which enshrine the underlying principles behind the hate crime movement and which give explicit recognition to the distinction between hate offences and 'ordinary' offences. In this respect, there is consistency in the message conveyed both by the law and by official policy documents in alerting criminal justice agencies, sentencers and the general public to the harms of hate crime.

Core features

It is worth pausing a moment at this stage to reflect upon what we know about hate crime from this inspection of definitions and legal provisions. Certainly, the range of policies, laws and campaigns that have emerged over the past thirty years or so is indicative of the increased diversification of British society and the affirmation of the right to be different. But aside from conveying society's condemnation of hostility directed towards such 'difference', why has hate crime policy assumed such significance? What does the term 'hate crime' represent, and what are its key characteristics?

In many respects the emergence of the concept of hate crime is synonymous with the rise to prominence of 'the victim'. While victims of crime as a generic group are widely recognised as being important, newsworthy and deserving of public and criminal justice support, their concerns have only relatively recently formed a central feature of academic and political discourse, having spent years on the fringes of criminological and sociological debate (Goodey, 2005). Although early studies of victimology were typified by a tendency to attach some degree of blame or responsibility to victims of crime through their reliance on notions of victim-precipitation and victim-proneness, recent decades have seen the emergence of a more critical stance which has examined in greater depth the wider social and cultural context of victimisation (see, *inter alia*, Walklate, 1989; Zedner; 2002).

This increased standing for victims has implications for the development of hate crime policy, for it is within this context that we have begun to appreciate the differential impact of certain forms of crime upon particular groups of victims. Indeed, this would appear to be one of the key underlying premises of hate crime policy: that crimes motivated by hatred or prejudice towards a person's core identity or 'difference' hurt more than 'ordinary' crimes. The reasoning behind this line of argument will be explored within subsequent chapters. But there are several other important features worth noting at this stage. First and foremost, most definitions of hate crime are consistent in arguing that the individual victim is interchangeable as he or she is chosen on the basis of their perceived or actual membership of a particular group. In this context hate crimes are seen as 'message crimes'; crimes that are designed to tell not just the victim but the entire subordinate (as perceived by the perpetrator) community to whom the victim belongs that they are 'different' or unwelcome. This thereby extends the impact of hate crime beyond the actual victim, transmitting a sense of apprehension and vulnerability to other members of that particular community.

By implication and as discussed above, it is commonly assumed that hate crimes are acts perpetrated against strangers with whom the offender has had little or no personal contact, and that the victim simply represents the 'other' through their membership of the subordinate group (see, for instance, Perry, 2001). However, whilst this construction of hate crime helps us to understand the way in which the commission of hate crime may act as a way of reinforcing social hierarchies, it is wrong to suggest that victims and perpetrators will invariably be strangers to each other. Mason (2005a), for instance, contests this assumption by drawing from British Crime Survey data and other research evidence to show that a substantial proportion of racially motivated and homophobic incidents are committed by perpetrators who are in fact *not* strangers to their victims (see also Moran, 2007; Ray and Smith, 2001). Using this evidence as a backdrop to her own research data, Mason's findings challenge the popular image of hate crime as a form of 'stranger-danger' and the 'one size fits all' method of describing perpetrator–victim relationships (2005a: 856). Clearly, hate crimes may often take the shape of message crimes directed at the wider subordinate community, but by the same token they may also include acts where the perpetrator is familiar to the victim. This reality is an important but often overlooked feature of hate crime perpetration that will also be explored further in the chapters that follow.

It is also worth underlining that the presence of hate is not central to the commission of a hate crime. Rather, most credible definitions are consistent in referring to broader notions such as prejudice, hostility or bias as key factors in the classification of a hate crime. However, we also know that the criminal justice system regards certain prejudices as more 'punishable' than others. As noted previously, domestic hate crime policy refers to five monitored strands of hate

or prejudice, namely race, sexual orientation, faith, disability and gender identity. By implication therefore, the damage or 'hurt' associated with offences
perpetrated on such grounds is distinct from that created by other 'ordinary'
crimes, and this justifies the 'special attention' that comes with their inclusion
under the umbrella category of hate crime. But as with other core issues in the
'hate debate', this reasoning has the capacity to divide opinion. Do offences
based on these monitored strands 'hurt' more than other crimes? Are there other
targets of prejudice who deserve the special protection afforded to the recognised groups of hate crime victims? And if so, what implications does this have
for the development of meaningful hate crime research and policy?

Conclusion

As this chapter has illustrated, understanding the concept of hate crime is a
harder task than might at first be imagined. We have seen that the term 'hate' is
a problematic, ambiguous and in many cases inaccurate descriptor of the offences
with which it is commonly associated, and there is considerable disparity
between the various interpretations used to define what constitutes a hate crime.

Equally, we must not lose sight of the positive developments that have
emerged with the maturation of hate crime discourse within the UK. A number
of laws have been passed during recent years which provide added protection to
groups especially vulnerable to acts of hate and prejudice, and these have underlined the significance of hate crime to criminal justice agencies, sentencers,
researchers, the media and the general public. This process has been important
to the governance of diversity and community cohesion and should not be
under-valued. Therefore, when seeking to make sense of the concept of hate
crime we should be mindful of its origins, and continued utility, as an umbrella
construct designed to combat a range of prejudices. How to maintain its social
and political relevance in the face of the difficult conceptual and practical challenges facing hate crime scholars, practitioners and policy-makers is something
that we consider over the course of this book.

Guide to further reading

Until recently the subject of hate crime had been explored much more exten-
sively in North America than anywhere else. In particular, Jacobs and Potter,
Hate Crimes: Criminal Law and Identity Politics (1998), Perry, *In the Name of Hate:
Understanding Hate Crimes* (2001) and Gerstenfeld, *Hate Crimes: Causes, Controls*

and Controversies (2013) all retain a strong influence on the development of hate crime discourse within this country. However, hate crime is now a burgeoning area of study amongst British scholars. Hall, *Hate Crime* (2013), Chakraborti (ed.), *Hate Crime: Concepts, Policy, Future Directions* (2010) and Iganski, *'Hate Crime' and the City* (2008) are all excellent texts for readers seeking a domestic overview of hate crime policy and scholarship.

Links to online material

The stance of the current (at the time of writing) UK government on hate crime policy and prevention is captured in their 2012(a) Action Plan entitled *Challenge It, Report It, Stop It: The Government's Plan to Tackle Hate Crime*. This is available at www.gov.uk/government/uploads/system/uploads/attachment_data/file/97849/action-plan.pdf

The Office for Democratic Institutions and Human Rights (2009a) produced guidance in 2009 on the drafting and reviewing of hate crime legislation for members of the Organization for Security and Cooperation in Europe (OSCE) region. Entitled *Hate Crime Laws: A Practical Guide*, it offers an accessible framework for understanding hate crime and the justifications for legislation, and is available at www.osce.org/odihr/36426?download=true

2

RACIST HATE CRIME

Chapter summary

Offences motivated by hate or prejudice towards the victim's ethnic identity are the most common type of hate crime in terms of sheer numbers, and also the most familiar in terms of political, public and academic recognition. As such there is an extensive body of literature devoted to issues of race and ethnicity, to the relationship between race and the criminal justice system, and to the needs and experiences of victims of racist crime.

This chapter seeks to address some of the key points from this body of literature which have implications for our understanding of racist hate crime. It begins by examining race within the context of its emergence as an issue of significance in the UK, before moving on to explore the problem of racist hate crime in greater depth. The chapter then examines the scope and dimensions of this problem, together with the legal framework in place to address racist victimisation and the ways in which research in this field has shaped constructions of racist hate crime.

Introduction

Racist hate crime remains the strand of hate crime with which commentators are most familiar; indeed, politicians, journalists, practitioners and academics sometimes fall into the trap of describing hate crime exclusively in terms of racist crime. The sheer weight of literature devoted to issues of race, ethnicity and racist prejudice in comparison to the relatively small (but growing) number of texts on alternative strands of hate crime is illustrative of how academic studies have prioritised racist victimisation over other forms of targeted hostility, at least until recently.

The breadth, depth and scale of race-related research conducted over the past thirty years or so are far too extensive to summarise within the confines of this particular chapter. There are a number of excellent sources that offer a comprehensive overview of the salient points from this research, and these are acknowledged in the guide to further reading that follows this chapter. However, in terms of developing our understanding of hate crime, we need to consider the links between racism and crime and the way in which ethnicity is used as a tool to victimise people on the basis of their 'difference'.

The term 'racism' is used fairly expansively within this chapter as a way of describing the beliefs and practices that can result in people being discriminated against on the basis of their perceived ethnic origin. Problems of racism and perceptions of ethnic difference are complex, constantly evolving and contingent on global, national and local contexts. As Mason (2012) acknowledges, terms such as 'racism' and 'racist' are subjective and can sometimes shut down debate rather than open up solutions, but nonetheless it is through these 'crude linguistic instruments', to use her words, that we can 'challenge and resist the very real forms of inequality, injustice and violence that are embedded in hierarchies of difference' (2012: 41). Although the label of racism should be used cautiously and responsibly, its application should not be limited to extreme thought and behaviour; rather, it should be conceived of in a way that helps us to identify and denounce those subtle and indirect practices that give rise to racist hate offences.

Racism in the UK

Whilst differentiation on the grounds of skin colour, bodily features or cultural practices has a long history, it is only relatively recently that the idea of 'race' has emerged as an explanatory device to justify such differentiation. As Bowling and Phillips (2002) observe, the concept can be traced back to the philosophies of the European Enlightenment and to the ascendancy of science and reason within the work of writers such as Hume, Kant and Hegel. For many of these philosophers race was seen as a way of distinguishing the cultural superiority of white Europeans from the savagery associated with non-whites from outside Europe, a view that became entrenched during the expansion of the transatlantic slave trade over the course of the seventeenth and eighteenth centuries (Bhavani et al., 2006). Similar lines of thinking developed during the nineteenth and twentieth centuries, most notably through the form of the eugenics movements, which forcibly sought to control the perceived purity of the races, and through the widespread promotion of laws across many countries designed to enforce racial segregation.

However, it is the post-Second World War context that has the most significant implications for the way in which the UK's contemporary 'race agenda' has developed. Although migration to and from the country had occurred quite extensively prior to this point, the post-war influx of migrants into the UK quickly resulted in a noticeably different demographic profile. Approximately 11,000 West Indians arrived in Britain in 1954, with the figure more than doubling the following year, while the rate of migration from India and Pakistan rose dramatically from the comparatively low figure of 7,350 in 1955 to equal that from the West Indies after 1960 (Hiro, 1992).

Whilst immigration during this post-war period was not confined solely to incomers from the Caribbean and Asia, it is the migration of former inhabitants of New Commonwealth countries that appears to have shaped subsequent debates and policy-making on race relations.[1] Specifically, it was the racial disturbances of 1958, first in Nottingham and then in Notting Hill, that were the trigger for the now-familiar politicisation of race and its association with crime, the economy and nationhood (Bowling and Phillips, 2002). The sustained violence directed towards black people during these disturbances, together with the sizeable increase during the late 1950s and early 1960s of New Commonwealth immigrants, resulted in a much tougher political stance on issues of immigration, and in effect a set of provisions within successive pieces of legislation that differentiated unashamedly between the rights of white and non-white settlers (for further details see Hiro, 1992).

Case Study 2.1

Early signs of the politicisation of race

In spite of tighter controls introduced through the Commonwealth Immigrants Act 1962, anti-immigrant sentiment remained strong amongst many sections of the public, as the Labour party learned to its cost during the general election campaign of 1964. In the West Midlands constituency of Smethwick, Patrick Gordon Walker, a Labour Shadow Cabinet Minister, lost what had been assumed to be a safe seat for his party to the Conservative candidate and local headmaster Peter Griffiths, whose campaign had been largely based around the threats posed by immigration to the local white population. Griffiths' campaign is perhaps most infamous for its use of the slogan 'If you want a nigger neighbour, vote Liberal or Labour', a rhyme that was described by the victorious MP as a 'manifestation of popular feeling' (Hiro, 1992; Solomos, 1993).

Not long after this episode, the notorious 'rivers of blood' speech of Conservative MP Enoch Powell in 1968 helped to shape the future direction of immigration policy in the UK. Within this speech Powell used highly emotive language to plead for an end to immigration and to criticise the government's perceived betrayal of the 'British' electorate through its open-door policies. He cited the supposed case of one of his own Wolverhampton constituents, an elderly white woman who was too scared to leave her own home, and when she did, was followed by 'charming, wide-grinning piccaninnies' (Sandbrook, 2007: 679). Utilising provocative language that echoed images of slavery, Powell predicted that: 'In this country in fifteen or twenty years' time the black man will have the whip hand over the white man'. If existing levels of 'coloured' immigration were maintained, he continued, then: 'Like the Roman, I seem to see the River Tiber foaming with much blood' (2007: 679).

Though the speech resulted in his removal from the Conservative Shadow Cabinet, Powell's continued influence as an active back bencher, allied with the extensive media coverage of issues he raised, laid the platform for further restrictions on the rights of migrants in the Commonwealth Immigrants Act 1968 and the Immigration Act 1971. Similar lines of rhetoric came a decade later from the Conservative administration led by Margaret Thatcher, whose publicly declared fears of Britain being 'swamped' by an 'alien culture' were reflected in a series of legislative moves that signified the continuing racialisation of immigration policy on the lines of skin colour (Sales, 2007).

These developments are important in the context of our understanding of racist hate crime. Despite the extensive levels of violent racism directed towards minority ethnic communities from the Second World War to the late 1970s – a phase described by Bowling and Phillips (2002: 13) as being 'among the most viciously racist periods in British domestic history' – depictions of these communities tended be framed mainly in terms of their disorderly characteristics, with little attention given to their experiences as victims of racist hate (see also Hall et al., 1978). Even when the fractious relationship between the police and black communities collapsed with the outbreaks of public disorder and rioting during 1981 in St Paul's, Brixton, Toxteth and other inner-city neighbourhoods across the country,[2] explanations for this disorder gave relatively little consideration to black experiences of oppressive policing and social and economic exclusion.

Although the public inquiry into the disturbances chaired by Lord Scarman acknowledged problems of minority ethnic deprivation and disadvantage, it stopped short of explicitly locating black communities' grievances within their experiences of racist stereotyping and oppression. It also failed to stave off the potential for future rioting, which duly occurred in the areas of Handsworth in Birmingham and the Broadwater Farm estate in London during 1985.[3] Crucially, the Scarman Report did not accuse the police service of being institutionally racist, favouring instead the 'bad apples' explanation that located the problem of racism within the domain of a small number of low-ranking prejudiced officers. Consequently, some of the key policing concerns of minority ethnic communities persisted, including the feeling that the service did not take racist victimisation seriously; that minority ethnic communities were disproportionately targeted by officers for stop and search procedures; and that the organisation itself was racist and was populated by racially prejudiced officers.

However, if 1981 was a landmark year in the context of British race relations because of the inner-city rioting, in other ways it was also an equally significant year for the recognition of ethnic minorities as victims. In this year the Home Office published *Racial Attacks*, its inaugural report highlighting evidence of the racist harassment directed at minority ethnic communities. This laid the foundations for the systematic collection of evidence on various facets of racist victimisation that has taken place since; indeed, it is only from 1981 that local and central government agencies have kept records of racist violence and have begun to develop policies in response to the problem (Bowling, 2003: 64). Equally, the murder of Stephen Lawrence in 1993, or more specifically the lessons learned from the flawed Metropolitan Police investigation into his murder, has had a profound impact upon the way in which racism is perceived and policed. The tragic circumstances of Lawrence's murder – an unprovoked, racially motivated attack on a defenceless teenager – attracted widespread (and unprecedented in the context of victims of murderous racism) media coverage, even from papers such as the *Daily Mail* whose concerted campaign to name and shame the killers ran in stark contrast to their traditionally antipathetic stance towards issues of antiracism.

Described by many commentators as a 'watershed moment', Sir William Macpherson's report into the issues arising from the murder of Stephen Lawrence gave rise to an extensive package of reforms whose implications have been discussed extensively within the wider literature (see, *inter alia*, Bourne, 2001; Hall et al., 2009; Rowe, 2007; Rowe, 2012).[4] Unlike the riots of 1981, the Lawrence case acted as a catalyst for change in the context of police–minority relations, public attitudes towards issues of race and in relation to the definition, reporting and recording of racist incidents. However, this progress – and the sense of justice, albeit belated, that followed the conviction of two of Lawrence's killers some nineteen years after his murder – should not be allowed to overshadow the damaging problems that continue to be posed by racist discrimination and violence. Recent figures, for instance, illustrate that black people are six times more likely, and Asians twice as likely, to be stopped and searched by the police than white people,[5] while the Metropolitan Black Police Association used the 20th anniversary of the Lawrence murder to declare its belief that the Metropolitan Police Service was still institutionally racist (Muir, 2013). Burnett (2013) has also challenged the fallacy of assuming that violent racism is a throwback to a previous, pre-Macpherson age, referring to the way in which racist attacks have widened in scope to incorporate new targets and intensifying levels of violence.[6] These points will be considered at greater length in the following section.

The scale and scope of racist hate crime

Official interpretations of racist victimisation are invariably informed by the broad definition of a racist incident provided through Recommendation 12 of the Macpherson Report which was subsequently adopted by the police and other criminal justice agencies. The recommendation sees a racist incident as 'any incident which is perceived to be racist by the victim or any other person' (Macpherson, 1999: 328). This definition acts as a refinement to the one previously used by the police by giving primacy to the interpretation of the victim, as opposed to the judgement of the recording or investigating officer, which was the case with the earlier definition.[7] Racism itself is also defined in fairly broad terms in the Macpherson Report as consisting of 'conduct or words or practices which disadvantage people because of their colour, culture or ethnic origin' (1999: 20)

The relatively wide-ranging scope of such definitions is illustrated by the substantial number of racist incidents recorded each year by the police, which rose from 4,383 in 1985 (when such figures were first collected) to a pre-Macpherson high of 23,049 in 1999 (Phillips and Bowling, 2002: 583). The latest figures for 2013/14 show that 47,571 racist incidents were recorded by the 43 police forces in England and Wales, a figure that has remained relatively stable for the past three years (Creese and Lader, 2014). It is well documented that police-recorded racist incidents tell only some of the story when it comes to measuring levels of racist crime on account of the twin problems of under-reporting among ethnic minorities and under-recording by the police (Webster, 2007).

In addition to recording racist incidents, the police are also obliged to record racially and religiously aggravated offences under the penalty enhancement provisions introduced by the Crime and Disorder Act 1998.[8] According to recent published statistics, the police recorded 30,234 racially or religiously aggravated offences in 2012/13, a 21% fall from 2008/09 (Home Office et al., 2013). While this source of data provides us with useful supplementary information about the extent of police-recorded racism, it rather crudely conflates racist and religious aggravation despite the important distinctions between the two (as discussed more fully in Chapter 3) and again tells us little about those offences which are not reported to the police. Successive sweeps of the British Crime Survey (BCS), or more recently the Crime Survey for England and Wales (CSEW),[9] have facilitated a more detailed examination of the different dimensions of racist victimisation. Recent estimates suggest that 124,000 racially motivated incidents took place in 2012/13 (Home Office et al., 2013), a significant drop from the previous year's figure of 185,000 but a considerably larger figure than the equivalent police-recorded figures for that year, as noted above.

Measures such as these have gone some way towards assessing the scale of racist offending. However, they – and other attempts to quantify levels of racist hate and prejudice – have tended to bracket together ethnic minorities as one seemingly homogeneous group, thereby dismissing, or at best underplaying, the differences in experience and perception of racism between the persons grouped together within such a framework, or for that matter persons typically excluded from such a framework. This can be the case even where attempts have been made to analyse victimisation by ethnicity, for the influence of various other factors, be they socio-demographic, religious or geographic, may not be sufficiently appreciated.

Consequently, attempts to measure racist hate crime must be wary of assuming that the patterns and trends identified by a particular study are collectively applicable to all who fall under the umbrella of minority ethnic group 'membership', without acknowledging the differences in individual experiences. Gunaratnam (2003), for instance, has noted how the research process itself can sometimes merely reproduce dominant constructions of race and ethnicity as a result of the common tendency to 'essentialise' the experiences and practices of individuals and groups into neat categories. An appreciation of the broader dimensions of racist hate crime is also necessary to recognise the experiences of groups who can often be overlooked by researchers and policy-makers. The experiences of mixed-race families and relationships are a case in point, with what little research evidence there is suggesting that those from a mixed heritage background face a higher risk of victimisation (Home Office et al., 2013) and that white partners in mixed-race relationships face a real, but seldom recognised, risk of being the target of racist abuse (Garland et al., 2006).

The experiences of Gypsies, Travellers and Roma have also remained peripheral to most studies of racism. The stigmatisation of these communities through restrictive policy and public resentment has been evident throughout Europe for centuries, and is rooted in cultural stereotypes that depict them as dangerous 'others' to be feared rather than as normal people living an alternative lifestyle to much of the population. This has resulted in their continuing marginalisation in many spheres of public life, including access to public services, health care, education and employment, and their experiences of oppressive and discriminatory policing in states across Europe (ODIHR, 2010b; Stewart, 2012). Although Gypsies, Travellers and Roma are the largest minority in Europe, research has shown that they are subjected to disproportionally high levels of hate crime, prejudice and hostility which are rarely acknowledged or challenged in the way that similar acts towards other 'recognised' minority ethnic groups would be (James, 2014).

Certainly, it is important to be aware that there is a diverse range of less familiar, less visible targets who can fall victim to racist hate. Racism experienced within white working-class communities has received relatively little academic attention and is likely to have a quite different qualitative dimension from that experienced by visible minority ethnic groups. The failure to recognise prejudice directed towards 'undesirable forms of whiteness' (Neal, 2002) is also evident in the case of asylum seekers and Eastern European migrant workers (see Case Study 2.2). Equally, violence experienced by overseas students can often have a racist element to it. In this context – and as with many of these examples – the racist sentiment may not be based exclusively on a sense of racial superiority but rather on a sense that the victims 'don't fit in' or 'don't belong' within communities characterised by discomfort with and/or resentment towards visible outsiders (Mason, 2012).

Case Study 2.2

The targeting of asylum seekers and new migrant communities

Since the late 1990s, press hysteria has generated a succession of headlines warning against the supposed dangers of allowing asylum seekers to enter the country. This has triggered punitive political responses to the entry, freedom and public acceptance of the asylum seeker. Similarly, following the expansion of the European Union on 1 May 2004, the migration of workers from Eastern Europe reignited age-old debates about Britain's allegedly 'soft' immigration policies and the supposed erosion of national identity, which have since intensified following the lifting of transitional restrictions on the freedom of movement of Bulgarian and Romanian migrants at the start of 2014. In addition to – or perhaps partly because of – national and local vilification from politicians and the press, asylum seekers and new migrant communities are often the targets of racist attacks, many of which have seen 'children being hounded from schools, adults being hounded from their homes and families being hounded from the towns and cities where they have sought safety' (Burnett, 2013: 11). Very few of these acts of racism are reported to the police or other agencies, often because of an understandable wariness of authorities born from previous negative encounters (Iganski, 2011).

A more responsible political and media response – focusing, for instance, on the plight of new arrivals or the role of Western nations in contributing to the economic struggles and conflicts in developing countries – could arguably have helped to alleviate some of the underlying tensions surrounding asylum and immigration (Philo et al., 2013). Instead, a process of continued political and media scapegoating has given rise to what Burnett (2013) describes as a new 'common sense' racism – a pragmatic form of prejudice that is legitimised as economically and culturally necessary and that fosters an environment in which targeted hostility is allowed to prosper. And yet at the same time, the notion of Britain being a tolerant, 'anti-racist' society remains largely unchallenged within popular thought. Kundnani (2001: 50) uses the distinction between racism and xenophobia to suggest how such a situation has arisen:

> ... whereas racism denotes a social process of exclusion based on colour (or, latterly cultural) difference, xenophobia suggests a natural psychological reaction against 'strangers' ... Hence it appears that those who propound the view that 'too many are coming' are not racists to be cast out of the political mainstream – they are merely fearful of the impact that large numbers of new

(Continued)

(Continued)

arrivals will have on the nation, and that is considered a legitimate political viewpoint. As such, xenophobia provides an alibi for racism, legitimating it by making it seem natural.

Recent figures released by the *Guardian* newspaper suggest that these processes have contributed to a worrying increase in hate crimes directed towards Polish people living in the UK. Using freedom of information requests to identify numbers of police arrests for hate crimes against Polish people, the *Guardian* figures revealed a tenfold increase from 2004, which they attribute to anti-Polish feeling that is fuelled by political stereotyping and negative media coverage, and given legitimacy with a climate of austerity and dwindling job opportunities (McDevitt, 2014). Similar concerns and explanations have been noted by the College of Policing (2014) and Chakraborti, Garland and Hardy (2014a) with reference to targeted hostility directed towards asylum, refugee and new migrant communities.

It would appear that the cloak of 'common-sense', 'legitimate' prejudice enables the hegemonic state of affairs that perpetuates the demonisation, and in some instances criminalisation, of particular 'undesirables'. Not surprisingly, the hostility directed towards these groups – be they asylum seekers, economic migrants or Roma, Gypsy or Traveller communities – has tended to receive little mainstream public or political sympathy, and yet it seems perverse not to recognise this process of demonisation alongside other forms of racist hate within academic and criminal justice policy frameworks.

Legal protection from racist hate crime

In light of the points raised thus far, establishing robust legal protection is a pivotal way of demonstrating society's condemnation of racism and offering support to victims. As noted above, the main impetus for legislative change was the murder of Stephen Lawrence in 1993, itself the third killing in a sequence of racist attacks committed in the area of south-east London around that time,[10] and the subsequent inquiry and report into the circumstances that led to that murder. The Macpherson Report was hailed as a watershed in British race relations, not least for placing the issue of racist crime high upon the agenda for criminal justice, political and other organisations by officially recognising the problem of 'institutional racism', for broadening the definition of a 'racist incident', and for supposedly leading the way for a more victim-oriented approach to dealing with racist incidents (Bridges, 2001; Burney and Rose, 2002).

It is important to remember that legislation addressing the promotion of racial hatred existed long before the Stephen Lawrence case in the form of the Race Relations Acts of 1965 and 1976, and more recently the Public Order Act 1986. Section 18 of the Public Order Act prohibits the use of words or behaviour which is 'threatening, abusive or insulting' and which is either intended 'to stir up racial hatred' or where 'having regard to all the circumstances racial hatred is likely to be stirred up thereby'. More recent provisions governing the stirring up of religious hatred were introduced under the Racial and Religious Hatred Act 2006, and will be the subject of closer scrutiny in Chapter 3. For present purposes, however, the most significant legal developments came through changes introduced by the Crime and Disorder Act 1998 which established a series of new racially aggravated offences. Under section 28 of that Act, offences are classed as racially aggravated if:

(a) at the time of committing the offence, or immediately before or after doing so, the offender demonstrates towards the victim of the offence hostility based on the victim's membership (or presumed membership) of a racial group; or

(b) the offence is motivated (wholly or partly) by hostility towards members of a racial group based on their membership of that group.

A 'racial group' under the 1998 Act refers to persons defined by reference to their race, colour, nationality or ethnic or national origins and now, following the amendment introduced by section 39 of the Anti-Terrorism, Crime and Security Act 2001, section 28(3) covers membership of any religious group (the implications of which are considered in Chapter 3). Central to these Crime and Disorder Act provisions is evidence of hostility, which can be expressed in a variety of ways including words, gestures or the singing of particular songs. As the wording suggests, aggravated offences can be committed either through a demonstration of hostility towards a victim's actual or presumed race or religion, or where the offence is fully or partially motivated by hostility towards their actual or presumed race or religion.

A number of concerns have been raised about these provisions, mainly in relation to the notion of 'hostility'. As Walters (2013) observes, the term has been under-theorised and subjected to different interpretations in the absence of a legal definition or any standard direction on its parameters. This can result in ambiguity and accusations of unfairness from all sides. From one perspective, this ambiguity allows the Crime and Disorder provisions to cast their net too wide by capturing a different type of offender from that originally envisaged through the creation of aggravation laws. Dixon and Gadd (2006), for instance, suggest that convictions for racially aggravated offences are not necessarily reliable indicators of racist attitudes, noting that some of those who came across as the least racist interviewees amongst their sample of perpetrators had prior convictions for racially aggravated crimes whereas some of the most racist had none. Similarly, Gadd (2009), Burney (2002) and Jacobs and Potter (1998) all note that aggravation provisions, if interpreted literally, run the risk of capturing low-level, superficial expressions of racism which may accrue from hostility conveyed in the heat of the moment and not deep-seated ideological hatred.

But equally there are those who feel that the provisions have been interpreted too narrowly and in a way that often fails to recognise the presence of a racial motivation. For example, Athwal and Burnett (2014) use their analysis of post-Macpherson race-related deaths in the UK to suggest that the racially motivated element to cases is commonly filtered out by the police, the CPS and the courts because of a variety of factors.[11] These include a failure to recognise racial motivation and the broader context in which racist attacks are committed, and the reclassifying of racist attacks as disputes, robberies or other forms of hostility (2014: 10).

All of these concerns have merit and are illustrative of the 'grey areas' that envelop much hate crime policy and theory. However, Walters (2014a: 4) makes a compelling case for believing that expressions of hostility in this context should be construed to include 'not just conscious attempts to vanquish "difference" (i.e. hate motivation) but any physically expressed prejudice or bigotry which the offender is *aware* [italics in original] is likely to have a subjugating effect on the victim's identity'. For Walters this broad interpretation is necessary, first to ensure that offenders who intentionally subjugate their victim's identity during the course of an offence are held legally culpable, irrespective of whether their expression of hostility is born from genuine hatred or is more tangential; and second, to recognise the increased emotional and social damage that these offences cause to victims, their families and to more general levels of community cohesion. According to this stance, when interpreting the Crime and Disorder Act provisions it should be the perpetrator's awareness that he or she is targeting the victim's 'difference' which carries relevance, and not any sense of hatred or deeply felt animosity towards the victim's group identity.

Also relevant in this context is McGhee's (2005: 29) support for the declaratory value of the racially aggravated provisions, as noted below:

> This legislation also performs a symbolic role in attempting to modify or correct undesirable behaviour in society not only in the name of greater protection for certain groups who are 'injured' by hate, but also in the name of protecting wider society from the negative impacts of a hate incident in the form of institutional mistrust, and the potential polarization between social groups. The legislation also emphasises the destructive and often marginalizing impact of hate crimes such as racist incidents on the victim, family, neighbourhood, community and ultimately the nation.

Through highlighting the symbolic importance of the laws on racial aggravation, McGhee makes reference here to one of the central justifications for hate crime laws in general: namely, that the higher sentences awarded to perpetrators are an important way of denoting society's condemnation of such crimes, preventing future attacks upon the individual victim and their broader community, and protecting society at large from the destructive elements associated with the commission of hate offences. As alluded to previously, this line of argument has been contested by critics of hate crime laws. Dixon and Gadd (2006: 324), for example, have cast doubt over the capacity of the racial aggravation provisions to deliver a symbolic message to the criminal justice system and to the general public without unnecessarily criminalising significant numbers of already marginalised people whose 'racism' has surfaced not from a commitment to racist beliefs or ideology but through an inability to control their language in moments of stress and/or inebriation. Debates over the effectiveness of hate crime laws in terms of their declaratory and deterrent impact have been a recurring theme in academic discourse, and we shall return to these debates later in the book.

Conclusion

While there has been welcome progress in recognising and responding to problems of racist hate in the UK, there remain grounds for concern in a number of contexts. Following an initial examination of the emergence of race as an issue of political and criminological significance, this chapter went on to discuss the scope of racist hate and suggested that official accounts paint an incomplete picture of the true extent and nature of this problem. It was argued that some groups' experiences can be overlooked as a result of oversimplified attempts to quantify racist hate crime, and through the narrow frameworks and terms of reference used by researchers and policy-makers. This chapter has also drawn attention to some of the problems inherent in legislative provisions covering racist hate which have affected the potential effectiveness of these laws.

The sheer scale of progress reports, internal reviews and policy developments issued in the years following the publication of the Macpherson Report is illustrative of the ongoing efforts being made by the police and other criminal justice agencies to respond to the challenges raised in this chapter. Nevertheless, and as we have seen, research continues to highlight worryingly high levels of racism and increasing fear and vulnerability on the part of many minority ethnic groups. In some respects, much of the difficulty surrounding official responses to racist hate stems from the continued reliance on 'incidents' as a means of distinguishing racist behaviour. For Bowling (1999), an incident-driven approach detaches the lived experience from its wider context of racist exclusion and fails to appreciate the impact of racism on victims' lives beyond the actual incident itself. This goes some way towards explaining why victims can feel unprotected despite apparent improvements in policy, as he notes below in his analysis of violent racism (1999: 285):

> Becoming a victim of any crime – particularly one as complex as violent racism – does not occur in an instant or in a physical or ideological vacuum. Victimisation – with the emphasis on the suffix 'isation' – denotes a dynamic process, occurring over time. It describes how an individual becomes a victim within a specific social, political, and historical context.

As we saw in Chapter 1, understanding the process, as opposed to simply the singular event, of racist victimisation requires an examination of the lived experiences of those affected, including the nature, extent and impact of racist behaviour, the wider context that gives rise to different forms of racism and the effectiveness of support provision for victims. It also requires an understanding of the routine, everyday nature of many experiences of racism; experiences that in themselves may not appear especially serious but that cumulatively, and when considered in the context of repeat victimisation and broader patterns of 'othering', can impact upon the victim (and their community) in a variety of corrosive ways, be it as Spalek (2006: 68) describes 'psychologically, emotionally, behaviourally, financially and physically'.

A succession of studies have shown that 'low-level' racist harassment – such as verbal abuse, intimidatory staring, the throwing of eggs or stones, the blocking of driveways with cars, being sprayed with air freshener or being the subject of racist 'humour' – is a regular feature of day-to-day life for many ethnic minorities; moreover, it has a 'drip-drip' effect that magnifies feelings of vulnerability and imposes severe constraints upon the victim's quality of life, despite seldom being fully recognised as racist behaviour by other members of local communities or by agencies and policy-makers (see, *inter alia*, Burnett, 2013; Chahal and Julienne, 1999; Chakraborti, 2010; Garland and Chakraborti, 2006; Mason, 2012). Recognising the significance of these more everyday experiences is a key challenge for those responsible for supporting victims and responding to hate crime, as we shall see in later chapters.

Guide to further reading

The body of literature on issues relating to racist hate and victimisation is very sizeable indeed, particularly when compared with the availability of texts on other forms of hate crime. Readers are therefore advised to use the references within the chapter as a guide to areas of specific interest. For an insightful overview of early perspectives and the history of race relations in the UK readers should refer to Hiro, *Black British, White British: A History of Race Relations in*

Britain (1992) and Bowling and Phillips, *Racism, Crime and Justice* (2002). The latter text and Rowe, *Race and Crime* (2012) also provide comprehensive accounts of the relationship between race and crime and the criminal justice response to racist crime. Hall et al.'s classic text *Policing the Crisis: Mugging, the State and Law and Order* (1978) has shaped our understanding of racist stereotyping and criminalisation while Bowling, *Violent Racism: Victimisation, Policing and Social Context* (1999) remains a seminal text on core aspects of racist victimisation.

Links to online material

Section 95 of the Criminal Justice Act 1991 requires the government to publish statistical data to assess whether any discrimination exists in how the criminal justice system treats individuals based on their ethnicity. The most recent set of statistics is available at www.gov.uk/government/uploads/system/uploads/attachment_data/file/269399/Race-and-cjs-2012.pdf

The Institute of Race Relations is a UK-based independent educational charity which carries out research and collects resources on race relations throughout the world. A wide range of material, including research reports and a free news service on race and refugee issues in the UK and Europe, is available through their website at www.irr.org.uk

Notes

1 In excess of 121,000 former Polish soldiers came to the UK with their families following the 1947 Polish Resettlement Act, and these numbers were augmented by the arrival of 24,000 German, Ukrainian and Italian former prisoners of war and over 25,000 other immigrants (Somerville, 2007).

2 The sheer scale of the 1981 disorders is highlighted by Hiro (1992: 88–89), who notes that as many as a third of the Metropolitan Police Force – approximately 7,000 officers – had been required to quell the Brixton disturbances which took place in an area comprising less than a square mile in total, with the damage costing around £6.5 million. Moreover, the four-day disturbances in Toxteth only a few months later resulted in 705 arrests, 781 police officers being injured and property damage amounting to nearly £15 million.

3 The riots of September 1985 in the Lozells Road area of Handsworth resulted in the deaths of two Asian men, injuries to 74 officers and 35 local people and just under 300 arrests. A month later the death of a black woman during a police raid on her home triggered the disturbances on the Broadwater Farm estate in north London during which more than 250 people were injured and a police officer, PC Keith Blakelock, was fatally stabbed.

4 The Macpherson Report was published in 1999 and produced 70 recommendations designed to reform relationships between the police and minority ethnic communities. This wide-ranging set of recommendations, which covered, for instance, issues relating to police diversity training, recruitment and retention policies and the handling of racist incidents, was endorsed by the government and the police, thereby bringing, as Webster (2007: 68) observes, 'the issue of racist violence from the periphery to the centre of law and order policy in Britain'.

5 It is important to note that only a small proportion of police stops and searches result in an arrest. Ministry of Justice figures show that between 2008/09 and 2011/12 approximately 10% of stops and searches of black people resulted in arrests, which is similar to the proportion for white people and higher than that for Asian people (7%) (Home Office, Office for National Statistics and Ministry of Justice, 2013).

6 A number of prominent campaigners have continued to express doubts over the reliability of police recorded figures, attributing the decrease in official levels of racist hate to failings in police recording practices and to victims' lack of faith in the criminal justice system (Wright, 2014).

7 Prior to the Macpherson Report, the police had relied on the following definition since 1985: 'A racial incident is any incident in which it appears to the reporting or investigating officer that the complaint involves an element of racial motivation, or any incident which includes an allegation of racial motivation made by any person'.

8 As amended by the Anti-Terrorism, Crime and Security Act 2001.

9 The British Crime Survey covered England, Wales and Scotland but the survey has since been restricted to England and Wales, hence the change of name. The Scottish Crime and Victimisation Survey (SCVS) offers a bespoke survey of victimisation in Scotland.

10 Two high-profile racist murders which occurred in south-east London prior to the death of Stephen Lawrence involved the killings of Rolan Adams in 1991 and Rohit Duggal in 1992.

11 Athwal and Burnett's (2014) research identified 93 deaths between February 1999 and December 2013 with a known or suspected racial element. Over half of those killed were Asian or Asian British, with the majority of those from Pakistani (22) or Indian (14) backgrounds. Sixteen victims were black or black British. In 69 cases (74%) the attacker or attackers were white British.

3

RELIGIOUSLY MOTIVATED HATE CRIME

Chapter summary

Since the turn of the millennium, and fuelled in the main by reactions to the threat of extremism and acts of terror, we have seen greater scrutiny over the extent to which particular religious identities and practices are compatible with the values of secular societies. Although this growth in attention has helped to promote an enhanced awareness of religious diversity and distinctions between religious and ethnic identity, it has also had rather more negative implications for faith communities targeted on the basis of their religious beliefs.

To begin, this chapter examines the relationship between religious identity and British criminology and discusses events that have seen religiously motivated hate crime emerge as a source of academic and political concern. As we shall see, the level of legal protection available to defend faith communities from attacks upon their religious identity has increased significantly over the past decade and the chapter seeks to explore the underlying factors behind the introduction of this legislation. In so doing, attention is given to two particular examples of religious intolerance – Islamophobia and antisemitism – to illustrate the escalating challenges posed by religiously motivated hate.

Introduction

Although issues relating to faith may in the past have been overshadowed by the propensity to focus predominantly, and sometimes exclusively, upon 'race' and ethnic identity, events over the past decade or so have seen religion occupy a much more significant role within political and academic thought. In an age in which the terrorist attacks of September 11 2001 in the United States and July 7 2005 in the UK loom large in the public imagination, religious identification – and specifically the extent to which such identification is reconcilable with the values associated with British national identity – has been the source of extensive conjecture. This has given rise to what Hunt (2005: 123–4) has described as a perceived clash of cultures between the visibility of faiths and the values of a secular culture, as evidenced, for instance, through disputes over faith schools, religious dress and custom and intra-faith attitudes towards gender and sexuality. In terms of criminological literature, researchers' propensity to view diversity through an ethnic lens may have resulted in the marginalisation of faith issues and of important divisions within ethnic communities: for instance, use of the secular term Asian to describe people from the Indian subcontinent may lead us to neglect the differences in history, perception and experience between the Hindu, Sikh or Muslim faiths, while Caribbean communities are often divided by their respective loyalties to various Christian traditions (Hunt, 2005; Spalek, 2008).

Distinguishing religious from ethnic identity is all the more important within a plurally constituted society such as that of the UK. According to the 2011 Census, Christianity remains the most common religious affiliation in England and Wales, with 59.3% of the population (33.2 million people) declaring themselves to be Christian. The second largest religious group is Muslim at 4.8% of the population (2.7 million) while the Hindu and Sikh faiths are followed by 1.5% (817,000) and 0.8% (423,000) respectively. The numbers of people describing themselves as Jewish (0.5%, 263,000) and Buddhist (0.4%, 248,000) are slightly lower (ONS, 2012). Whilst these figures highlight the comparatively high proportion of people identifying themselves as Christian, it is interesting to note that this proportion has dropped significantly – from 71.7% to 59.3% – since 2001. Correspondingly, the proportion of people practising each of the other main religions has increased during this period, most notably in the case of Muslims, whose numbers have risen from 3.0% to 4.8% of the population. At the same time there has been a large increase in the number of people stating that they have no religion – from 14.8% in 2001 to 25.1% in 2011 (ONS, 2012).

Analysis of the geographic distribution of faith communities conducted by Furbey et al. (2006) revealed a varied picture with regard to the extent to which people of different faiths connect with one another. They note that there can be a significant degree of neighbourhood separation between different faith communities and a risk of these communities leading 'parallel lives', a theme that chimes with the fears raised by Trevor Phillips in 2008 (speaking in his capacity as head of the Equality and Human Rights Commission) about there being a 'cold war' between Britain's different minority communities due to their inability or reluctance to interact with others of different faiths and ethnicities (BBC News, 2008a). These kinds of concerns relating to a perceived lack of inter-faith connectivity, together with the heightened tensions surrounding debates over religious ideology, citizenship and extremism, have inevitably placed greater scrutiny upon members of faith communities, and in particular British Muslims, as will be discussed shortly.

'Faith-hate' and existing legal protection

Whilst Britain has a long history of conflict between different religions, the specific issue of religiously motivated hate offending has become an area of growing concern to criminologists. According to the Crime Survey for England and Wales (CSEW) for 2011/12 and 2012/13, an average of 70,000 religiously motivated hate incidents take place each year (Home Office et al., 2013) and a variety of factors are relevant to the commission of these offences. The post-9/11 and -7/7 climate of mistrust surrounding religious extremism has acutely affected Muslim communities who have seen their identity repeatedly challenged as a result of public misapprehension and misrepresentation. Equally, the number of attacks perpetuated against South Asians in general – and not just against Muslims – has risen steeply, prompting fears that anyone ostensibly 'looking Asian', for instance through wearing a turban, sporting a beard or simply by virtue of being 'dark-skinned', has become increasingly susceptible to the risk of physical assault or verbal abuse. Jewish communities too have experienced growing levels of harassment, while other forms of inter-faith friction have indicated that religious intolerance should not be seen as a problem perpetuated exclusively by the majority white British community against minority faith groups.[1]

With faith being such a central, and in many instances *defining*, feature of people's self-identity, the need for effective legislative protection against attacks upon religious identity is extremely important. Until relatively recently the main source of protection for faith groups in the UK could be found in the blasphemy provisions of the Criminal Libel Act 1819. To quote McGhee (2005: 96), these provisions preclude 'the publication of contemptuous, reviling, scurrilous or ludicrous matter relating to God as defined by the Christian religion, Jesus, the Bible or the Book of Common Prayer, intending to wound the feelings of Christians or to excite contempt and hatred against the Church of England or promote immorality'. However, while these provisions cover the Christian faith, they do not extend to those from other religious denominations.

As such, the blasphemy laws of 1819 have limited application to today's multi-faith society. With respect to more recent legislation, the Public Order Act 1986 and the Crime and Disorder Act 1998 have some relevance with, respectively, their incitement to racial hatred and racially aggravated provisions. Though these Acts were designed to cover ethnicity and not religious identity *per se*, case-law has extended the scope of this definition to include religious groups commonly described as mono-ethnic, such as the Sikh and Jewish communities; communities whose membership, it is argued, has historically been drawn from just one cultural group (McGhee, 2005).

More significant in the context of this chapter is the Anti-Terrorism, Crime and Security Act 2001, which signalled the introduction of new religiously aggravated offences. As a result of this Act, the aggravated provisions of the Crime and Disorder Act 1998 were extended to all faith groups, allowing the courts to impose higher penalties in cases where the offender either demonstrates or is motivated by hostility towards someone's religious identity (see Chapter 2 for further details on aggravated offences and the enhanced sentencing provisions of the Crime and Disorder Act). The conflation of racial and religious aggravation in official figures makes it difficult to be precise about the use of these provisions in the context of faith-hate. Recent data show that the number of offenders convicted at all courts for racially or religiously aggravated offences nearly tripled over a ten-year period, from 2,300 to 6,500 in 2012 (Home Office et al., 2013), although it is important to consider this conviction rate alongside the 185,000 racially or religiously aggravated offences committed each year according to the latest CSEW estimates.

Further legislation offering protection to faith communities came in the form of the Racial and Religious Hatred Act 2006, which introduced provisions to guard against the stirring up of hatred on the grounds of religion. The passing of these provisions followed a fractious and protracted period of debate on the issue; indeed, prior to 2006 there had been six attempts within the previous twelve years to make the incitement of religious hatred unlawful, with each attempt in turn greeted with fierce criticism (Goodall, 2007).[2] It is worth reflecting briefly upon specific points of contention and the way in which these influenced the legislation now in place.

Prior to the passing of this Act there had been earlier calls to create an offence that would give faith communities the same level of protection as provided under the provisions of the Public Order Act 1986. The Runnymede Trust (1997: 60), for example, had called for the Public Order Act to be amended to outlaw the incitement of religious hatred, making reference to the disparity between the treatment of Jews and Sikhs on the one hand and that of Muslims perpetuated under the existing incitement legislation. This point relates to the fact that groups such as Jews and Sikhs are regarded as mono-ethnic religious communities – and therefore covered under the Public Order Act – as opposed to multi-ethnic religious communities such as Christians and Muslims whose membership is drawn from numerous ethnically and culturally diverse groups.

In addition to addressing this anomaly, a further justification for extending the laws on incitement lay in the message conveyed by such a move. For McGhee (2005) the declaratory value associated with incitement of religious hatred legislation resides in its capacity to send out a clear and unambiguous message to society denouncing faith-hate as not only unacceptable, but also criminal. This has particular relevance for Muslim communities in the context of the alarming levels of anti-Islamic propaganda circulated by groups such as the BNP and EDL over the past ten years or so. However, as well as deterring Islamophobic hatred, the potential for incitement of religious hatred provisions to influence the activities of extremists *within* Muslim communities may have been an equally persuasive factor behind the then government's determination to press ahead with the legislation. Introducing provisions that would help to deter and prosecute incitement from so-called Muslim 'hate clerics' was especially relevant in the post-7/7 climate where allaying public fears over the preaching of anti-Western sentiment and the radicalisation of Muslim youth assumed greater political significance.

These were some of the central justifications for introducing incitement of religious hatred provisions, incitement that under the original framework of the Religious and Racial Hatred Bill would have included words, behaviour or material which were threatening, abusive or insulting, and which would constitute a criminal offence if the words, behaviour or material were likely to be seen or heard by any person in whom they were likely to stir up such hatred. However, from the outset the Bill was subjected to a barrage of criticism from MPs of all parties, large sections of the media and freedom of speech campaigners. Among the most potent criticisms directed towards the original proposals was that they unfairly curtailed freedom of speech, and in so doing criminalised 'fair comment' and 'religious humour'. Fears over the extent to which these proposals – and in particular the criminalisation of not just threatening but also abusive or insulting words, behaviour or material – would stifle freedom of expression formed a central component of the powerful (and ultimately successful) lobbying effort to derail the proposals.

Following House of Lords amendments, the incitement of religious hatred provisions introduced by the Racial and Religious Hatred Act 2006, and enshrined within a new Part 3A of the Public Order Act 1986, represent a watered-down version of those originally proposed. The amended provisions restrict the scope of the original proposals in several key ways. For an offence to have been committed the prosecution need to prove that the perpetrator's words or conduct were threatening (and not merely abusive or insulting) and that the perpetrator intended to stir up religious hatred. In both respects the provisions represent a departure from the equivalent protection against the stirring up of racial hatred, which as we have seen follows a significantly broader model. In addition, the 2006 Act inserts an explicit defence clause for freedom of expression into the Public Order Act through the creation of section 29J, which makes it clear that the 'discussion, criticism or expressions of antipathy, dislike, ridicule, insult or abuse of particular religions' is not enough to constitute an offence.

Allied with the practical necessity of finding a compromise solution that would appease critics of the original proposals, the new provisions in their more restricted guise offer protection from hatred to faith communities whilst adhering to the principles of free speech. However, some important issues remain unresolved. By limiting the scope of the legislation to threatening words, behaviour or material the Act is clearly intended to govern the more extreme forms of incitement, and yet incitement does not need to be framed in explicitly 'threatening' terms to convey its message. Moreover, the inclusion of a subjective burden of purposive intention (and the removal of the more objective 'likely to' test of intention) makes the prospect of successful prosecutions more remote. As Goodall (2007: 111) observes, the 'likely to' test was included as part of the racial hatred provisions precisely because research had shown that prosecutions were likely to flounder under the restrictive threshold of proving purposive intention.

'Faith-hate' in action: anti-Muslim hate

Though it may be tempting to conceive of Islamophobic, or anti-Muslim prejudice as a relatively new phenomenon that emerged in the aftermath of the 9/11 attacks in the United States, it is important to recognise that Muslims have faced forms of prejudice based upon their religious identity over the course of many centuries. There has been a Muslim presence in Britain for at least 300 years, though the bulk of today's British Muslim population has its roots in the post-war patterns of migration that began in earnest during the 1950s from places such as the districts of Azad Kashmir in Pakistan, the Sylhet area of north-eastern Bangladesh, and from Gujarati districts of India (Runnymede Trust, 1997). Subsequent decades have seen further Muslim migration from Turkey, the Middle East and North Africa, while more recently the British Muslim population has been supplemented and diversified further still through the establishment of Somalian, Kosovan, Kurdish, Iranian and Bosnian communities.

Most other ethnic faiths, as Hunt (2005: 126–7) observes, lend themselves rather more readily to assimilation when transplanted to alien soil, and historically Muslims have seldom found it easy to adapt to the challenges of living within Western societies characterised by political and moral change, pluralism and a culture of disbelief and doubt. Key difficulties include the widespread misunderstanding and misrepresentation of Islam which has served to accentuate the differences between Muslims and non-Muslims; the extensive economic, political and social marginalisation suffered by Muslim communities; and the publicity given to the more extreme and purportedly barbaric practices of south Asian Muslims, such as forced marriages and honour killings, as opposed to positive elements of their faith.

The term 'Islamophobia' – defined by the Runnymede Trust (1997: 4) as the expression of unfounded hostility towards Islam (including Muslims' experiences of unfair discrimination and political and social exclusion) – gained salience towards the end of the 1980s. However, the term 'anti-Muslim hate' (or prejudice) is often used in its place in recognition that 'many attacks on Muslims appear to be motivated by a crude political belief that Muslims are a security threat rather than any fear or hatred of Islam *per se*', to use the words of Githens-Mazer and

Lambert (2010: 17). The Tell MAMA (Measuring Anti-Muslim Attacks) project[3] – a national monitoring project set up in 2012 to record anti-Muslim hate crime and to offer support to victims – defines anti-Muslim prejudice as 'a dread, fear, dislike and hatred of Muslims, and also can include the practice of discrimination against Muslims by excluding them from the economic, social and public life of the nation'.

Clearly, the problem of anti-Muslim prejudice should not be linked exclusively to the post 9/11 era, although the terrorist attacks of the past decade accelerated the process of what Werbner (2004: 464) terms the 'spiralling progressive alienation' of Muslims in the West. McGhee (2005: 102) notes that there was a four-fold increase in the number of racist attacks reported by British Muslims and other Asian, ostensibly 'Muslim-looking' groups in the UK during the months immediately after 9/11, with Asians based in the Tower Hamlets district of London experiencing a 75% increase in attacks during the same period. Similarly, in the three weeks following the July 7 2005 bombings police figures showed a six-fold increase in the number of religiously motivated offences reported in London, the vast majority of which were directed against Muslim households and places of worship, while during the same three-week period over 1,200 suspected Islamophobic incidents were recorded by police forces across the UK (BBC News, 2005; Dodd, 2005). Other evidence to illustrate the links between the terrorist attacks and the 'othering' of Muslim households has come from Spalek's (2002) research into British Muslim women's fear of crime, where she found that all of her research participants had felt more vulnerable to harassment and victimisation as a result of the 9/11 terrorist attacks, and from the similar contentions made by Muslim households in Garland and Chakraborti's (2004) studies of racism in rural England and in Zempi's (2014) research with veiled Muslim women.

Levels of anti-Muslim violence have continued to escalate in recent years, both in terms of physical attacks against Muslim communities, mosques and other Islamic institutions and with respect to online hate and prejudice expressed through social networking sites (Awan, 2013b; Copsey et al., 2013). Many of these incidents are not reported (Allen et al., 2013) and as with other strands of hate crime it is often those more extreme, violent and shocking cases that tend to generate news coverage: the attempts in 2011 by Anders Behring Breivik to trigger a European war against Islam through the killing of 77 Norwegian innocents, mainly teenagers (see Case Study 10.1), or the murder and bombings of British mosques committed by Ukrainian white supremacist Pavlo Lapshyn in 2013, are just two examples. Moreover, evidence shows that Muslims can often experience a surge of hate offences in the aftermath of high-profile events linked to Islamic extremism, as illustrated in Case Study 3.1 (see also Perry, 2003a; Poynting et al., 2004). This exacerbates the sense of persecution, marginalisation and vulnerability felt within Muslim communities.

Case Study 3.1

Seven days of anti-Muslim violence

In the week following the brutal murder of British soldier Lee Rigby on 22 May 2013 outside Woolwich barracks in south-east London, as many as 200 anti-Muslim incidents were recorded by Tell MAMA, the government's monitoring body. A small selection of these attacks is described below:

27 May 2013: A non-league footballer, Shaun Tuck, encouraged people to 'bomb and gas every mosque in England' on Twitter. His tweets went on to say 'Am raging in here in me loft yno … Got the balaclava out, dusted down an ready for the meet — I'd be going through there door mate an taking there kids head off an killing whoever was in site!!' (*Daily Mirror*, 28 May 2013)

27 May 2013: Racist graffiti was daubed on a door, bin and the pavement in a street in Burnley, alongside the initials 'EDL' and 'BNP'. (*Lancashire Telegraph*, 28 May 2013)

26 May 2013: Petrol bombs were thrown at a mosque in Grimsby whilst a family with young children were praying inside. Two ex-soldiers were later charged with arson and intent to endanger life. The same mosque had been attacked a few days earlier. (*Grimsby Telegraph*, 28 May 2013)

25 May 2013: A former soldier stuffed a tissue into a bottle of alcohol and tried to burn down a mosque with it in Rhyl, Wales. (Wales Online, 27 May 2013)

24 May 2013: A girl in east London was confronted by a gang who tried to rip off her niqab. (Engage, 24 May 2013)

23 May 2013: At about 11.30pm, someone threw a burning bottle onto the roof of a mosque in Bletchley. About 30 people were inside praying at the time. (*Independent*, 24 May 2013)

23 May 2013: The words 'Islam = evil' were sprayed onto a mosque in Bolton, and a car nearby was daubed with graffiti saying 'terrorist inside'. (*Asian Image*, 23 May 2013)

23 May 2013: Milk bottles filled with paint were hurled at a mosque in Belfast. Two teenage boys were seen fleeing from the area. (*Belfast Telegraph*, 30 May 2013)

23 May 2013: A Muslim woman on a train from Bolton to Blackburn was spat on and abused by a white passenger. (Tell MAMA, 23 May 2013)

22 May 2013: A man threw a smoke grenade into a mosque in Essex and then stormed into the building. Brandishing two knives, he asked, 'Where is your Allah now?' (*Essex Enquirer*, 29 May 2013)

22 May 2013: A 48-year-old man took to Twitter to incite people to attack Muslim businesses, including a shop owned by Muslims near his home. (*Manchester Evening News*, 29 May 2013)

Source: Burnett (2013), reprinted with the permission of the author and the Institute of Race Relations

In some respects these problems are illustrative of the suspicion that surrounds the 'alien' characteristics of the Islamic faith and its perceived threat to secular, and often monoculturalist, images of national identity. Said's writings on Islam (1978, 1997) refer to a process of 'Orientalism' to describe the sweeping generalisations made about the Islamic faith, based upon extravagant, media-driven distortions that are connected with terms such as fundamentalism, radicalism or extremism rather than any enlightened or scholarly understanding of the subject. Consequently, Islam presently finds itself conceived of in a way unlike that of any other religious identity whereby its meaning goes beyond that of personal faith and instead takes the shape of a fiercely politicised construct.

For commentators such as Kundnani (2002) and Fekete (2004), Muslims now find themselves in a position not dissimilar to that of black communities in 1970s Britain, whereby alarmist media narratives have combined with punitive political rhetoric to amplify the threat posed by Muslims and to create a new folk-devil, an object of hostility who bears the brunt of social anger and whose alien character-istics concretise moral anxieties. Research on the impact of counter-terrorism measures on Muslim communities offers further confirmation of the way in which Muslims can often feel like a 'suspect community' targeted by authorities simply on the basis of their faith (Awan, 2013b; Chakraborti, 2007; Choudhury and Fenwick, 2011; Pantazis and Pemberton, 2009). Crucially, this climate of hostility has implications not just for Muslim men as the likely 'suspect group' but for women too (see Case Study 3.2).

Case Study 3.2

Muslim women and the veil

Muslim women are disproportionately targeted as victims of anti-Muslim hate, often because of the way in which visual identifiers such as the hijab or niqab readily demar-cate veil-wearers as 'different' and ostensibly anti-Western and act as a stimulant for the venting of anger towards Muslims (Allen et al., 2013). Within Western countries the wearing of the veil in public places is routinely perceived as a symbol of female subordination and segregation and a metonym for the perceived backwardness of Islam, but rarely as a sign of personal autonomy and an expression of faith. These negative constructions create an environment that legitimates the demonisation, and by consequence the targeting of veil-wearers because of their failure to conform to conventional expectations of gender performance or assimilation.

Several European countries have passed legislation to make it illegal for Muslim women to wear the veil in public, including France and Belgium, whilst at the time of writing others such as The Netherlands, Italy, Switzerland and the Spanish region of Catalonia have all taken steps in the same direction. Justifications in favour of veil bans have tended to take three forms: namely, that covering the face is irreconcilable with

(Continued)

(Continued)

Western values; is an impediment to communication and integration; and is a risk to security (Zempi and Chakraborti, 2014). However, veil bans – and indeed the wider rhetoric around veiling – merely exacerbate the social exclusion of Muslim women by stigmatising them as 'deviant' and thereby legitimising expressions of hostility and violence towards them (Chakraborti and Zempi, 2013). These expressions can take a variety of forms, including verbal and violent attacks as well as persistent and aggressive staring and stalking, all of which have grave implications for the physical and emotional well-being of victims, families and wider Muslim communities (for a fuller account see Allen et al., 2013; Zempi, 2014; Zempi and Chakraborti, 2014).

'Faith-hate' in action: antisemitic hate

The escalating level of prejudice directed towards Muslim communities has not surprisingly given a higher profile to faith-hate, and has been a significant factor in the creation of explicit legislative protection against attacks upon religious identity. However, Muslim communities are not the only faith group to have experienced rising levels of prejudice. That there has been a discernible rise in the number of antisemitic incidents within the UK and other European countries may come of something of a surprise: Jewish communities have been settled in many Western societies for a much longer period than most other religious groupings and have been found to be less stringent – and by implication less 'different' – in sustaining religious beliefs and practices than other minority groups (Hunt, 2005). Nonetheless, antisemitism remains a particularly significant and pervasive problem.

Antisemitism has a strong historical legacy that has been heavily influential upon the nature of prejudice directed towards Jewish communities in the present day. Gerstenfeld (2013: 187–9) offers a number of examples of how antisemitism has flourished over time, citing, for instance, the persecution of Jews by Egyptians, Greeks and Romans during the pre-Christian era, the massacre of Jews who refused to convert to Christianity during the Crusades and the demonisation of Jews advocated by Martin Luther, the founder of Protestantism, and by the Catholic church. She suggests this history of antisemitism is largely attributable to the fact that Jewish communities were a minority in every country in which they lived, and notes that their perpetual 'outsider' status, reinforced by their different religion, customs, language and manner of dress, has been particularly significant in Europe where ethnic identity has been regarded as especially important. The persecution of Jewish communities has also taken the form of expulsion from, and refusal of entry to, numerous countries and even large-scale extermination: for example, estimates indicate that as many as 100,000 Jews were killed in Eastern Europe between 1648 and 1658 alone (Gerstenfeld, 2013: 188).

The most infamous illustration of antisemitic persecution in recent history is undoubtedly the Holocaust, a period that began in Nazi Germany with a carefully crafted campaign of bigoted rhetoric that escalated during the 1930s and culminated in the mass slaughter of Jews in the 1940s. As part of this systematic process of demonisation, millions of European Jews were stripped of citizenship and property and subjected to widespread sanctions and forms of discrimination as a way of enforcing their economic deprivation and social castigation, before being forced into ghettos and then concentration camps during the later stages of the Nazi atrocities. Approximately 6 million Jews – two-thirds of Europe's Jewish population and one-third of the global Jewish population – lost their lives during this period, prompting some scholars to describe the Holocaust as the most significant hate crime of modern centuries (Gerstenfeld, 2013; Levin, 2004). Equally, Holocaust denial – the denial or distortion of the historical facts of the Holocaust – has commonly featured within the antisemitic rhetoric expressed by extremist groups and far-right political parties and has helped to promote anti-Jewish sentiment in both America and Europe (Iganski, 1999; Levin, 2004).

Recent figures suggest that there has been a decrease domestically in levels of antisemitic activity over recent years. A total of 529 antisemitic incidents were recorded by the Community Security Trust (CST) in 2013, an 18% drop from the previous year's figure of 649 incidents and the lowest annual total recorded by CST since 2005 (CST, 2014). The CST attributes this decrease to an absence of trigger events – such as the shooting of three children and a teacher at a Jewish school in Toulouse in May 2012 and the escalation in fighting between Israel and Hamas in Gaza and southern Israel during November of that year – which precipitated a spike in levels of antisemitic activity during 2012. At the same time the CST acknowledges that under-reporting continues to be a significant problem, citing survey findings obtained by the European Union Agency for Fundamental Rights which showed that 72% of British Jews who had experienced antisemitic harassment during the previous five years had not reported it to the police or any other organisation (FRA, 2013b). Like other forms of hate crime, antisemitic incidents are significantly under-reported, particularly when the victims are minors, where the incident is considered to be of 'lesser' impact, and in cases that take place on social media (CST, 2014).

Explanations for antisemitic hate crime have often been based around the ideologies and activities of far-right groups. Motivated by their belief in the superiority of the 'white' (Aryan) race over all 'others', many far-right groups and white supremacists have promoted violence against Jewish communities on the basis of the perceived threat that such communities pose to the sanctity of the white race; indeed this threat is seen not only to legitimate but also to require the violent repression or elimination of Jews as enemies of the white race (Perry, 2003b). This line of thinking has been present within the ideology of a number of established neo-Nazi groups and extremist movements across the world, and has unquestionably been a factor behind the expression of antisemitic hate and hostility.

In recent times incitement against Jewish communities from the far-right has decreased to some extent, with the focus of far-right hatred shifting as a result of successful criminal prosecutions and a post-9/11 change of strategy towards the Muslim community (McGhee, 2005). Sibbitt (1997) has questioned the influence of far-right groups in the UK, arguing that such groups play a marginal role in the perpetration of hate offences in terms of direct involvement, while Levin and McDevitt (2002) have also suggested that extremists are likely to be responsible for only a small proportion of antisemitic incidents.

For Iganski, Kielinger and Paterson (2005), antisemitic incidents tend to occur as part of the unfolding of everyday life as opposed to being a result of political extremism, with their analysis of incidents recorded by the Metropolitan Police Service indicating that most experiences of antisemitism take the form of so-called 'low-level' or ordinary crime such as damage to property, theft and name-calling committed during the course of everyday interactions. As discussed in the previous chapter, the cumulative impact of these 'everyday' encounters should not be underestimated, nor should they be disassociated from the wider cultural context of hostility in which they occur. But equally, we should not overlook the commission of acts of terrorism against Jewish people which continue to be a significant source of concern. The CST's annual review of 2012 outlines a series of British cases involving planned terrorist acts on Jewish targets by radicalised Muslim extremists, and describes 2012 as a year notable for numerous terrorist attacks and plots explicitly targeting Jews in Britain, France and elsewhere (CST, 2013).

Anti-Jewish sentiment may be embedded within the cultural fabric of many societies across the world and Gerstenfeld (2013: 187–9) identifies a range of factors that have shaped such ill-feeling, including the deep-rooted religious mistrust between Jews and other faith groups, resentment of the perceived socio-economic success enjoyed by Jewish communities in the West, and a confusion between anti-Zionism and antisemitism. This last point is particularly significant in the context of recent events, such as the ongoing Israeli–Palestinian conflict, and may be an especially telling factor behind the rise in levels of prejudice directed towards Jews. Whilst those opposed to the basic proposition of Zionism – namely, support for a political movement to establish a national homeland for Jews in Palestine – should be distinguished from those who are opposed to Jewishness *per se* or who advocate the persecution of or discrimination against Jews, in practice the two positions may often become conflated.

This 'transfer of tensions' from the Middle East to Britain and an increase in anti-Zionist or anti-Israeli sentiment have been referred to as major factors behind the rise in antisemitic activity within the UK during the mid-part of the last decade (Jinman, 2005; Vasagar, 2007). However, the profile of incidents reported to the CST in 2013 is indicative of the multifaceted nature of contemporary antisemitism. In 143 out of a total of 529 antisemitic incidents the offenders employed discourse based on the Nazi period, including swastikas and references to the Holocaust. Of those, 87 cases showed evidence of a far-right motivation or beliefs.

Discourse related to Israel or the Middle East was evident in 49 incidents, of which 37 showed evidence of anti-Israel motivation or belief; and discourse relating to Islam or Muslims was present in seven incidents, with five incidents showing evidence of Islamist motivation or beliefs. The CST goes on to observe that there was a 35% decrease from 2012 in the number of antisemitic incidents showing some degree of ideological motivation or belief, and that few of those incidents involving ideological motivation showed any link to extremist activity on the part of the offender (CST, 2014: 22–3).

Conclusion

We have seen in this chapter how the problem of religiously motivated hate crime has become an issue of considerable academic, political and social significance. Far from being simply an adjunct to issues of 'race', religious identity – and more specifically the perceived threat posed by particular faith communities to secular constructions of cultural and national identity – has become a major source of debate, concern and misrepresentation. Especially contentious in this post-9/11 age has been the position of Islamic identity within British society, with British Muslims becoming ever more vulnerable to attack (both metaphorically and literally) not only through organised Islamophobic campaigns and far-right activity but also through more routine and legitimised forms of prejudice and demonisation. Whilst this chapter has focused primarily on anti-Muslim and anti-Jewish hate, research has highlighted the importance of protecting all faith communities from violence, from the desecration of religious buildings and monuments, harassment and from other attacks upon their religious identity (see, *inter alia*, ODIHR, 2013).

In this context we have seen that establishing legal provisions to protect faith communities against acts of hate has become a priority. As outlined above, the level of such protection has been significantly bolstered since the turn of the millennium through the introduction of legislation covering religiously aggravated offences and the incitement of hatred on the grounds of religious identity. Whilst to all intents and purposes this statutory recognition puts faith communities on the same footing as minority ethnic communities in terms of safeguarding their identity and rights in the eyes of the law, the controversies surrounding the incitement provisions – and the amendments made to these provisions – show how difficult it is to strike a balance between the prohibition of hatred and freedom of expression. Arguably, the value or otherwise of hate crime laws is measurable not so much in terms of their capacity to lead to successful prosecutions, but rather in their symbolic capacity to reassert society's condemnation of hate crime and to convey a sense of solidarity with, in this context, faith communities. We shall return to this point in later chapters.

Guide to further reading

Readers seeking to develop a broad understanding of the role of religion in contemporary Britain will find useful insights in the works of Furbey et al., *Faith as Social Capital: Connecting or Dividing* (2006) and Hunt, *Religion and Everyday Life* (2005), while more specific accounts of faith-hate can be found in McGhee, *Intolerant Britain? Hate, Citizenship and Difference* (2005) and Spalek, *Communities, Identities and Crime* (2008).

The McGhee text also provides a very useful account of issues relating to anti-Muslim hate crime, as does Zempi and Chakraborti, *Islamophobia, Victimisation and the Veil* (2014); Copsey et al., *Anti-Muslim Hate Crime and the Far-Right* (2013); Fekete, 'Anti-Muslim Racism and the European Security State' (2004); and Ahmed, *Islam under Siege* (2003). The topic of antisemitic hate, meanwhile, is discussed insightfully by FRA, *Discrimination and Hate Crime against Jews in EU Member States: Experiences and Perceptions of Antisemitism* (2013b); Iganski, Kielinger and Paterson, *Hate Crimes Against London's Jews* (2005); and Iganski, 'Legislating Against Hate: Outlawing Racism and Antisemitism in Britain' (1999).

Links to online material

The Tell MAMA (Measuring Anti-Muslim Attacks) website allows people from across England to report any form of Anti-Muslim abuse online. It also contains links to relevant reports and other resources and to a news feed. The website can be accessed at http://tellmamauk.org.

The Community Security Trust (CST) website offers a similar service for victims of antisemitic incidents. A wide range of material, including a full list of publications, is available through their website at www.thecst.org.uk.

Notes

1 For instance, tensions amongst different British Asian communities, and most significantly conflicts between Sikh and Muslim youths and Hindus and Muslims, have risen in recent times, to the extent where groups such as the British National Party and the English Defence League have used prominent Sikh members to actively promote anti-Muslim sentiment (Kundnani, 2002; Muir, 2012).

2 As Goodall (2007: 89) notes, two attempts to introduce incitement to religious hatred legislation were made in the Criminal Justice and Public Order Bill 1994, and again with the introduction of a Religious Offences Bill 2001. The Labour government that

came to power in 1997 made three further attempts: in the Anti-Terrorism, Crime and Security Bill 2001, the Serious Organised Crime and Police Bill 2004 and the Racial and Religious Hatred Bill 2005.

3 The Tell MAMA project was launched in February 2012 by Eric Pickles MP, the incumbent Secretary of State for the Department for Communities and Local Government, and based on the model of the Community Security Trust.

4

HOMOPHOBIC HATE CRIME

Chapter summary

This chapter presents an analysis of the nature, extent and impact of homophobic hate crime. After discussing definitions of homophobia, the chapter assesses how the historical outlawing of sex between males, and its concomitant over-policing, has adversely affected the relationship between gay communities and the police. The lack of trust and confidence between the two parties has been a major factor in the reluctance of victims of homophobia to report incidents to the police. The chapter then outlines how legislative developments, such as the Criminal Justice Act 2003 and the Criminal Justice and Immigration Act 2008, have brought more equality under the law for gay people and may have helped to improve the confidence that such communities have in the criminal justice system.

The nature, extent and location of homophobic hate crime are then examined. It is suggested that low-level forms of harassment are commonplace and damaging, and that violent homophobic incidents, while rare, may be more extreme than those evidenced in other forms of hate crime. The use of homophobic language within educational settings and via social media can be especially impactful upon young people. The chapter concludes that whilst there have been some improvements in the way that the criminal justice system responds to homophobic hate crime, its levels are still worryingly high.

Introduction

Over the last decade or so there have been a number of cases of homophobic hate crime that have made national headlines in the United Kingdom. In October 2005, for instance, barman Jody Dobrowski was killed after being assaulted by two strangers on Clapham Common as he made his way home one evening. His assailants, Scott Walker and Thomas Pickford, were heard screaming homophobic insults as they rained punches and kicks upon their victim 'as if trying to kill an animal' (Kennedy, 2006: 4). Both men were convicted of Dobrowski's murder and received enhanced prison sentences through the provisions contained in section 146 of the Criminal Justice Act 2003 (discussed below). Just four years later, another brutal attack on a gay man in London also resulted in the victim's death. In September 2009 Ian Baynham was attacked while walking in Trafalgar Square by a group of teenagers who subjected him to homophobic abuse while violently assaulting him. He later died of his injuries. His assailants, Ruby Thomas and Joel Alexander, were convicted of manslaughter, with the former receiving an enhanced sentence due to the hostility she had displayed towards Baynham's sexual orientation (BBC News, 2011a). The extreme nature of these cases reflects Perry's (2001) contention that homophobic attacks tend to be more violent than other forms of hate crime. The forms and extent of verbal and physical homophobic harassment will be assessed below.

One key characteristic of the historical relationship between gay communities and the criminal justice system is that of mistrust, born of the historical over-policing of the sexual behaviour of gay men. This over-zealous 'policing of the closet' was symptomatic of the criminal justice system's discriminatory practices towards homosexual men and women in the decades following the Second World War. An understanding of how this has influenced reporting rates of hate victimisation is vital for a full perspective of gay communities' experiences, but before offering a brief historical analysis of policing issues, this chapter will consider definitions of homophobia and homophobic hate crime.

Definitional issues

'Homophobia' is a contested term. It appears to imply a deep-rooted fear of homosexuals: a psychological condition that is involuntary and irrational but which denies a role for wider societal causes for the targeted hostility faced by gay men and women. As a descriptor for the 'everyday' harassment that many gay people face it may therefore be misleading, for, as Tomsen and Mason argue, 'few perpetrators of the violence directed at lesbians and gay men suffer from an exceptional and literal "phobia"' (Tomsen and Mason, 2001: 270). The *Oxford English Dictionary* (2014) uses slightly different concepts to define homophobia in stronger but simpler terms, as: 'Fear or hatred of homosexuals and homosexuality', while McGhee (2005: 119) offers a broader understanding that also includes ideas of 'fear' and 'hatred' by suggesting that: 'Homophobia is the umbrella term used to describe the form of prejudice expressed by societies, institutions and individuals who hate (and fear) homosexuals.'

The significance of broader institutional and societal prejudices – such as the dominant heterosexist popular culture in the UK – for the development of individual and institutional homophobia should not be underestimated.[1] Herek (2009: 56–7) invokes the concept of sexual stigma to establish the link between them:

> Sexual stigma is a cultural belief system through which homosexuality is denigrated, discredited, and socially constructed as invalid relative to heterosexuality ... As with other forms of stigma, sexual stigma is expressed through society's institutions (e.g., through discriminatory laws and policies) and by its individual members. Individual enactments of stigma can range from personal ostracism to criminal attacks against people perceived to be homosexual or bisexual.

Thus, through the idea of 'sexual stigma' Herek shows how homophobia can manifest itself via structural and individual agencies that reflect and reinforce social values and processes that normalize heterosexuality to the detriment of other forms of sexual behaviour. Within the criminal justice system though, definitions are primarily focused upon evidence of bias within the offender's motivation. For example, those provided by the Crown Prosecution Service (CPS) suggest that homophobia (and transphobia) do not have to be predicated on hatred of gay (or trans) people, but instead can be based merely upon dislike:

> 'Homophobia' and 'transphobia' are terms used to describe a dislike of LGBT [lesbian, gay, bisexual and transgendered] people or aspects of their perceived lifestyle. In other words, homophobia and transphobia are not restricted to a dislike of individuals; the dislike can be based on any sexual act or characteristic that the person associates with a LGBT person, whether or not any specific LGBT person does that act or has that characteristic. That dislike does not have to be as severe as hatred. It is enough that people do something or abstain from doing something because they do not like LGBT people. (CPS, 2007a: 6)

The CPS's definition posits that homophobia can be evidenced not just by someone's actions but also by their *inactions*, an interesting idea that has echoes in Macpherson's view that institutional racism can be the result of *unwitting* attitudes or actions that disadvantage minority ethnic people (Macpherson, 1999: para 6.34). Furthermore, in the immediate aftermath of the 1999 Macpherson Report the police service revised its definitions relating to hate incidents in order to give priority to the perceptions of the victim, rather than those of attending police officers, meaning that, in the case of an alleged homophobic incident, if the victim or any other person perceived it to be homophobic, then the police were obliged to record and investigate it as such (ACPO, 2005: 11). Subsequently, the College of Policing (2014: 4) produced a definition of a sexual orientation hate crime as:

> Any criminal offence which is perceived, by the victim or any other person, to be motivated by a hostility or prejudice based on a person's sexual orientation or perceived sexual orientation.

Legal protection from homophobic hate crime

As mentioned above, the historical criminalisation of gay male sexual relations, which for decades led to the intrusive policing of the private space of gay men, created an atmosphere of mutual mistrust and suspicion between the two groups. This existed within a society characterized by heteronormative cultures and homophobic prejudices (exhibiting Herek's (2009) 'sexual stigma') that acted both to justify the criminalisation of a sexual minority's behaviour and to fuel substantial levels of homophobic harassment. However, between the early 1950s and the present day there have been a number of key milestones that have challenged these attitudes, and a necessarily brief review of them begins with the Wolfenden Report, which paved the way for the decriminalisation of homosexuality in England and Wales.

The Report was produced by a committee appointed by the government (chaired by Sir John Wolfenden) to examine the law and practice relating to homosexual offences (Home Office and Scottish Home Department, 1957: 1). At that time (the mid-1950s) all gay male sexual activity was illegal, although sex between females was left untouched by the law. The Report, which appeared in 1957, was a progressive document that made a number of key recommendations in this area. For example, it argued that, as homosexuality was 'a state or condition' then it 'as such does not, and cannot, come within the purview of the criminal law' (1957: 11), and concluded, rather bravely for the times, that:

> Unless a deliberate attempt is made by society, acting through the agency of the law, to equate the sphere of crime with that of sin, there must remain a realm of private morality and immorality which is, in brief and crude terms, not the law's business. We accordingly recommend that homosexual behaviour between consenting adults in private should no longer be a criminal offence. (1957: 24-25)[2]

The eventual outcome of the Report was that Parliament passed the 1967 Sexual Offences Act which made homosexual acts between two adult males (over the age of consent of 21) in private no longer a criminal offence (it would take until 1980 for similar legislation to be passed in Scotland and 1982 in Northern Ireland). It was not until the Sexual Offences Act of 2003 that the offences of buggery and gross indecency were finally removed from the statute book, effectively ending discriminatory law dating from the Victorian era that punished certain homosexual activities but not their heterosexual equivalents.[3]

Also in 2003, and significantly for the study of hate crime and its prosecution, section 146 of the Criminal Justice Act conveyed upon courts the capacity to enhance sentences for offences that:

> at the time of committing the offence, or immediately before or after doing so, the offender demonstrated towards the victim of the offence hostility based on (i) the sexual orientation (or presumed sexual orientation) of the victim .... or

(b) that the offence was motivated (wholly or partly) (i) by hostility towards persons who are of a particular sexual orientation... [4]

(3) The court—

(a) must treat the fact that the offence was committed in any of those circumstances as an aggravating factor, and (b) must state in open court that the offence was committed in such circumstances.

(4) It is immaterial for the purposes of paragraph (a) or (b) of subsection (2) whether or not the offender's hostility is also based, to any extent, on any other factor not mentioned in that paragraph.

(HM Government, 2012b)[5]

Importantly, the wording of the Act implies that the offender need demonstrate hostility *or* motivation based upon hostility. This means that proving motivation (something notoriously difficult to verify) is not necessary in order to gain a conviction as long as there is evidence that hostility was demonstrated in the commissioning of the offence. Also of note is the insistence of section 146 that hostility towards sexual orientation need only be *part* of the reason for the commissioning of the offence for the sentence to be enhanced.

Prior to this Act, although statistics were collated annually relating to the targeting of someone due to their sexual orientation, there was no legal provision for this type of offence to have an enhanced sentence.[6] Section 146 (which came into effect on 4 April 2005) was therefore an important development for gay victims of hate crime, although the Act did not create specific aggravated offences in the way that the Crime and Disorder Act 1998 had with those that were 'racially or religiously aggravated'.[7] This meant that, unlike the case for these racially or religiously aggravated offences where the offence and the aggravation are inseparable, the defendant can still be found guilty of the 'basic', non-aggravated offence under Section 146 provisions. In Scotland, meanwhile, Section 2 of the Sentencing of Offences Aggravated by Prejudice (Scotland) Act 2009 gives courts similar sentencing powers to those in England and Wales with regard to offences motivated by 'malice and ill-will towards persons who have a particular sexual orientation'.

In 2013 the Law Commission embarked upon an extensive consultation regarding the disparities in provisions under the existing suite of hate crime legislation, including whether to extend the aggravated offences provisions contained in the Crime and Disorder Act 1998 to include sexual orientation. In May 2014 it published the results of its investigations, recommending that a further, government-sponsored review into the aggravated offences be undertaken. The Commission added the proviso though that if the government did not support this review then, as a 'less valuable' option with 'limited benefits', the aggravated offences should be extended to include sexual orientation (Law Commission, 2014: 126). The Commission also recommended that the Sentencing Council provide clear guidance on the sentencing approach for any crime where hostility on one of the five grounds was proven and that, in cases where an enhanced sentence was applied in cases aggravated by hostility, then this should be noted on the offender's record on the Police National Computer (2014: 126).

Another important piece of legislation is section 74 of the Criminal Justice and Immigration Act 2008, which amended Part 3A of the Public Order Act 1986 to include a new offence of inciting hatred based upon a person's sexual orientation, thereby achieving broadly similar legal provision for gay people to that already provided to minority ethnic and religious communities. The Act has a high threshold for prosecutions, which means that only words, behaviour or material that are *threatening* are liable to legal sanction (similar to the incitement of religious hatred provisions): abusive or insulting language directed against gay people is not considered to be illegal under the Act. Also, the Act allows for successful prosecutions only if it can be proved that there was an *intention* to stir up hatred, unlike the provisions for inciting racial hatred that also allow for conviction if it can be proved that there was a *likelihood* that hatred was stirred up, something which, some argue, renders offences relating to sexual orientation extremely difficult to prosecute successfully (Law Commission, 2013: 44).

Setting this high threshold reflected concerns expressed during parliamentary debates regarding section 74 that those whose religious views caused them to find homosexuality unacceptable would be subject to arrest and prosecution under the proposed new law, thus threatening their freedom of speech (House of Lords Hansard, 2008). These objections prompted the insertion in the final version of the Criminal Justice and Immigration Act 2008 of '29JA Protection of Freedom of Expression (Sexual Orientation)', which states 'for the avoidance of doubt, the discussion or criticism of sexual conduct or practices or the urging of persons to refrain from or modify such conduct or practices shall not be taken of itself to be threatening or intended to stir up hatred' (Office of Public Sector Information, 2008). However, despite concerns that these concessions could result in extremists citing a 'religious defence' when facing accusations of inciting homophobic hatred, the 2010 Derby incitement case examined in Case Study 4.1 revealed that this type of defence is not enough by itself to avoid conviction.

Case Study 4.1

The Derby incitement convictions

In January 2012 the first trial under s74 of the Criminal Justice and Immigration Act 2008 occurred at Derby Crown Court. The three men on trial – Ihjaz Ali, Kabir Ahmed and Razwan Javed – were accused of distributing hundreds of copies of a leaflet in July 2010 in the lead up to Derby's gay pride event that were both threatening and

(Continued)

(Continued)

designed to stir up hatred against the city's gay communities. The leaflet in question, 'The Death Penalty?', depicted a mannequin hanging with a noose round its neck and debated by which method – stoning, flinging from a high place or burning – gay people should be executed. It argued: 'The only debate among classical authorities about how to punish homosexuality was the method of carrying out the execution ... [because] the death sentence was the only way that the immoral crime [of homosexuality] can be erased from corrupting society' (Law Commission, 2013: 44). Two other leaflets that were also distributed by the three men, but were not part of the prosecution, were entitled 'G.A.Y. God Abhors You' and 'Turn or Burn', which contained a picture that appeared to show someone – with the implicit suggestion that it was a gay person – burning (Judiciary of England and Wales, 2012).

Four witnesses at the trial stated that they had felt threatened by the leaflets, with one worried that he might be 'burned' (Addley, 2012). In their defence, Ali, Javed and Ahmed argued that they had not meant to threaten anyone but felt it was their duty to express Islam's stance on homosexuality and to urge people not to commit 'sin'. Despite this, all three were found guilty of distributing written material that was threatening and intended to stir up hatred on the grounds of sexual orientation. The judge, John Burgess, stated: 'Much has been said during the course of the trial about freedom of expression, and the freedom to preach strongly held beliefs; beliefs which may have some foundation in scripture. Freedom of speech is a cornerstone of democracy and a basic ingredient of any free society. Parliament clearly had this very much in mind when this legislation was passed' (Judiciary of England and Wales, 2012: 2). All three men were given jail sentences of at least 15 months each. To date, this case remains the only successful prosecution under the incitement provisions of the Criminal Justice and Immigration Act 2008.

Nature and extent of homophobic hate crime

Police figures for 2012/13 show that out of 42,236 recorded hate crimes in England and Wales, 4,267 (or 10%) were classified under 'sexual orientation', the second highest total for the monitored strands. Interestingly, the Crime Survey for England and Wales (CSEW) combined dataset for 2011/12 and 2012/13 puts the figure much higher, at 39,000 sexual orientation hate crimes per year on average (or 14%), but places sexual orientation fourth in the monitored strand rankings (Home Office et al., 2013: 22). However, as is discussed below, the true extent of homophobic harassment is difficult to discern as it is estimated that only around one-in-four to one-in-five homophobic incidents is reported to the police (Guasp et al., 2013). However, victimisation surveys provide an indication of the extent to which LGB people are targeted by this form of hate crime. For example, one in five gay or lesbian people had experienced a hate incident 'in the last three years' (HM Government, 2011) while Stonewall's 2013 analysis of the experiences of 2,544 lesbian, gay and bisexual people put the figure at one in six for the same time period (Guasp et al., 2013: 7). The EHRC indicated that just over 60% of gay survey respondents had experienced some form of verbal abuse while four out of ten gay men and three out of ten lesbians had been bullied (EHRC, 2009a: 30).

Whilst methodological differences regarding how victimisation surveys are carried out may explain some of the variance in findings between them, there are nevertheless broadly similar trends that can be picked out. For example, levels of harassment are consistently high for both sexes, with commonly around two-thirds to nine-tenths of respondents in various studies reporting being the victim of verbal abuse, something that can be a persistent fact of life for many lesbians and gay men (see, for example, EHRC, 2009a). Figures for being a victim of violence are much lower but also significant, with one in ten victims reporting being physically assaulted in Stonewall's study and one in fourteen experiencing violence in Galop's (Antjoule, 2013: 5; Guasp et al., 2013: 10).

Different groups within LGB communities experience hate crime in varying ways too, with lesbians and gay men more likely to be victimised than bisexual men and women, and black and disabled groups also more likely to be subjected to violence (Guasp et al., 2013: 8, 10). Perry (2001) suggests that lesbians suffer homophobic violence at a lower rate than males, something borne out by Herek (2009) and also Stonewall, whose survey revealed that gay and bisexual men were almost twice as likely to be threatened with violence than lesbians and bisexual women (Guasp et al., 2013). Perry (2001) explains that same-sex affection and physical contact between women are more acceptable for the general public than similar acts between men, making them less of a target for homophobic harassment. Herek (2009) concurs with this while also pointing to broader factors, such as men generally being more likely than women to be victims of violent crime anyway, and especially violence perpetrated by strangers. In addition, fear of victimization also varies, with black and minority ethnic (BME) and disabled gay and bisexual groups twice as likely to feel homophobic attacks are a problem in their local neighbourhood than white groups or those without disabilities respectively (Guasp et al., 2013: 8).

It is also important to note the types of homophobic harassment experienced. Of the third of Herek et al.'s (2003: 243) sample of 450 lesbians and gay men who had experienced an actual or attempted bias crime, one in nine were victims of property crime and just under a quarter had experienced an assault or rape. Other forms of victimisation reported by Stonewall's respondents included burglary and robbery, being threatened with violence and experiencing unwanted sexual contact (Guasp et al., 2013: 10). As discussed in Chapter 2, a key aspect of understanding hate-related harassment is recognising that incidents form part of a continuum of such victimisation. Drawing upon Kelly's (1987) study of sexual violence, this continuum should not be seen as one with the most minor events at one end and the most violent at the other, for, as Kelly argues, *all* such incidents cause alarm, hurt and distress to the victim. Instead, such a continuum of victimisation is based on the *frequency* of such events, and for many gay people these can be part of their daily lived experience.

As with other forms of hate crime, the Internet has become a significant site for harassing or abusing gay people, with around one in twenty reporting being victimised within the previous 12 months and those aged between 18 and 24 especially at risk (Guasp et al., 2013: 9). Antjoule (2013: 5) notes that the homophobic word 'faggot' was featured in over 13 million tweets in a single year (from July 2012 to June 2013), something which could help to normalise such language back in the 'real world', as one victim commented to Stonewall:

> I do see the internet as a place where people feel safer to indulge this hate without any real repercussions. I think this is a problem because it's helping to normalise this behaviour again, and that may translate to a shift backwards in real world behaviour over time. (Michelle, 31, quoted in Guasp et al., 2013: 9).

Over the past decade the term 'gay' has 'become embedded in popular usage, particularly amongst adolescents, as a term of insult or as a reference for things deemed 'rubbish' or 'lame' (Johnson et al., 2007: 31). Such misuse of the term can damage the self-worth of gay people and has been a significant factor in low educational achievement or truanting amongst LGB pupils (2007: 31). These studies also revealed that gay pupils often felt that teachers were unsympathetic to their homophobic victimisation and indeed there were occasions when pupils had witnessed teachers themselves being homophobic (see Case Study 4.2).

Case Study 4.2

Homophobia in educational settings

Although schools, colleges and universities are often seats of 'progressive' learning with their own equal opportunities policies they unfortunately also appear to be environments in which gay and lesbian students, and gay parents, can experience homophobic harassment. This can come not only from fellow pupils and students but also from those in authority, such as teachers and tutors (Perry and Dyck, 2014). Guasp's (2012: 3–4) large-scale survey of young lesbian, gay and bisexual people at secondary schools revealed that:

- More than half of lesbian, gay and bisexual pupils had experienced homophobic bullying.
- Over nine out of ten had heard homophobic remarks in school.

- More than half had been subjected to verbal harassment and one in six to physical abuse.
- Three out of five gay pupils who had experienced homophobic bullying stated that teachers who had witnessed it never intervened (2012: 4).

The impact of homophobic bullying can be devastating, as one female student reported: 'I feel awful all the time. It eats away inside you and sometimes knowing what they'd do to me if they knew makes me lose the ability to breathe' (Guasp, 2012: 5). Such bullying can lead to feelings of isolation, depression and a sense of helplessness, particularly when it goes unchallenged or is tacitly endorsed by teachers (METRO Youth Chances, 2014). Hunt and Jensen's (2007) work also uncovered the varied and complex forms that homophobic harassment can take in schools, ranging from verbal abuse to death threats, sexual assault and being ostracised. Typical of the experience of many lesbian and gay pupils is that of a female in Trotter's (2006: 295) research, who, in the words of one of her contemporaries, '… got tortured for it [her sexuality]. She ended up sitting on the front [alone] at dinner times and breaks for being called lesbian.'

The four most frequently experienced types of harassment in Trotter's research – verbal abuse, malicious gossip, intimidating looks, and being ignored and isolated – are the so-called 'low-level' forms of abuse which can nevertheless be so damaging. In addition, the seemingly routine pejorative use of the word 'gay' by pupils, to mean something "rubbish" or "bad" … promotes negative feelings of isolation and fear' (Hobson, 2012: 5–6) and can prevent gay pupils from coming out. Yet this is rarely recognised as bullying by teachers, something that may reflect the fact that less than one in ten schools has developed specific policies to counter and deal with homophobia (Hobson, 2012).

A relatively new but increasingly important form of homophobia is cyberbullying, which can occur via Internet message boards or apps such as Viber and Snapchat, on social networking sites like Facebook, forums such as LittleChat or via text. It can take a variety of forms, from 'trolling' (posting malicious abuse or gossip about someone), setting up groups to bully others, sharing embarrassing videos, 'sexting', or hijacking someone's online identity in order to humiliate them. Almost a quarter (23%) of the gay pupils surveyed by Stonewall had experienced cyberbullying (the fourth most common form of abuse reported) and a tenth had been bullied by text (Guasp, 2012: 4). Being targeted in this way can cause anxiety, depression, loneliness, health problems and self-harming (NSPCC, 2014).

However, there are some signs that the situation in schools may be improving, with Stonewall reporting that levels of homophobic bullying have fallen by 10% between 2007 and 2012 while the number of schools explicitly stating that homophobic bullying is wrong has more than doubled, to 50% (Guasp, 2012). There is also evidence that in some educational settings the use of homophobic language among pupils has become unacceptable, although cultures of heteronormativity still dominate (McCormack and Anderson, 2010).

Meanwhile, victim surveys suggest that just under one in five gay victims of hate crime have experienced a homophobic assault, making them more at risk of being a victim of violence than heterosexual people (Dick, 2009: 10). It is also worth noting that the CSEW estimates that 42% of the offences under the 'sexual orientation' strand were classified as 'violence against the person', a higher percentage than for any of the other monitored strands. A higher percentage of these offences resulted in injury than for any of the categories too (Home Office et al., 2013).[8] Perry (2001: 107) argues that homophobic attacks tend to be amongst the most brutal acts of all hate crimes, citing work by the National Gay and Lesbian Task Force in the United States which found that over half of gay-related homicides show evidence of 'rage/hate-fuelled extraordinary violence ... such as dismemberment, bodily and genital mutilation, use of multiple weapons, repeated blows from a blunt object, or numerous stab wounds'. This graphic violence reveals a frightening kind of 'overkill' typical of manifestations of violent homophobia. Research has also shown that on a significant number of occasions these violent episodes also involve an element of humiliation, perhaps revealing evidence of real *hatred*, rather than just prejudice, on behalf of the perpetrator(s) (as in the murder of Jody Dobrowski, for example).

The issue of the murder of gay people is a complex one.[9] Tomsen's (2002) study of homophobic murders of gay men found two distinct categories: attacks on those perceived to be homosexual by groups of people in public spaces, and one-on-one attacks in private spaces, which give rise to allegations of unwanted sexual advances that somehow triggered the assailant's actions. Bartlett's (2007) detailed examination of gay sexual homicide (an analysis of CPS files relating to the deaths of 77 people from 1976 to 1981) found that, in almost all of the cases, there had been no prior intent to kill; usually, only the victim and the perpetrator were present at the time of death, but exceptional violence in the deaths was commonplace (Bartlett, 2007: 582).

Katz-Wise and Hyde note that there is a higher prevalence of mental disorders in the LGB population, something which can be explained within the broader conceptual framework of 'minority stress', in which 'stigma, prejudice, and discrimination create a hostile or stressful social environment that causes subsequent mental health problems' (Katz-Wise and Hyde, 2012: 144). Homophobic harassment can exacerbate these issues, creating a heightened sense of vulnerability and insecurity, feelings of helplessness and isolation, increased insecurity amongst other members of the local gay community, and a lack of self-esteem and confidence (EHRC, 2009a; Herek et al., 2003). These can have a long-term effect on mental health, which can lead to greater risk of suicidal behaviour, relationship difficulties, depression, anxiety and sleeplessness (METRO Youth Chances, 2014), and can cause victims to restrict their movements and behaviour, and conceal their identity (Mason, 2009; Williams and Tregidga, 2013).

Reporting incidents to the police

As discussed above, gay communities' perception of the police has been negatively affected by the over-zealous policing of the sexual behaviour of gay men. This wariness has helped to create a situation whereby despite being more likely to be victims of crime, lesbian and gay communities are less likely to report crime to the police than the general population (Dunn, 2012). There is also a feeling amongst LGB communities that institutional and individual police homophobia will manifest themselves in active hostility towards them, with officers not taking their hate incident seriously nor pursuing any investigations with urgency (Dick, 2009). In the context of the United States, the reluctance of victims to report to the police is worsened by the suggestion that over a quarter of gay males had been victimized *by* the police (Katz-Wise and Hyde, 2012: 152). In the UK, Jones and Williams (2013: 2) relate that within the organisation itself, gay officers report 'being subjected to derogatory discourse; professional humiliation; physical violence and the refusal from some heterosexual officers to work in close proximity with LGB officers'.

Such evidence helps to clarify why concerns about police attitudes are so often behind the reluctance of victims of homophobia to report incidents to the police (Chakraborti et al., 2014a; Herek et al., 2003), although other factors, such as a belief that the police could not have done anything to help, or that the victim was fearful of reprisals, should also be noted (Guasp et al., 2013; Williams and Tregidga, 2013). These concerns may vary between different groups, with Dick (2009) finding, for example, that reporting rates were much lower amongst gay men and young people than lesbians and older people respectively. However, one group that passes 'under the radar' by rarely reporting homophobic incidents is that of ostensibly heterosexual men, who are victimised while having sex with other men but do not want to disclose this secret 'other side' to officers or anyone else (Williams and Robinson, 2004).

Despite the historically troubled relationship between gay communities and the police, there is evidence that since the publication of the Macpherson Report in 1999 the police have been trying to purge the service of homophobia while also placing increased emphasis on the investigation of homophobic hate crimes (Rowe, 2014). However, how effective these developments have been in raising trust and confidence in the police (and hence increasing reporting rates of hate crime) is a moot point, with Stonewall reporting that the levels of gay people who would expect discrimination from the police when reporting a hate crime in 2013 had remained unchanged (at around one in four) over the five years since their previous survey in 2008 (Guasp et al., 2013: 10). In addition, Galop's survey of LGBT Londoners recorded a drop in confidence in the police in the years from 2008/09 to 2012/13 (Antjoule, 2013: 6) while analysis of British Crime Survey data from 2007 to 2010 by the EHRC revealed that over half of all homophobic hate crimes were still not being reported to the police (Botcherby et al., 2011). Whilst these statistics obviously do not show the whole picture of police–LGB relations they do suggest that there is still considerable scope for improvement in this regard.

Conclusion

This chapter has explored the nature, extent and effects of homophobic hate crime. It traced the history of problematic relations between gay communities (and especially gay males) and the police, and in particular the over-zealous 'policing of the closet' that has damaged the trust and confidence that gay men have in the police. The nature and extent of homophobic hate crime were also assessed, and it was suggested that so called 'low-level' harassment was common-place for LGB groups. Evidence was also cited of a worryingly high frequency of violent homophobic assaults, and it was argued that not only are lesbian and gay men more likely to be the victims of such attacks than their heterosexual coun-terparts, but that these assaults were likely to be of a more extreme nature than other forms of violent hate crime.

The chapter argued that legislative developments, such as the Criminal Justice Act 2003 and the Criminal Justice and Immigration Act 2008, coupled with the criminal justice system's re-evaluation of its LGB policies in the post-Macpherson climate, may have created an improved atmosphere within police–LGB relations. The successful prosecution of the perpetrators of high-profile homophobic crimes, such as the murders of Jody Dobrowski and Ian Baynham, may also have helped to reassure gay communities that the police are now according the investigation of homophobic hate crime with the resources that it deserves. However, sugges-tions that levels of homophobic hate crime are rising, and that homophobic bul-lying is still commonplace in schools and the workplace, serve as a timely reminder that these are still very serious contemporary issues.

Guide to further reading

Antjoule's *Hate Crime Report* (2013) is a comprehensive overview of homophobic, biphobic and transphobic crime in London. Katz-Wise and Hyde (2012) provide a useful statistical overview of the extent of homophobic hate crime and Mason's (2009) examination of the 'visibility' of homosexuality, and how this relates to the risk of homophobic victimisation, offers important perspectives on the issue.

The *Journal of Homosexuality* makes for informative reading and the 1957 Wolfenden Report is a fascinating historical document (HOSHD, 1957).

Links to online material

There is a wealth of information available online for scholars of hate crime wishing to specialise in contemporary LGB issues and the study of homophobia. The Pink News site at www.pinknews.co.uk/home/ is a valuable source of up-to-date news stories, as is that of Stonewall (the lesbian, gay and bisexual charity) at www.stonewall.org.uk/. This site also provides guidance on broader LGB issues, including those relating to hate crime victimisation. Further informative advice can be found at the Equality and Human Rights Commission's 'Sexual Orientation' pages at www.equalityhumanrights.com/advice-and-guidance/your-rights/sexual-orientation/.

Notes

1 In 2013 the ONS estimated that just 1.5% of adults in the UK identify themselves as gay, lesbian or bisexual – approximately 765,000 people (ONS, 2013: 2), although other estimates put the figure much higher, at 5–7% of the population or 3–4 million people (Antjoule, 2013: 5).

2 At the time of the publication of the Wolfenden Report the *Sunday Express* was moved to refer to it as the 'Pansies' Charter' (Sandbrook, 2007: 487).

3 Sections 12, 13 and 32 of the Sexual Offences Act 1956 (covering gross indecency, buggery and soliciting by a man) were all abolished under the Sexual Offences Act 2003. The Home Office acknowledged that these sections had been used in a discriminatory way in the past against gay men (McGhee, 2005: 202).

4 Ministry of Justice (2010: 2) guidance makes it clear that, in this legal context, sexual orientation 'covers only groups of people who are gay, lesbian, bisexual or heterosexual' and is therefore not defined by, for example, preferences for certain sexual practices.

5 Although Section 146 does not define sexual orientation, the CPS guidance sees it as 'a term used to describe a person's emotional and/or physical attraction to another' (CPS, 2007a: 43).

6 The first full set of annual CPS statistics relating to such incidents covered the year 2004/05, when the CPS prosecuted 317 offences identified as having a homophobic or transphobic element: by 2012/13, this figure had risen to 1,096 (CPS, 2014).

7 Other significant legislation includes the Civil Partnerships Act 2004, which entitles same-sex couples to a union of 'civil partnership', the Equality Act 2010, which prohibits discrimination or harassment on grounds of sexual orientation in the workplace,

and the Marriage (Same Sex Couples) Act 2013, which made the marriage of same sex couples lawful.

8 The next highest were 32% of 'disability' offences and also those for 'gender identity' (Home Office et al., 2013: Appendix Table 2.03).

9 Thankfully, murders of gay people in any context are very rare. For example, there were no homophobic murder investigations recorded by the Metropolitan Police Service during 2007/08, 2010/11, 2011/12 and 2012/13, with just two each in 2008/09 and 2009/10.

5

TRANSPHOBIC HATE CRIME

Chapter summary

This chapter discusses transphobic hate crime, which, despite being one of the recognised 'five strands' of monitored hate crime, has received comparatively little scholarly attention. The chapter begins by discussing the complexities of gender and gender identity, and outlines some of the key debates relevant to the analyses of the nature of transphobic victimisation that follow. It then proceeds by examining the intersection of gender with sex and sexuality, and assesses the importance of their complex relationship within the context of understanding the rationale behind perpetrators' actions. Following a necessarily brief summary of these theoretical ideas (and those relating to queer and feminist theory) the chapter examines the nature and extent of hate crimes where the victim is a transgendered person. Various forms of this harassment are outlined, and it is proposed that transphobic hate crime can be more frequent, and have a deeper impact, than other forms of recognised hate crime.

Discussions of transphobic victimisation have often been included with those relating to the targeting of lesbian, gay and bisexual communities under the 'LGBT' label, suggesting implicitly that the experiences of these groups are similar. The chapter challenges this assumption by unpicking the differences between transphobic and homophobic hate crime. We observe that while the broad LGBT label helps to highlight the commonalities and histories of discrimination and stigmatisation suffered by lesbian, gay, bisexual and transgendered groups, the differences in the characteristics and impacts of their targeted victimisation highlight the need for distinct lines of analysis.

Introduction

Within the study of hate crime it is important to recognise the complexities of the relationship between gender, sex and sexuality, especially when the victim is of a minority sexual orientation or is someone who does not conform to 'standard' ideas of gender. Within this context, understanding how these facets that are so central to a person's identity and sense of self inter-relate can help uncover any commonalities between homophobic and transphobic victimisation.

A useful starting point in this discussion is an analysis of the concepts of 'gender' and 'sex'. For Namaste (2006: 587) 'gender' refers to societal expectations of the 'roles and meanings assigned to men and women on their presumed biological sex'. Whittle (2002: 253) cites Zucker and Bradley's (1995) idea that gender roles are 'behaviours, attitudes, and personality traits that a society, in a given culture and historical period, designates as masculine or feminine'. 'Sex', on the other hand, refers to someone's biological characteristics at birth, with especial reference to their genitalia, which usually means that they are defined as being either 'male' or 'female'. Gender identity is a more complex concept, however, being someone's 'deeply felt internal and individual experience of gender, which may or may not correspond with the sex assigned at birth, including the personal sense of the body ... and other expressions of gender, including dress, speech and mannerisms' (Turner et al., 2009: 42). This conceptualisation provides the necessary space for the construction of a plurality of gender identities, rather than just the oppositional binary of male and female, and also challenges 'accepted' and traditional ideas of how men and women behave, function and present themselves (see Case Study 5.1).

'Sexuality' is itself a concept distinct from both gender and sex, and refers to the 'human focus of attraction, and on related identities (such as LGBT or heterosexual)' which can include 'sexual conduct [and] eroticism' (Richardson and Monro, 2012: 7). Again, though (as discussed in Chapter 4), there are dominant ideas and expectations within most Western societies regarding sexuality and sexual behaviour that are usually based upon 'acceptable' conceptions of heterosexuality. This in turn can breed a climate of heteronormativity (the institutional privileging of heterosexuality) which devalues or denigrates other forms of sexuality, such as homosexuality. Just as with gender, though, sexuality can have a myriad of permutations that exceed hegemonic and rather restrictive societal expectations of sexual behaviour (see Richardson and Monro (2012) for an extended discussion of sexuality).

Linked with these discussions of gender and sexuality are the influential ideas of 'queer theorists' like Judith Butler, who argue that gender is 'performative' and is not based upon physical characteristics nor restricted to binary, oppositional classifications like male and female (see Butler, 1990). The aim of their work is therefore to 'disrupt categories *per se*, to disrupt the fixity of identity by showing up its non-natural incoherence' (Beasley, 2005: 105). Butler's work concentrates upon those who may feel that they belong to neither gender or perhaps even to both, and are therefore marginalised from traditional gendered constructions of society. It questions the 'taken for granted' assumption that male bodies, for example, automatically produce a certain kind of heterosexual masculinity. Instead, queer theory offers a model that allows for the fluidity and permeability of gender and sexual boundaries whilst questioning associated hierarchies, and thus includes many of those that are the victims of homophobic and transphobic violence.

Case Study 5.1

What do we mean by 'transgender' and 'transsexual'?

The lack of a consensus in the definitions of 'transsexual' and 'transgender' is due to the sheer complexities of the concepts involved – sex, gender, identity and sexuality – and the wide range of disciplines, from gender studies to feminism and from sociology through politics to psychology and psychiatry, in which they are discussed.

Often the debate centres upon the significance of gendered behaviour rather than the physical or surgical details of what actually constitutes a male or a female. There is therefore scope for someone who is physically male to behave and dress in a feminine fashion, and consider themselves female, and yet also for someone to have hormone treatment and surgery and *physically* become female.[1] One term for the former person could be 'transgendered' and for the latter, 'transsexual'.

Turner et al. extend these ideas (2009: 5) [bold added for emphasis]:

Transgender is an umbrella term ... which describes the identities of a range of people whose lifestyles appear to conflict with the gender norms of society. In the broad sense of the term, a transgender person crosses the conventional boundaries of gender by dressing and presenting themselves as their preferred gender role. It can include those who may describe themselves or be described by others as transvestite or cross dressers.

People who may be described as **transsexual** have a deep conviction that their gender identity does not match that of their appearance or anatomy and they wish to present to the world in a different gender to that assigned at birth. The majority will wish to undergo hormone therapy, oestrogens or testosterone depending upon their birth gender and the gender they wish to acquire legally. Most will also wish to undergo some surgery to bring their bodies in line with their gender identity. The term transsexual can be misleading and many assume that it is about sexual orientation but it is an issue of gender identity.[2]

Cisgender, or **cissexual**, meanwhile, refers to those whose gender identity matches the one they were biologically born with, while cissexism refers to the belief that the gender identities adopted by trans people are not equal to, or authentic as, those of cissexual people (Perry and Dyck, 2014: 186).

(Continued)

(Continued)

Abbreviations are often used to denote those who have 'transitioned' from one gender to another. A person who was male but has become female is often denoted as MTF ('male-to-female') whilst someone who has undergone the opposite experience is frequently cited as FTM ('female-to-male'). This and all related terminology need to be used with care and sensitivity, which is why surveys of such communities can include gender categories such as 'crossdresser, drag queen, drag king, transsexual man (FTM), transsexual woman (MTF), transgender man, transgender woman' (GenderPAC survey in Lombardi et al., 2002: 93). Juang (2006: 711) goes further, citing Stryker's (1998) assertion that there is a 'wild profusion of gender subject positions', including 'FTM, MTF, eonist, invert, androgyne, butch, femme, nellie, queen, third sex, hermaphrodite, tomboy, sissy, drag king, female impersonator, she-male, he-she, boy dyke, girlfag, transsexual, transvestite, transgender, cross-dresser'. Furthermore, a trans person may move from one trans identity to another over time (Whittle et al., 2007).

The sheer multitude of these positions can complicate discussions of transgender issues enormously. What is clear, though, is that transsexuality should not be confused with homosexuality, although this error is not uncommon amongst the general public. Whilst issues of sexuality are important and are inter-woven with gender, transsexual people can, of course, be gay, straight or bisexual, just like members of other communities.

A contentious aspect of queer theory, though, is that in some respects it does *not* offer space that incorporates transgendered perspectives, but rather excludes them. It does this because it challenges the very notion of clearly defined genders, and yet for many in the transgendered communities the identification with a certain gender is the most important facet of their lives. Their sense of gender identity is so strong that it defines not only who they are but also who they want to become, i.e. it may be the catalyst for the process of transitioning from one gender to another. Thus, rather than 'queering' gendered boundaries, for some commentators, transgendered people actually reinforce them (see Koenig (2003) for further discussion).

However it is not just queer theory that offers challenges to the very notion of transsexualism. Feminism has offered a number of critiques of transsexuality for reflecting patriarchal norms by reinforcing gender stereotypes, with trans women accused of reinforcing a 'stereotypical model of uber femininity' and trans men of being 'renegades seeking to acquire male power and privilege' (Hines, 2007: 18). Some of these feminist critics, such as Janice Raymond, argue that it is patriarchal society that has generated these clearly defined notions of masculinity and femininity and yet transsexuals, rather than offering a new and 'queered' version of gender, find themselves 'bound' by those patriarchal notions of masculinity and femininity, and merely move from one clichéd version of gender to another

(Elliot, 2010). Raymond controversially argues that 'All transsexuals rape women's bodies by reducing the real female form to an artefact, appropriating this body for themselves' (1979: 49). She also sees MTF transsexuals as 'pastiches' of women that invade female spaces while reinforcing male domination.

Such a rejection of MTF transsexuals by some radical feminists may undermine attempts to find similarities between different forms of targeted victimisation, such as transphobic violence and domestic abuse. In the case of transphobic violence, if its victims are viewed as reinforcing the patriarchal society that is seen by many feminists as being the root cause of much domestic abuse, then perhaps victims of transphobic and domestic violence have little in common.

Definitional issues

Historically, the phenomena of transphobia and homophobia have been regarded by many academics and practitioners as having a significant number of shared characteristics: so much so, in fact, that they have often been grouped together. However, within the last decade transphobia has begun to receive attention in its own right, and is now more readily acknowledged as a separate phenomenon from homophobia. Bettcher (2007: 46) sees transphobia as 'any negative attitudes (hatred, loathing, rage, or moral indignation) harboured toward trans people on the basis of enactments of [their] gender' and Bornstein's (2006: 238) definition equates to the fear and hatred of anyone seen as a 'border-dweller' (someone who occupies a gender position that may be on the margins of the 'accepted' male/female dichotomy). Lombardi (2009: 980) suggests that behind this prejudice is a 'heterosexism, authoritarianism, a belief in only two sexes, and a belief that gender is biologically based', while Hill and Willoughby (2005: 533–4) offer a more detailed explanation:

> [Transphobia entails] … emotional disgust toward individuals who do not conform to society's gender expectations; [and transphobia] … involves the feeling of revulsion to masculine women, feminine men, cross-dressers, transgenderists, and/or transsexuals. Specifically, transphobia manifests itself in the fear that personal acquaintances may be trans or disgust upon encountering a trans person … the 'phobia' suffix is used to imply an irrational fear or hatred, one that is at least partly perpetuated by cultural ideology.

These ideas are developed via Hill and Willoughby's own 'Genderism and Transphobia Scale', which suggests that this irrational fear or hatred towards trans people is made up of three strands: genderism (an ideology that subordinates those who do not conform to gender norms), which causes transphobia (fear and disgust of trans people) which, in turn, results in what they term 'gender bashing' (the abuse and harassment of gender 'non-conformists' (2005: 533–4 – see Case Study 5.1). The scale is particularly helpful as it incorporates the importance of wider societal attitudes and prejudices that dominate as a form of 'cultural ideology'. Meanwhile, a very succinct practitioner-oriented definition is supplied by the College of Policing (2014: 4) which classifies a transphobic hate crime as: 'Any criminal offence which is perceived, by the victim or any other person, to be motivated by a hostility or prejudice against a person who is transgender or perceived to be transgender'. Those covered by this definition include 'People who are transsexual, transgender, transvestite and those who hold a gender recognition certificate under the Gender Recognition Act 2004' (2014: 4).

Nature and extent of transphobic hate crime

Transphobic hate crime has been recognised as one of the monitored strands of hate crime by police forces in England and Wales since 2008 and has been covered by the Crime Survey for England and Wales (CSEW) since 2009. However, reliable data regarding transphobic hate crime are still surprisingly hard to come by, with the CSEW, for example, admitting that the numbers of transphobic offences showing up in its survey are so low as to make accurate estimates of them impossible, even though anecdotal evidence suggests that victims of transphobia can be targeted over 50 times per year (Antjoule, 2013: 3). Police figures show that there were 309 transphobic hate crimes during 2011/12 and 361 for 2012/13, just one per cent of the total of recorded hate crimes (Home Office et al., 2013: 19). Of the 361, just under half were recorded as 'lower-level' public order offences while nearly a third were violence against the person (Home Office et al., 2013: Appendix Table 2.03).

The incidence of transphobic victimisation may be higher than for other forms of hate crime, with many transgendered people experiencing the 'pervasive and everyday presence of violence' that often goes unreported to the police (Moran and Sharpe, 2004: 396). Like other forms of hate crime, the prevalence of transphobic incidents is hard to gauge as trans victims are reluctant to engage with the criminal justice system (Duggan, 2014; HM Government, 2011). Community surveys have therefore been useful in developing a picture of trans victimisation, although it is interesting to note that a number of the surveys discussed in Chapter 4 were of 'LGBT' people (and not solely gay groups), meaning that the transgender experience is often subsumed under the LGBT umbrella and its specificities lost. It therefore makes direct comparisons between these different minorities – based on sexuality on the one hand, and gender/sex on the other – difficult.

There is also less research on the transgendered experience of hate crime compared to other hate victim groups. A useful starting point though is Turner et al.'s finding, from their online survey of around 2,700 trans people from across Europe, that nearly 80% had 'experienced some form of harassment in public, ranging from transphobic comments to physical or sexual abuse', with 83% of English respondents being victimised in this way (Turner et al., 2009: 1). The most common forms of harassment were verbal, including unsolicited comments (44%) and abuse (27%). Similar high rates of victimisation were uncovered in Morton's survey (2008) of the experiences of transgendered people in Scotland, which found just over 60% of respondents reported being a victim of harassment. The study also revealed that just under a fifth had endured violence, four out of ten had been subjected to threatening behaviour and one in twenty had been sexually assaulted (see Case Study 5.2 for an analysis of transphobic murder). Bettcher's work (2007: 46) found that around 80% of transgendered people have been victims of verbal transphobic abuse and 30% to almost half had suffered some form of physical assault, slightly higher than some of the surveys of homophobic harassment mentioned in Chapter 4. Furthermore, evidence suggests that trans people can be victimised on almost a daily basis (Chakraborti et al., 2014a), while the Government Equalities Office's (2011) survey of nearly 1,300 trans people revealed that nearly half (47%) said they were most worried about being a victim of a violent crime or harassment, and that they feared most for their safety on the streets and using public transport.

There is also the suggestion that rates of victimisation can vary according to social class, income, education and ethnicity, with minority ethnic trans people or those more economically marginalised or with less formal qualifications suffering higher rates of victimisation (Lombardi, 2009). Furthermore, participants in Turner et al.'s (2009) research felt that MTF transsexuals had worse experiences of transphobic hate crime than FTM, which could be due to the fact that they pose a more significant challenge to society's ideas of both heteronormativity and gender hierarchies than FTM transsexuals. It may also be due to them having more difficulty passing in their chosen gender, meaning that, for some, they 'stand out', even if they were not aware of it themselves. This is evident in the comments below, expressed by a trans woman during the course of the Leicester Hate Crime Project (Chakraborti et al., 2014a):

> The idea that people are shouting abuse at you, or that you are being labelled, [means that] it does play on your mind that you're clearly standing out. And that's the thing that will play, that I must stand out. I'd thought that I'd actually disappeared into the background, but I must stand out.

Typical of the experiences of trans people are those of a transgendered woman in Liverpool, who reported being verbally abused, threatened, having her windows smashed and her car set on fire (Kidd and Witten, 2008). Suffering such harassment can cause trans people to leave where they live, as one victim told the Scottish Transgender Alliance:

I had to move out of the town I was staying in due to violent, intolerant people in the area, including my immediate neighbours. I had people physically accost me in the street in the middle of the day, comments made in the supermarket when minding my own business, things smashed up in my back garden. I feared for my own personal safety so much I was restricted to my flat on many occasions for weeks or even months on end. (Morton, 2008: 11)

Thus, whilst being 'out' carries a greater risk of violence for all LGBT groups, this risk may be higher for those transsexual individuals who do not visibly conform to society's accepted notions of how males and females should look, and therefore experience 'regular and extreme levels of physical and verbal abuse' (Johnson et al., 2007: 18). Such harassment may go unrecorded in official statistics as transphobic incidents may be misrecorded as homophobic ones or the victim's transgendered status may be misunderstood or ignored. As Bettcher (2007: 54) argues:

It is precisely the fact that transpeople often do not have their self-identifications taken seriously that is so deeply bound up with transphobic hostility and violence. How can we ignore the fact that often 'transgender woman' simply means 'man disguised as a woman' to so many people?[3]

The impact of being targeted may be deeper for trans victims than for those of other forms of hate crime, with those in Williams and Tregidga's research ten times more likely to have had suicidal thoughts after being abused than other hate crime victim groups (Williams and Tregidga, 2013: 10, 19). As a trans woman in Perry and Dyck's (2014: 192) research stated, being constantly victimised can severely damage mental health:

My feeling was that I was never safe anywhere and that led to being very reclusive, isolating, which then tied in with severe depression and suicide attempts ... the subjective experience of safety is radically altered by those experiences you have ... even just harassment, bullying, ridiculing and mocking takes a tremendous toll on us.

These difficulties can be compounded by other factors that are unique to the transgender experience. For example, a victim's sense of self-worth can be further dented by the fact that those who want gender reassignment surgery are classified as having gender identity disorders, and therefore psychiatrists still regulate gender reassignment processes, which can damage self-esteem and self-acceptance (Johnson et al., 2007). The victim therefore has to cope with the trauma of experiencing a hate incident whilst also coping with the stigma of being 'pathologised'. It is no surprise therefore to note that studies that focus specifically on transgendered people have found elevated rates of suicide and self-harming behaviour in adolescents and adults (Haas et al., 2010).

Case Study 5.2

Transphobic murder

In October 2013 28-year-old Romy Maynard was jailed for life after being convicted of murdering 22-year-old Chrissie Azzopardi in Finsbury Park, north London, in April 2012. Azzopardi, who was due to undergo gender reassignment surgery, was found dead in her flat after being stabbed twice by Maynard in what the prosecuting counsel described as a 'swift and brutal killing' (Press Association, 2013). The murder had chilling echoes of another that occurred in London, this time in 2009, when 29-year-old trans woman Destiny Lauren was the victim of a murder described by the Metropolitan Police as 'brutal and pre-meditated' (BBC News, 2011b).

Both these killings highlight the extreme nature of violent transphobic incidents and also the worrying prevalence of the murder of trans people internationally (Kidd and Witten, 2008). For example, the Trans Murder Monitoring Project reported 238 killings of trans people worldwide in the 12 months between November 2012 and November 2013 and that, in total, from January 2008 to March 2014, it had recorded 1,509 similar murders, prompting the project to suggest that the word 'transcide' be employed to denote the 'continuously elevated level of deadly violence against trans people on a global scale' (Transgender Europe, 2014: 1). The same organisation also noted an alarming number of cases in 2013 in which victims had been under 18 years old, including two separate murders of 13-year-old trans girls in Brazil and that of a 16-year-old in Jamaica, who had attended a party in female clothing only to be chased and then brutally killed by a mob who violently objected to her trans status (Transgender Europe, 2013: 1).

Juang (2006) estimates that there are roughly two killings of transsexuals reported each month in the United States, while attacks upon, and murders of, trans people are 'regular' in North America (Hill and Willoughby, 2005: 531). Some of these killings have gained international attention, with perhaps the most infamous of these (as it inspired the 1999 film *Boys Don't Cry*) being the 'execution style' shooting of Brandon Teena (a FTM transgendered person) in rural Nebraska in 1993. It is of deep concern, though, that while this film brought the victimisation of trans people welcome global recognition, the types of prejudice featured within it, that fuel the violent victimisation of trans communities worldwide, are still very evident over fifteen years on.

Legal protection from transphobic hate crime

Until relatively recently there was a stark disparity between the protection offered to transgendered victims of hate under the law and that provided to other recognised hate victim groups. However, from December 2012 section 65 (9) of the Legal Aid, Sentencing and Punishment of Offenders Act 2012 amended Schedule 21 of the Criminal Justice Act 2003 so that enhanced sentences can be applied to offences that are aggravated by hostility on the grounds of transgender identity, putting punishment for these crimes on the same footing as those aggravated by hostility towards disability and sexual orientation. No provision was made, though, for the creation of separate 'aggravated offences' like those that exist for racist or faith-hate crimes. The amendment also provides for a starting point of 30 years for the minimum term for a life sentence for murder aggravated on the grounds of the victim's transgender identity, offering the same protection as that afforded to the other recognised strands. In Scotland, the Sentencing of Offences Aggravated by Prejudice (Scotland) Act 2009 provides for additional sentencing tariffs if the hostility towards the victim is based upon their transgendered status.

However, an anomaly still exists with regard to offences relating to 'stirring up hatred' against trans people. While section 74 of the Criminal Justice and Immigration Act 2008 makes the incitement of hatred on the grounds of someone's sexual orientation an offence, this section does not cover incitement based upon someone's transgendered status.[4] Interestingly, the Law Commission's (2014) review into the existing protection offered by the various strands of hate crime legislation concluded that it had not been persuaded of the practical need to extend the stirring up hatred provisions to include transgender identity. The Commission justified this decision by arguing that 'the type of hate speech typically found in relation to ... transgender status is far less likely to satisfy the requirements for a stirring up offence than that found in relation to race and religion', meaning that there would be 'still fewer' successful prosecutions under this strand than for the already existing ones (2014: 209). In relation to aggravated offences, the Commission recommended that a further, government-sponsored review of existing aggravated offences legislation should be undertaken, rather than suggesting that the aggravated offences be extended to include transgender identity. Only if the government declined to undertake this commitment did the Commission recommend, very much as an 'option two', that those offences be extended that way (2014: 126).

Transphobic and homophobic victimisation compared

As noted above, the specificities of the transgendered experience of hate crime have often been lost due to the propensity of practitioners and academics to employ the broad 'LGBT' category under which sexual and gender minorities are subsumed.[5] This practice carries the inherent assumption that lesbian, gay, bisexual and transgendered populations have sufficient commonalities to be thought of as a unified LGBT 'grouping', and that by extension the nature of their victimisation is also similar. Indeed, there is some evidence that, by not 'doing gender properly', LGB and transgendered people may be victimised for broadly the same reason: that they do not conform to gender or sexual norms. Namaste

(2006) argues that the public often confuses gender and sexuality, and that if the perception of gender dissidence informs homophobic harassment, then those individuals who live outside of normative sex/gender relations, whether they be lesbian, gay or transgender, will be most at risk of assault. Furthermore, Namaste contends that gay men behaving effeminately are at a much higher risk of homophobic violence than those who behave in a 'masculine' way (2006: 588).

Tomsen and Mason (2001) suggest that much homophobic violence directed against lesbians and gay men is *gendered* and is mainly perpetrated by men seeking to preserve the dominant status of masculinity within society's gendered hierarchy. Violence directed against lesbians and gay men is fuelled by perceptions that they are not performing gender roles 'correctly' (either by being 'butch' lesbians or effeminate men, for example), rather than by hatred against gay people *per se*. These types of biases can fuel transphobia too, with those who are prejudiced against lesbians and gay men also exhibiting similar but even stronger feelings towards trans people (Norton and Herek, 2012).

As the evidence in this chapter and Chapter 4 has shown, the effects of transphobic and homophobic harassment may also be similar, with LGB and transgendered victims feeling isolated, depressed and anxious. However, Johnson et al. (2007) suggest that these feelings can be heightened for transgendered victims, who are more likely to be homeless, to self-harm or to feel suicidal. Moreover, for those transgendered people who have difficultly passing in their chosen gender, the risk of hate-related harassment may be higher than for gay groups and incidents may be more extreme (Turner et al., 2009).

Therefore, whether it is appropriate to employ an all-inclusive LGBT banner under which the experiences of victims of homophobic and transphobic hate crimes can be grouped has been the subject of much debate, especially as such a broad label may mask the complexity and diversity of those communities subsumed within it, and the 'ableism, ageism, biphobia, "fatphobia", racism and transphobia' that may exist in and between groups (Formby, 2012: 5). Importantly, there is some survey evidence to suggest that around one in five trans people have experienced discriminatory behaviour *from LGB people* (Keogh et al., 2006; our emphasis). Other research suggests that each individual subgroup within the LGBT bracket experiences different forms of prejudice from within that grouping, and that this prejudice is most evident in lesbian feminist circles directed toward trans women (Morrison, 2010).

Social and political pressures may also create tensions, with some gay rights activists viewing bisexual and transgendered individuals as being detrimental to their pursuit of gaining wider societal acceptance and equality for gay people. Part of this campaign involves, in some instances, the constructing of 'more acceptable' gay identities that are sold to wider society as being 'just like everyone else but with a same sex partner', and that individuals who identify as transgendered or bisexual are an unwelcome challenge to this 'safe' image (Weiss, 2003). Stone

(2009), meanwhile, found that gay men were less likely than lesbians to be empathetic towards transgendered individuals while lesbians were ambivalent to the inclusion of the 'T' within the LGBT acronym. Therefore, while a certain amount of security can be found under the LGBT banner, this feeling of like-mindedness and solidarity does 'not necessarily mean similarity' (Formby, 2012: 5) and can be accompanied by the ostracising of those, like transgendered people, who may challenge the group's notions of harmony (Bornstein, 2006).

Richardson and Monro (2012) also suggest that the 'B' and 'T' populations within the LGBT 'whole' are 'marginalised', and that 'some lesbians and gay men attempt to disassociate from trans people, and/or refuse to accept that bisexuality exists, or are overtly transphobic or biphobic' (2012: 43). This biphobia can be rooted in, among other things, perceptions that bisexuals can access 'heterosexual privilege' (that is denied to lesbians and gay men), that they are 'parasitical' to gay communities, or that they are, in the eyes of lesbian feminists, apolitical and a 'cop out' (2012: 18). However, for all the divisions that may exist between certain parts of the LGBT 'community', the commonalities in the nature of the hate-related victimisation suffered by the different lesbian, gay, bisexual and transgendered groups should not be forgotten. Their experiences, though, can best be understood if the multiple facets of their identities (including sexuality, age, disability and ethnicity) are fully acknowledged when considering an individual's risk of being targeted. For example, Bettcher (2007) suggests that minority ethnic transsexuals suffer higher rates of transphobic victimisation than their white equivalents, an interesting point that also raises the issue of intersectionality: the idea that individual identities should not be understood and defined solely under one label based upon one facet of that person (such as their sexuality or transgendered status), but rather it is the *intersection* of their many different identity aspects that is most important. By acknowledging this, simplistic assumptions about the nature of transphobic victimisation can be avoided.

Conclusion

The chapter began by assessing issues of gender, sex and sexuality, and how their multifaceted relationships can have implications for the study of transphobic and homophobic hate crime. Of particular relevance was the idea that gender might not be a natural 'given' based upon biology, but instead may be a socially constructed and performative phenomenon that can be lived or enacted in many different ways. The challenge posed by queer theorists to traditional notions of gender, sex and sexuality was also discussed, especially within the context of those 'gender variants', like transgendered and transsexual people, who do not conform to conventional understandings of gendered and sexed roles. The impact of transphobic hate crime was then outlined, and it was suggested that it can be more severe than other forms of hate crime, and an especially pertinent problem for those male-to-female transsexuals who have difficulty in passing as female.

Some commentators feel that gender is central to the perpetration of homophobic and transphobic violence, encapsulated in the concept of the perpetrator as a 'gender defender', whose fear and hatred of anyone who contravenes gender norms cause them to 'lash out' at gender or sexual 'outsiders', thus perpetuating 'the violence of male privilege and all its social extensions' (Bornstein, 2006: 237). Both Perry (2001) and Willoughby et al. (2010) also identify perpetrators' desire to assert their own aggressive heterosexual masculinity as a motivating force behind homophobic and transphobic hate crime, a notion that has some resonance in discussions of domestic abuse (see Chapter 7).

Important though these ideas are, they do not paint the whole picture of transphobic victimisation, as it was noted earlier that some trans victims experience hostility and harassment from those within their own LGBT 'community'. This is not to suggest that the vast majority of hostility that trans people face does not come from those outside this grouping and nor is there any sense of 'blaming' already marginalised and targeted groups for the daily abuse that blights the lives of trans people. Rather, hostility originating from within the LGBT grouping merely reflects the complexities of these 'communities within communities' which can sometimes manifest themselves in suspicion and resentment that undermines notions of unity generated through shared experiences of hate crime victimisation. For trans victims, whose experience of hate can be particularly relentless and on rare occasions extreme, it must be especially disappointing to realise that even some fellow 'outsiders' may not welcome their presence.

Guide to further reading

Elliot's *Debates in Transgender, Queer, and Feminist Theory* (2010) and Richardson and Monro's *Sexuality, Equality and Diversity* (2012) provide an excellent overview of research and theoretical debates in this area. The campaigning organisation Press for Change has produced a very useful overview of transphobia in the EU in *Transphobic Hate Crime in the European Union* (2009).

Links to online material

The Gender Identity Research and Education Society (GIRES) provides a wealth of very useful information and advice regarding gender identity concerns at www.gires.org.uk/. Two other similar organisations, Press for Change at www.pfc.org.uk/ and The Beaumont Trust at www.beaumont-trust.org.uk/, also offer help and guidance on a range of transitioning and legal issues. Meanwhile, some fascinating insights on trans issues can be found within Juliet Jacques' blog at http://julietjacques.blogspot.co.uk/.

Notes

1 It is estimated that although around 12,500 people have sought medical care for gender variance in the UK the number of adults who experience some degree of gender variance could be as high as 500,000 (GIRES, 2011: 1).

2 As the debate surrounding these terms is so complex, and remains unresolved, they will be used interchangeably.

3 In 2014, for example, senior executives at the *Sun* newspaper agreed to meet with Dr Kate Stone, a trans woman, after she had lodged a complaint with the Press Complaints Commission following references in the press to her as 'Sex-swap Kate' and the 'Sex-swap Scientist' after she inadvertently hit the headlines after being gored by a stag in 2013 (Conrad, 2014).

4 Other legal developments have undoubtedly provided further steps forward in the trans communities' struggle for equal rights under the law, including the Gender Recognition Act 2004, which enables trans people to obtain a birth certificate in their new gender and also marry in that gender, and the Equality Act 2010, which makes it unlawful to discriminate against someone while they are in the process of gender reassignment and when they have fully transitioned.

5 It should be acknowledged here that 'LGB and T' is the preferred term for some as it highlights the 'separate but linked' social circumstances of transgendered people, while others favour 'LGBTQ' (with the 'Q' standing for 'queer' or those 'questioning' their sexuality) or even LGBTQI (where the 'I' denotes 'intersex' – see Richardson and Monro, 2012).

6

DISABLIST HATE CRIME

Chapter summary

This chapter assesses the forms and impact of disablist victimisation, a type of hate crime that has only recently started to receive the attention it deserves from the criminal justice system and academics. Prior to this, disablist harassment and violence were routinely misunderstood by agencies within the criminal justice system, who misinterpreted these as 'motiveless' anti-social behaviour. Through its assessment of the nature of disablist hate crime and its impacts upon those with physical disabilities, learning difficulties and those who suffer mental ill-health, the chapter notes that disablist hate crime has a number of distinguishing features that set it apart from other forms of hate victimisation.

The chapter goes on to discuss the concept of vulnerability and how it relates to disablist victimisation. The troubling problem of 'cuckooing', which can especially affect those with learning difficulties, is also examined. Developments in legal provisions relating to disablist hate crime are assessed, and it is argued that while gains have been made in this regard the inequalities that still exist are an unfortunate reminder of the relative position of victims of disablist hate crime within the broader hate debate.

Introduction

The Equality Act 2010 defines a person as disabled if they have a 'physical or mental impairment and that impairment has a substantial and long-term negative impact' on someone's ability to perform normal day-to-day activities.[1] As we have seen with the other recognised hate crime 'strands' in earlier chapters, the terminology and nomenclature employed when discussing minority communities and their victimisation are hotly contested. In the field of disability studies, scholars commonly employ the social model of disability, which 'distinguishes between impairment – the difference between body, brain and intellect – and disability, which is seen as the range of barriers that confront people with impairments' (Roulstone and Mason-Bish, 2013: 2), including structural disadvantage and discrimination, negative and aggressive attitudes and media hostility. In other words, possessing impairments does not in itself make someone disabled, but society's prejudice coupled with the barriers that those with impairments face can make them so. The range of negative attitudes and actions towards disability contained within this framework is captured in the term 'disablism', defined as:

> the social exclusion, marginalisation, prejudice, and discrimination experienced by disabled people ... [I]t occurs through stereotypical attitudes and prejudices and is reproduced in social institutions such as the media, the built environment, educational institutions, religions, and even the family. (Sherry, 2010: 22–3)

The term 'disablist hate crime' is therefore preferred here to 'disability hate crime', as it moves the focus away from the victim's impairments and the implicit suggestion that they somehow precipitated their victimisation, towards the prejudice behind the action. It is worth noting here too that disabled communities are diverse, complex and multi-layered, and that individuals may be subject to hostility targeted towards not just their disability but other aspects of their identity, such as ethnicity and sexual orientation, too. Any discussions of disablist hate crime therefore need to be informed by this understanding.

Nature and extent of disablist hate crime

Disabled people are at greater risk of hate-related victimisation than the non-disabled population, and are more likely to be victims of other crimes and to have a higher fear of crime (Coleman et al., 2013). In a similar fashion to the other officially recognised forms of hate crime, the criminal justice system's understanding of disablist hate crime is victim orientated, with the College of Policing (2014: 21) defining it as:

> any criminal offence which is perceived by the victim or any other person, to be motivated by hostility or prejudice based on a person's disability or perceived disability.

Therefore (and in common thematically with the other definitions of officially recognised hate incidents) if the victim or anyone else believes an incident to have been motivated by disablist hostility, then the police are obliged to record and investigate it as such. In 2012/13, and within the context of an austerity climate in the UK that had seen disabled people labelled as 'benefit scroungers' by a sometimes hostile tabloid press and some politicians, the police recorded 1,841 disability hate crimes, compared with 1,757 offences the previous year (a 5% increase).[2] Disablist hate crimes accounted for 4% of all hate crimes recorded by the police in 2012/13, although, interestingly, they were represented much more significantly in the Crime Survey for England and Wales, as 22% of all hate crimes at around 62,000 incidents per year for 2011/12 and 2012/13 (Home Office et al., 2013: 22).

The figure from the Crime Survey for England and Wales may offer a more accurate estimate, as victimisation rates for people with disabilities are worryingly high. For example, more than half of the disabled people who responded to Scope's online survey said they had experienced hostility, aggression or violence from a stranger because of their condition or impairment (ComRes, 2011), while over nine out of ten disabled victims surveyed by the Leicester Hate Crime Project had suffered verbal abuse and a similar number had experienced bullying or threatening behaviour (Chakraborti et al., 2014b: 6–7). Half of this sample had been the victim of violent crime while a fifth had been subjected to sexual violence at least once, with those who had been targeted because of their mental ill-health especially at risk (2014b: 6–7).

It is worth noting, though, that disabled victims of hate crime may be targeted due to multiple identity markers or characteristics, including dress and appearance, ethnicity, age, faith, gender, health condition or illness, or sexual orientation. Women and younger people may suffer a higher risk of being victimised, as do those with learning disabilities or mental ill-health (Chakraborti et al., 2014b; Office for Disability Issues, 2011). In the face of this evidence it is of concern that many agencies view hate-related victimisation in a simplistic way, with victims categorised into discreet groups that fail to acknowledge any intersectional identities that may have been targeted by the perpetrator. Furthermore, as the EHRC reports (2011), when the Metropolitan Police reanalysed its data on racist and homophobic victimisation it discovered that a disproportionate number of these victims were also disabled.

Disablist hate crime can take many forms, ranging from murder, sexual violence and abuse to theft and fraud, bullying, domestic violence, property crime, verbal abuse and harassment. Those around disabled people, such as carers, family members and even assistance dogs can be targeted too, as well as their wheelchairs and other equipment (EHRC, 2011). Police figures show that a third of disablist hate crimes involved violence against the person, the second highest of the five monitored strands after sexual orientation. Compared to the other forms of hate crime, the 'other notifiable offences' category was much higher: 20% compared to an average of 4% across all strands (Home Office et al., 2013: 26), indicating the disproportionate way that disabled people suffer sexual abuse as well as theft and fraud, which are all included in this 'other' category.

At the extreme end of the victimisation 'scale' are murders of disabled people. Most of the murders investigated by the EHRC for its *Hidden in Plain Sight* report (2011) featured shocking cases of abuse and torture of the victims yet, worryingly, almost all were not prosecuted as disablist offences. These concerns are reflected in Quarmby's (2011) examination of a range of disablist killings which, she argues, were not 'motiveless' at all, but instead were 'reactive, angry crimes' (2011: 237)[3] that have a number of similarities, including the victim being burnt, scalded or otherwise tortured, or being urinated on or humiliated in other ways (see Case Study 6.1). Quarmby argues that in the majority of these cases the police, judges and journalists referred to them as 'senseless' and 'motiveless', seemingly unable, or unwilling, to acknowledge their disablist element. Importantly, evidence suggests that the trauma involved with being targeted for verbal abuse or harassment can be heightened due to victims' awareness of the murders of disabled people that have made the news headlines (Chakraborti et al., 2014a). That such cases are not flagged by the criminal justice system as hate crimes is therefore significant, as these decisions can affect a feeling of security and the well-being of the wider community.

Case Study 6.1

The persecution and killing of Bijan Ebrahimi

The murder of 44-year-old Bijan Ebrahimi in Brislington, Bristol, on 14 July 2013 was the culmination of years of bullying and harassment of Ebrahimi by many of those that lived on his estate. Ebrahimi, an Iranian national with physical disabilities who moved to Britain in 2001, was racially abused on a daily basis after he settled in Brislington in 2007, something that he reported repeatedly to Avon and Somerset Police (Morris, 2013). His property was also targeted, including the hanging baskets outside his flat that were his pride and joy. In an effort to collate evidence about this vandalism, Ebrahimi took a number of photographs of people gathering outside his flat, but this was misinterpreted by local residents as the actions of a paedophile taking pictures of children (disturbingly, disabled people are often the subjects of false allegations of paedophilia – Sin et al., 2009). Things came to a head in mid-July 2013 when a group of around 15 people, described as 'hostile ... raw and rabid' by a witness, gathered in a threatening manner outside his flat (BBC, 2013a).

The police were called but inadvertently exacerbated the situation by arresting Ebrahimi, supposedly for his own safety. Once released he returned to his home but was again the victim of sustained abuse, which he reported to the police, saying that he was being called 'nasty things and didn't feel safe' in an email that went unread by officers until after his death (Morris, 2013). Ebrahimi was effectively under siege in his own home. A few days later two members of the vigilante mob that had earlier terrorised him, Lee James and Stephen Norley, returned to his address. James targeted Ebrahimi with a vicious assault that knocked him to the floor, where he repeatedly stamped on his victim's head. Once Ebrahimi became unconscious, James was assisted by Norley in dragging his body to a piece of grassed land around 100 yards away, where it was set on fire. The post mortem revealed that Ebrahimi died either as a consequence of receiving multiple blows to his head, or from asphyxiation after inhaling blood. He was already dead when he was set on fire (*Bristol Post*, 2013).

At the subsequent trial James was found guilty of murder and given a life sentence with a minimum term of eighteen years, while Norley received four years after admitting to helping to burn the body. However, these sentences disappointed and frustrated disability campaigning groups, who felt that the court should have acknowledged that James' actions had been motivated by hostility towards Ebrahimi's disability and therefore he should have received a minimum tariff of 30 years for murder under the provisions of the Criminal Justice Act 2003. The CPS, however, felt differently, finding no evidence that James was motivated in such a way (BBC, 2013b).

One of the puzzling aspects of this awful case was the way that the police failed to protect someone who, by virtue of living alone on a troubled estate and being disabled and 'foreign', was in an extremely vulnerable situation. This is especially troubling as the police were aware that he had been the repeated recipient of racist harassment. Another disappointing aspect was the failure of the court to recognise the racist and disablist nature of the hostility directed towards Ebrahimi, something that has chilling echoes of the treatment of another man with disabilities, Brent Martin, who was murdered on a similarly poor and marginalised estate in Sunderland in 2005. In the eight years between the cases it seemed as though little had changed regarding the criminal justice system's (in)ability to recognise disablism, protect victims and sentence offenders appropriately.

A relatively new facet of disablist hate crime is cyberbullying, which includes the ridicule, abuse or harassment of disabled people via social networking sites, online forums or text messaging. The anonymity offered by online message boards, coupled with the possibility of 'performing' in front of a wider audience than would normally be the case when the perpetrator is sharing the same physical space as the victim, has led to a proliferation of disablist cyber abuse, with disabled young people experiencing more of it, over a longer period of time, than non-disabled people of the same age (EHRC, 2011).

Another form of cyberbullying is the physical and/or sexual abuse of the disabled victim which is then photographed or filmed on mobile phones for later posting on Facebook, Twitter or video sites such as YouTube. In a notorious case in Melbourne, Australia, in 2006, for instance, a girl with learning disabilities was indecently assaulted, urinated upon and then set on fire by 12 boys, who also forced her to perform oral sex on two of them. The whole episode was filmed and then posted later on YouTube. While the teenage victim was traumatised for months by the incident, all of the eight boys charged with various offences avoided a custodial sentence (Sherry, 2010: 5–6). In a number of disablist murders in the UK (including those of Brent Martin and Christine Lakinski) 'trophy' photos or videos have also been taken of the victim, further demeaning them.

Another recent manifestation of disablist hate crime that has received a degree of attention over the last few years is that of 'cuckooing', which involves a disabled person (usually someone with learning disabilities or mental ill-health) who is living on their own being 'befriended' by someone who appears to be a benign or even helpful influence, but in reality has targeted the person in order to use their home for criminal activity. The person selected is often socially isolated and deliberately chosen because of this, as they have no ready-made social network of family or friends who could conceivably step in and help them. Instead, the situation commonly escalates, with the 'target' being physically or mentally abused, or becoming the victim of theft or financial exploitation. They are also often threatened into being too scared to report their circumstances to housing authorities or the police (Doward, 2010).

Therefore, while (as previous chapters have shown) public spaces, buses and trains are common locations for acts of targeted hostility, a disproportionately high amount of disablist incidents occur in the home, and are perpetrated not by strangers but by those whom victims often trust or rely upon – 'friends', carers, health care professionals or family members. Victimisation often takes the form of 'the withholding of food, water, communication and travel aids, money, medication and sanitary aids by placing them out of reach; bullying; sexual assault and rape; violence; torture and murder' (EHRC, 2011: 82), and may be more frequently perpetrated by women than other types of hate crime.

Being targeted in their own home, where they should feel safe and secure, is especially traumatic for victims, who often feel isolated, alone and trapped as they fear that if they go to the police then they will either lose the support of someone they are reliant on, or they will be moved out of their specially adapted home to a care facility. For a number of commentators, moving victims into care homes is a flawed response as it categorises the abuse as a 'care issue' rather than a criminal justice one, and, as the shocking case of Winterbourne View exemplified, may inadvertently expose the victim to institutional abuse.[4]

The impact of these and other forms of disablist hate crimes is felt more severely by victims than those of other forms of hate crime, and especially by those who suffer mental ill-health. Commonly, victims of disablist hate report feeling anxious, mistrustful of others and vulnerable, and unable to participate fully in society in the ways that they would wish (Chakraborti et al., 2014b). Research suggests that disabled victims have a heightened fear of future victimisation too, and are more likely to have suicidal thoughts after being targeted than those in the other hate crime victim strands (Williams and Tregidga, 2013).

Support for victims

Critics of the responses of statutory agencies to disablist hate crime cases allege that that there is a general ignorance within the criminal justice system of the needs and life circumstances of disabled people, which has helped to create a climate between them characterised by a lack of trust and under-reporting of incidents (Sherry, 2010). Lane, Shaw and Kim (2009) suggest that the reluctance to believe that disabled people are victims of hate crime has damaged their trust and confidence in the criminal justice system. As disablist murders are often preceded by patterns of victimisation involving verbal abuse, harassment or bullying, it is paramount that victims are believed if they report hate incidents to the police or other organisations early on in this process.[5] However, as Quarmby (2011) notes, there have been an alarming number of cases, such as that of Michael Gilbert, when a lack of interventionist action by the police has had tragic consequences. Gilbert, who had learning disabilities, reported the abuse he suffered at the hands of a Luton family on at least eight occasions to three different police forces, but no effective action was taken by them (Quarmby, 2011). In the meantime he suffered years of physical and mental violence from the Watts family, which culminated in his murder in 2009.

As noted above, in cases such as these sometimes the victim can be reticent in reporting incidents when the perpetrator is someone close to the them – perhaps a family member, 'friend' or carer – and they fear being further victimised by them, losing care assistance if the perpetrator is apprehended or not being believed by the police or other agencies that they may want to report to (Sin et al., 2009). All too often, disabled people, and especially those with learning disabilities, are not seen as credible witnesses. This is something that victims find intensely frustrating and which, in the long term if no action is taken against those persecuting them, may seriously jeopardise their safety and well-being.

The fallout from the flawed handling by the police and other agencies of the victimisation of Fiona Pilkington and her family was supposed to precipitate a 'watershed' in the ways that victims of disablist hate crime were treated by statutory and voluntary bodies (see Case Study 6.2). Although there is some evidence of the police taking the issue more seriously by providing a better service to victims, these improvements have been somewhat sporadic and uneven, leading some to question the amount of progress that has been made since the Pilkington case (Chakraborti et al., 2014a). Others argue that responses have failed to recognise disablist hate crime for what it is, and instead of launching criminal investigations into incidents, agencies decide to take the health and social care route by restructuring the care offered to victims (Sheikh et al., 2010). While this may be helpful in some regards, in other ways it is not as it fails to result in the criminal prosecution of perpetrators of hate (Sin, 2012).

Case Study 6.2

The Fiona Pilkington case: a catalogue of police failings

The policing of hate crime is a complex and often controversial issue, with a number of victim communities historically reluctant to report incidents to the police (see Chapter 9). However, following the publication of the 1999 Macpherson Report (which severely criticised the Metropolitan Police Service for the way it had conducted its investigation into Stephen Lawrence's racist murder), there appeared to be a new determination within the police to provide a better service to hate crime victims. However, within a decade of the report's publication the police attracted further opprobrium over their treatment of a family experiencing hate crime victimisation in a case that 'sent out shock waves across police forces all over England and Wales' (HMCPSI et al., 2013: 10).

The case itself centred around the events of 23 October 2007, when 38-year-old Fiona Pilkington killed both herself and her daughter Francecca ('Frankie') Hardwick in a lay-by in Leicestershire by setting alight to the car they were both occupying. She had taken such drastic action after having endured seven years of constant verbal and physical disablist harassment from youths who lived in the same town as her, Barwell. Frankie had 'severe to profound multiple learning difficulties' and the 'functioning of a 3–4-year-old' while Fiona's son, Anthony, had special educational needs (IPCC, 2011: 22). Yet, while the family and neighbours contacted the police at least 33 times to report these incidents the police failed to adequately deal with them, failed to liaise properly with other local agencies that should also have been helping the family, and above all, failed to protect them. In the four suicide notes left by Fiona she spoke of how disillusioned she was with the police's treatment of her and her family.

Typical of the hate incidents targeted at the family, and how they were handled by police, was one that occurred on 13 October 2006, when Fiona's mother, Mrs Cassell, reported to the police that Anthony had been injured in a physical assault by local youths. After a series of phone calls from the police to Mrs Cassell cancelling, rearranging or apologising for not being able to make meetings with her, officers finally attended the Pilkingtons' house on 21 October. The police incident system was subsequently updated to say that the incident was 'not as reported' and was just 'neighbourhood problems with local kids' (IPCC, 2011: 67). Noting that the police took eight days to properly respond to the assault, the IPCC (2011: 68) concluded that there was no evidence that the police had generated a crime report or had even spoken to the alleged assailants. The IPCC continued by stating that: 'It is difficult to understand why this situation was allowed to occur bearing in mind Fiona Pilkington's son was a repeat victim of crime, [and also] his age and vulnerability' (2011: 68).

The despair that Fiona Pilkington felt, which eventually led her to take the tragic actions that she did, was driven by a feeling that the police, and other agencies, were not providing her and her family with the kind of protection that they needed. At the subsequent 2009 inquest into Fiona and her daughter's deaths the jury delivered a 'damning verdict' on Leicestershire Constabulary and the local borough council, ruling that they bore some responsibility for their deaths (Brookes, 2013: 131). The investigation into Leicestershire Police's handling of the case by the IPCC was very critical of many aspects of the force's conduct, noting that officers had failed to recognise that the family had repeatedly been targeted due to Frankie and Anthony's learning disabilities. The IPCC concluded that:

> Although Fiona Pilkington and her family were clearly vulnerable for a number of reasons it should not be overlooked in the first instance that Fiona Pilkington was a member of the local community who was reporting incidents of crime and anti-social behaviour and simply asking the police to carry out their responsibilities. Ultimately, Leicestershire Constabulary failed in delivering those responsibilities. (IPCC, 2011: 179)

Tied in with this, issues around disability and notions of 'vulnerability' have become an especially contested area within disability studies, with some commentators objecting to the conflation of disability with vulnerability as it can give the impression that disabled people are inherently 'weak', helpless and in need of sympathy and pity (Roulstone and Sadique, 2013; Thomas, 2011). Notwithstanding these concerns, problems surrounding the safeguarding of adults deemed to be vulnerable have become increasingly prominent within the hate crime debate in recent years. Safeguarding – the protecting of those with care and support needs from abuse and neglect – has traditionally been the responsibility of dedicated multi-agency teams that are under the aegis of local authorities. Policies relating to safeguarding have, however, been the subject of much criticism from disability rights campaigners who argue that they have failed to make the link between hate crime, safeguarding and the perpetration of such offences by those close to the victim, such as carers (Lane et al., 2009). This lack of understanding of the nature of disablist hate crime, coupled with confusion regarding the roles and responsibilities of those involved, has resulted in misguided and flawed approaches to dealing with hate crime cases. If a tragedy ensues, there has been no mandate for local authorities to undertake serious case reviews into the deaths of vulnerable adults.

The advent of the Care Act 2014 may, however, signal a change for the better in this regard, as for the first time it provides a legal basis under which the local authority Safeguarding Adults Boards can operate, making divisions of roles and responsibilities between agencies mandatory. Such boards also have a duty to enact a Safeguarding Adults Review in cases when an adult with care and support needs dies as a result of abuse or neglect and where there is concern about how one of the agencies with responsibility for their care behaved. Time will tell, of course, just how effective these new arrangements will be, but at least they are a signifier for progressive change in the way that victims of disablist hate crime are treated.

Legal protection from disablist hate crime

The last two decades have seen people with disabilities gain legal safeguards from discrimination which are now encapsulated in the Equality Act 2010.[6]

These groups also have some protection under hate crime legislation through section 146 of the Criminal Justice Act 2003. Whilst this Act does not create new and separate offences 'aggravated by disablism', it nevertheless does contain the provision for enhanced sentencing if hostility based on a victim's actual or perceived disability is seen as an aggravating factor in the commissioning of an offence.[7]

The CPS, in its *Guidance on Prosecuting Cases of Disability Hate Crime*, lists a number of circumstances to be considered when deciding whether hostility towards someone's disability is evident in the offence against them. These include 'serious aggravating factors' (CPS, 2007b: 24) such as 'deliberately setting the victim up for the purposes of humiliation or to be offensive', 'if the victim was particularly vulnerable' and 'if particular distress was caused to the victim or the victim's family'. Despite these provisions, section 146 has been utilised comparatively rarely. One explanation for this may be that there is another, less problematic legal route down which offenders who commit crimes against disabled people can be taken. Advice from the Sentencing Council (2011) encourages courts to impose stiffer sentences upon those found guilty of crimes committed against certain vulnerable groups, including disabled people. Therefore, offences committed against disabled people can be punished with longer sentences without recourse to section 146, which demands the more 'onerous' proof of evidence of disablist hostility. By taking this 'easier' course of action, however, sentencers' reluctance to utilise section 146 represents something of a missed opportunity to 'flag up' genuine acts of disablist hate crime to the wider society.

A further measure of equality under hate crime legislation was afforded by the Legal Aid, Sentencing and Punishment of Offenders Act 2012, which amended Schedule 21 of the Criminal Justice Act 2003 by providing for a starting point of thirty years for the minimum term for a life sentence for murder aggravated on the grounds of the victim's disability (previously it had been fifteen years), bringing it into line with other forms of hate-motivated murders. However, and somewhat perplexingly, there is no provision for protection under any incitement to hatred legislation for disabled people. As this anomaly has caused a degree of consternation amongst some disability rights campaigning groups it was included in the Law Commission's review of hate crime legislation that it undertook during 2013–14 (as noted in earlier chapters). Despite extensive input into the review from a number of academics, practitioners and campaigners who supported equal provision for victims of disablist hate crime, the Commission, perhaps rather disappointingly, decided not to extend the stirring up of hatred provisions to include disability as it had not been persuaded by the practical case to do so. Their decision was based on the arguments that such a provision would prove to be ineffective (as arguably some of the existing incitement provision has proved to be for other strands of hate crime); that the types of 'hate speech' used in relation to disabled people would not satisfy the requirements for such a 'stirring up' offence; that the 'deterrent and communicative effects of the new offences would be very limited indeed'; and that this problem was covered by existing legislation anyway (Law Commission, 2014: 210). A number of campaigning organisations disagreed with this reasoning, including the Disability Hate Crime Network (2014a: 1), who argued that the Commission had missed an opportunity to 'capture a unique, specific and grave type of wrong'.

Conclusion

This chapter has highlighted the nature and extent of disablist hate crime. It has shown that, while this form of hate crime has much in common with others – not least the pernicious effects of verbal abuse and harassment that can do so much to wear down those that suffer them – it also has differences. Some of these – such as the apparently higher rate of perpetration by those who are 'friends', relatives or carers of the victim than for other forms of targeted hostility – have been documented before. Others, such as the development of specific forms of crime, such as cyberbullying or the abuse and exploitation of those with learning disabilities who live alone, need further examination.

That disabled people have become society's scapegoats in the post-2008 austerity era, with a hostile tabloid press and some national and local politicians suggesting that they are 'undeserving' of the state benefits they receive, is a significant development. It is also a cause for concern that there still appears to be an inability amongst some who work within the criminal justice system to recognise the abuse that disabled people have received within this climate as hate crime, rather than 'mindless' anti-social behaviour. In addition, in the wake of the Pilkington case, the fact that only 640 disablist hate crimes were successfully prosecuted during 2012/13, just 6% of the overall total for the five hate crime strands (CPS, 2014: 9), is illustrative of continuing problems with the recognition of disablist hate crime by those within the criminal justice system. Bearing in mind the CSEW estimates that disablist hate crimes constitute 22% of the total for hate offences, this low conviction figure becomes an especially worrying anomaly.

In response to this, Sin (2014) proposes the development and adoption of what he calls a 'layers of influence' model which could result in the wider recognition and successful prosecution of disablist hate crimes. Within this model, Sin suggests that a holistic approach be taken in cases of disablist hostility that entails recognition of the complex interactions and relationships between structure and agency in such cases. This involves developing understandings of the disabled person's circumstances and how they relate to their family, friends and carers (and to the attitudes and behaviours of these people); to organisations and agencies who are responsible either for their care, service provision or for investigating

claims of victimisation; and lastly to the wider society and prevailing attitudes towards disablism. Fully comprehending how these different layers co-exist and influence each other, Sin (2014) argues, offers the opportunity for effective early intervention in cases where a disabled person is being targeted.

For some, however, the current lack of recognition and understanding of disablist hate crime reveals further evidence of the existence of a 'hierarchy of victims' within the criminal justice arena, with some victim groups apparently enjoying a more 'privileged' position than others when it comes to legal protection from hate crime and how their cases are dealt with by the police, CPS and courts. The discrepancies that still exist between the legal provisions offered to victims of racist and disablist hostility, for example, as well as the comparatively small number of convictions for disablist hate crime, may add some credence to this viewpoint. This is not to argue that progress has not been made, as evidenced by, among other things, the recognition given to the specificities of disablist hate crime in the government's Hate Crime 'Action Plan' of 2012, and by the CPS issuing further, detailed guidance on disablist hate crime in 2010. Rather, it is to suggest that despite the higher recent profile of disablist hate crime and the various interventions designed to tackle its causes and effects, the problem is *still* not getting the resources or recognition it requires – and that is a serious cause for concern.

Guide to further reading

While there is a wealth of literature on disability there is only a comparatively small, but growing, body of work on the topic of disablist hate crime itself. An overview of relevant issues is provided by Quarmby in *Scapegoat: Why We Are Failing Disabled People* (2011) and by Roulstone and Mason-Bish's edited collection *Disability, Hate Crime and Violence* (2013). There are also a number of research reports into discrimination and disablism, not least the Equality and Human Rights Commission's important *Hidden in Plain Sight* (EHRC, 2011) and *Crime and Disabled People* (EHRC, 2013). The journal *Disability and Society* provides an in-depth analysis of relevant issues.

Links to online material

Up-to-date news items and discussions of disability issues can be found at the Disability News Service at http://disabilitynewsservice.com/ and at Disability Now's site at www.disabilitynow.org.uk/. Those readers who would like to become more informed about the work of disability campaigning groups should visit the Disability Hate Crime Network site at http://dhcn.info/dhcn/ and Disability Rights UK at http://disabilityrightsuk.org/. More broadly, readers are encouraged to get involved with any of the campaigning groups discussed within this book that they feel are relevant to them. Reading about these issues is all well and good, but supporting the work of those who combat the hurtful effects of hate crime is something we would endorse.

Notes

1 This definition includes people living with HIV/AIDS, cancer or multiple sclerosis. The Disability Living Foundation (2012) states that there are over 10 million people registered as disabled in the UK, with the likelihood of someone becoming disabled increasing with age.

2 For example, Conservative MP Philip Davies argued in 2011 that disabled people should consider working for less than the minimum wage in order to 'help them get on their first rung of the jobs ladder' (Stratton, 2011).

3 Among others, Quarmby (2011) examined the murders of Sean Miles, Keith Philpott, Steven Gale, Michael Gilbert, Raymond Atherton, Barrie-John Horrell, Steven Hoskin, Brent Martin and Kevin Davies.

4 In 2011 a BBC documentary *Undercover Care: The Abused Exposed* revealed the neglect, violence, bullying and verbal abuse that residents (mainly with learning disabilities or autism) of the Winterbourne View care facility near Bristol were being subjected to. The programme resulted in the successful prosecution of 11 of the care workers involved but raised concerns that such abuse may be widespread in care homes (BBC News, 2012; Sin, 2014).

5 Findings from the Leicester Hate Crime Project indicate that victims of disablist hate crime may be six times more likely to report hate incidents to organisations other than the police compared to victims of other strands of hate crime (Chakraborti et al., 2014b).

6 Among the acts that have improved the protected from discrimination provisions for disabled people is the the Disability Discrimination Act 1995, which outlawed direct discrimination against disabled people, and this Act has since been subsequently significantly supplemented and strengthened by the Disability Rights Commission Act 1999, the Special Educational Needs and Disability Act 2001, the Disability Discrimination Act 2005 and the Equality Act 2010. These pieces of legislation now grant disabled people rights in areas such as employment, education, property and accesses to services and facilities.

7 In 2013 Labour MP Ian Mearns tabled the Hate Crime (People with Learning Difficulties and Learning Disabilities) Bill, which had the aim of requiring the police to specifically record hate crimes committed against people with learning difficulties and learning disabilities. Although well intentioned, it caused some controversy as it concerned only some forms of disability and not others. In any case, the Bill ran out of parliamentary time before it could be passed and was shelved.

7

VULNERABILITY, 'DIFFERENCE' AND
GENDERED VIOLENCE

Chapter summary

A significant feature of contemporary hate studies is a growing interest in those forms of harassment and violence that are motivated by hostility towards group identities but are *not* routinely viewed as hate crimes. This chapter examines the factors behind why these victim groups find themselves at the margins of the hate debate even though their victimisation appears to bear all of the hallmarks of that suffered by those groups officially accorded hate crime victim status by the criminal justice system.

After a necessarily brief discussion of relevant theoretical developments the chapter considers the nature of some of these different forms of targeted hostility. Beginning with attacks upon members of alternative subcultures, the chapter then examines the nature, extent and impact of domestic violence, elder abuse and attacks upon sex workers and the homeless. The social circumstances of these types of victimisation, and of the groups targeted, are also assessed. The chapter concludes by examining some of the arguments for and against the inclusion of these groups under an expanded hate crime 'umbrella' and suggests that a framework that reconstitutes the concept of hate crime as 'targeted victimisation' facilitates the necessary theoretical space for their inclusion.

Introduction

The origins of the concept of hate crime are rooted in the recognition in the 1960s in the United States of the shared suffering of those groups, like gay and minority ethnic communities, who found themselves routinely at the receiving end of discrimination, harassment and violence from majority communities

(Gerstenfeld, 2013). The concept was a way of developing a sense of shared solidarity between disparate groups whose historical disadvantage and exclusion were longstanding but who, by uniting behind a concept of hate crime, could draw strength from campaigning for civil rights and equality together.

In the UK the idea of hate crime took a little longer to develop, and has only been in currency for around the last twenty years or so. In this time a suite of legislation has developed which, while applying equally to majority or minority communities, is commonly understood to have been designed with the victimisation of minorities in mind (Hall, 2013). Currently, this legislation includes the 'five strands' of race or ethnicity, religion, sexual orientation, gender identity and disability. In parallel with these developments has been a growth in scholastic interest in the study of hate crime. This body of work has tended to regard the issue in a broadly similar way: that hate crimes 'hurt more' as they are an attack on the victim's identity; they are 'message crimes' as they can affect the victim's wider identity community too; and, importantly for this discussion, are perpetrated by those from dominant social groups against those from historically marginalised and disadvantaged communities that have suffered from discrimination and victimisation for decades, even centuries (Perry, 2001).

However, in the last few years there has been an attempt by some scholars to widen the parameters of the hate debate by considering those that have not been regarded as hate crime victim groups before, or have been pushed to the fringes of discussions. Among these 'new' groups under consideration are the homeless, the elderly, sex workers and members of alternative subcultures. Each of these groups and their experiences of targeted hostility are considered within this chapter. This is not an exhaustive list of these 'borderline' groups though, and indeed a number of the points made in this chapter can be applied to many other victims of hate and prejudice, such as new economic migrants or asylum seekers, of whom a lack of space regretfully prohibits discussion.

Walklate's (2011) broader work on victimisation and vulnerability helps to provide a backdrop for the consideration of the different forms of harassment experienced by these groups, via the concept of 'targeted victimisation'. This concept repositions the debate away from the arena of structural disadvantage and minority group membership towards the targeting of perceived difference and vulnerability (see Chakraborti and Garland, 2012; Walters, 2013). By doing this, priority is given to whether someone is targeted due to hostility towards their identity, or aspects thereof, and whether they are perceived to be in a vulnerable situation, rather than where they are positioned within society's hierarchies. Placed within a 'politics of justice framework' that 'limits protected attributes to forms of difference that have a justifiable claim to affirmation, equality and respect for the attribute that makes them different' (Mason, 2014a: 175 – see Case Study 10.2), it is suggested that targeted victimisation provides a way forward in reconceptualising hate-related harassment and violence.

After a brief discussion of relevant theoretical developments the chapter considers the nature of some of these different forms of targeted victimisation. Beginning with attacks upon members of alternative subcultures, the chapter then examines the nature, extent and impact of domestic violence, elder abuse and attacks upon sex workers and the homeless. The social circumstances of these types of victimisation, and of the groups targeted, are also assessed. The chapter concludes by examining some of the arguments for the incorporation of these groups under an expanded hate crime 'umbrella' and suggests that a framework that reconstitutes ideas of hate crime as 'targeted victimisation' facilitates the necessary theoretical space for their inclusion.

Issues at the margins of the hate debate

The targeting of 'alternatives'

Since the tragic murder of 'goth' Sophie Lancaster in August 2007 (see Case Study 7.1) the targeted hostility directed towards members of alternative subcultures – and the question of whether this hostility should be considered as hate crime – has become a growing topic of interest for hate crime scholars and practitioners alike. The notion of 'alternative subcultures' refers to a range of predominantly white music- and style-centred genres, like goth, emo, punk and metal, which involve strikingly different clothes, hair and body art that affirm these groups' sense of distance from 'mainstream' fashion and music. The moniker of 'alternatives' is often used as a collective descriptor of those involved (Garland and Hodkinson, 2014a).

This growth of interest has happened at a time when (as outlined above) academics have been questioning 'traditional' conceptions of hate crime by developing new perspectives, centred around ideas of risk, difference and vulnerability, that offer scope for groups other than just those of the five 'strands' to be included under the hate crime umbrella. In parallel with these theoretical developments, the 2012 UK Coalition government's Hate Crime Action Plan advised that, in relation to the Lancaster murder, 'although crimes such as this may fall outside of the nationally monitored strands, they are nonetheless hate crimes, and they should therefore be treated as such' (HM Government, 2012a: 6).

Case Study 7.1

The murder of Sophie Lancaster

A number of years on from her tragic murder in 2007 the fallout from the Sophie Lancaster case continues to grow in significance. Not only has the issue of the recognition of the targeted victimisation of those from alternative subcultures become an important part of the hate crime debate but it has also resulted in some important policing developments. The background to the case is as follows. Late on the night of 10 August 2007 Sophie (20) and her boyfriend Robert Maltby (21), both of alternative/gothic appearance, decided to cut across Stubbylee Park in Bacup, Lancashire, on their way home after a night at a friend's house. They bumped into a gang of youths and initially chatted with them amicably. Suddenly, and without provocation, one of the youths struck Maltby, precipitating a violent and savage assault upon him by the assailant and four other youths.

The attackers kicked and stamped upon Maltby until he lay unconscious. As she cradled her boyfriend's head in an effort to protect him, Lancaster pleaded with them to stop, only to become the subject of a vicious assault herself. A witness later told police: 'It looked like they were running over and just kicking her in the head, jumping up and down on her head' (Jenkins, 2008: 24). When paramedics arrived they found the victims lying side by side, unconscious and covered in blood. Both were in a coma and taken to separate hospitals and, whilst Robert eventually recovered enough to be able to leave hospital about two weeks later, Sophie died as a result of the brain injuries she suffered (Smyth, 2010).

After the assault the killers boasted to their friends that they had 'done summat good' and that: 'There's two moshers [goths] nearly dead up Bacup park – you wanna see them – they're a right mess' (Garland, 2010: 165). At the subsequent trial at Preston Crown Court it was established that the motivation behind the attack had been 'the fact that Sophie and Robert looked and dressed differently from their attackers ... they were known as "Moshers" and, therefore, a target' (College of Policing, 2014: 8). Interestingly, Judge Anthony Russell QC commented to the youths that 'This was a hate crime against these completely harmless people targeted because their appearance was different to yours' (BBC News, 2008b). The ringleader, 15-year-old Brendan Harris, was found guilty of murder and given an 18-year prison sentence while Ryan Herbert was also found guilty of murder and given a 16-year sentence.

Following Sophie's death her mother, Sylvia, founded the Sophie Lancaster Foundation, a campaigning charitable organisation which has the twin aims of challenging prejudice in all its forms, and getting attacks against people of alternative subcultures officially recognised as hate crimes. The Foundation has campaigned on multiple platforms, including online via Facebook and Twitter while also delivering hundreds of talks, lectures and training sessions (Garland, 2014b). It has garnered support from pop and rock stars, actors, politicians, academics and business entrepreneurs, and has been the driving force behind the decisions of Greater Manchester, Warwickshire and West Mercia police forces (in 2013 for the former and 2014 for the latter two) to record and investigate attacks against members of alternative subcultures as hate crimes.

However, while this development – and the subsequent decisions by three police forces to recognise 'alternatives' as a hate crime victim group – was warmly greeted by many commentators and those involved in 'darker' subcultures, others expressed scepticism, arguing that this belittled the experiences of recognised minority communities who had suffered centuries of discrimination and disadvantage. In addition, the concept of hate crime itself, some suggested, is rooted in recognition of the commonalities in the historical suffering of minority groups, and this would only be diluted by including those, like goths, who are considered to be generally middle-class and white and thus part of society's majority, dominant groups (Garland and Hodkinson, 2014a). Opponents to their inclusion also argued that to be a member of a subculture is a matter of personal lifestyle choice and also often a temporary 'phase' in the life course, and not an immutable part of someone's identity like physical characteristics such as skin colour. Furthermore, sceptics pointed to the difficulties in defining just what an 'alternative subculture' is, and where the lines of inclusion should be drawn (Garland and Hodkinson, 2014b).

To counter this, those in support of the inclusion of 'alternatives' as a recognised hate crime group highlight the patterns of harassment and prejudice suffered by such groups, which they argue is similar to that experienced by the more established sets of victims. For example, there is growing evidence that 'alternatives' can be the targets of verbal *and* physical abuse that forms part of a pattern of harassment that occurs on a regular and ongoing basis. Participants in Garland, Chakraborti and Hardy's (2015) study reported being the recipients of insults, such as 'dirty mosher', 'greb' and 'grunger', while also being spat upon and having missiles, eggs and drinks hurled at them from passing cars. They were also 'constantly' accused of being 'filthy', 'dirty' and 'lazy' by those who apparently linked alternative styles with fecklessness and messiness.

Other evidence points to an alarming level of violence perpetrated against alternative groups which resembles that suffered by recognised hate crime victim communities. Typical of these is the following incident, described by a participant in a study of the experiences of 'alternatives', which occurred outside a goth/alternative nightclub:

> Someone's walked up, [yelled] 'Fucking little Goth!'... shoved me, then punched me into a concrete pillar ... I went down, they then started kicking me in the head. And I've got a memory of crawling around on the floor with blood coming out the front of my face, asking where my glasses were, and I blacked out again. Then I remember going into an ambulance and I woke up in a neck brace. ('Jamie', cited in Garland and Hodkinson, 2014a: 620)

Other research into patterns of broader hate crime victimisation has also uncovered examples of brutal violence being meted out upon groups of 'alternatives' by gangs hostile to their appearance and perceived lifestyle, with attacks like this not uncommon:

> They came and shouted: 'What you grebs walking down here for?' and all that kind of stuff ... They then started to attack, they attacked my friend ... These people with bikes and golf clubs came and we just ran ... They ended getting my friend in the face with a golf club ... they were just tearing at his clothes, beating him up ... That was a very frightening experience. ('Adrian', in Garland et al., 2015)

Victims reported that these types of assaults, together with forms of 'lower-level' harassment, damaged their sense of self-worth and confidence. Many spoke of ongoing psychological problems that outlasted the effects of the physical injuries, including anger, anxiety, depression, fear and vulnerability, while a number altered their patterns of behaviour, including avoiding certain areas or groups of people. Pertinently, many alternative subcultural members related how news of attacks upon fellow 'alternatives' would ripple through their 'community', causing worry, uncertainty and upset, just as it does in similar circumstances in recognised hate victim groups (Garland et al., 2015; Garland and Hodkinson, 2014a; see also Morris, 2014).

Other research also explores the forms and effects of the targeted victimisation of alternative subcultural members. Leblanc, in her study of female punks, for example, draws parallels between the frequent harassment they suffered with that of recognised hate crime victim groups:

> Public harassment is a form of discrimination, whether it is directed at gays or lesbians, at people of colour, at persons with disabilities or at members of youth subcultures ... Although many forms of discrimination are illegal ... punks enjoy no such protection under the law. (Leblanc, 2008: 194)

Therefore, although there is some understandable opposition to the recognition of alternative subcultures as a hate crime victim group, the small but growing body of evidence on the nature, frequency and impact of their victimisation suggests that it does have commonalities with that of the recognised 'strands'. It has similar patterns (more frequent low-level' abuse and rarer, but significant, acts of violence), locations (such as on the street or in public spaces such as parks), and impacts (both upon the individual victim and their identity community).

Domestic violence

While the study of hate and prejudice suffered by members of alternative subcultures is relatively new, another form of targeted victimisation, domestic violence, has been the subject of much more extensive academic scrutiny. Much of this work has endeavoured to understand the nature, extent and impact of this 'hidden' form of crime as a gendered form of abuse that occurs as a result of unequal power relations between men and women within a patriarchal society (see Johnson, 2006). With this in mind, it is perhaps surprising that domestic violence has not received more attention within the field of hate studies. This section of the chapter will therefore undertake a necessarily brief overview of the topic of domestic violence against a backdrop of whether it should be considered a form of gendered hate crime.

There are a number of competing definitions of domestic violence and abuse, and a lack of space prevents them from being discussed here. However, Harne and Radford (2008: 1–2) offer a useful perspective on the issue, arguing that it is:

> ... a broad concept incorporating many forms of physical violence, sexual violence and a range of coercive, intimidating and controlling behaviours. Domestic violence can occur in any intimate or familial relationship, irrespective of whether the parties are living together or not, whether they are married or cohabiting or living in three-generational extended families.

Theirs is a wide understanding of domestic violence, taking in not just physical and sexual violence but behaviours which are intended to bully and control that occur in relationship or familial settings. In its breadth it is very similar to the UK cross-government definition of domestic violence and abuse (HMIC, 2014: 29), and thus will be adopted here.

As Maier and Bergen (2012) suggest, victims can be subjected to domestic violence over a number of years that has serious physical and emotional impacts. It can occur in any type of relationship, regardless of the sexual orientation, class or ethnicity of those involved. Both men and women are the perpetrators and the victims of it, although the Crime Survey for England and Wales (CSEW) has repeatedly shown that women are more likely than men to have been subjected to, or threatened with, domestic violence. The 2012/13 sweep revealed that 30% of women (aged 16 to 59) and 16% of men in England and Wales had experienced, or been threatened with, domestic violence since they were aged 16, and that 7.1% of women and 4.4% of men had reported having experienced it in the last year, equivalent to around 1.2 million female and 700,000 male victims (ONS, 2014: 1). Non-sexual partner abuse was the most common type of abuse among both women and men. In the same time period (2012/13) the police recorded 838,026 domestic abuse incidents (2014: 8), although direct comparisons with the CSEW figures are difficult as they measure different things (as the latter measures the number of victims and the former the number of incidents). Of the 269,700 domestic abuse-related crimes recorded by the police in England and Wales in 2012/13, around 96,000 were classified as 'assault with injury' (HMIC, 2014: 14; 28).

A number of feminist theorists have provided explanations for this abuse that utilise the concept of 'gendered violence'. This concept suggests that domestic violence occurs within patriarchal social structures that create and reinforce unequal power relations between men and women, with men the dominant party and therefore the most common perpetrators of violence, and women the frequent victims of it (Walby, 1990). These power inequalities 'not only make the choice to use violence more available to men than women, but also facilitate their ability to use a range of controlling strategies rarely available to women' (Harne and Radford, 2008: 7). Furthermore, perpetrators receive a form of what has been termed 'patriarchal peer support' from those men in their social network that helps them to justify their actions (DeKeseredy et al., 2006).

However, there have been a number of challenges to these feminist 'orthodoxies' that argue they are too deterministic and prescriptive. Some of this criticism has been prompted by survey findings which reveal a degree of 'gender symmetry' in rates of victimisation, with men as likely to be targeted as women (see, *inter alia*, Felson and Pare, 2005). Johnson (2006), however, argues that 'gender symmetry' explanations are too simplistic as they fail to acknowledge the qualitatively more severe nature of the violence that women suffer and the impact that it has upon them. He suggests that there are different forms of partner violence that illustrate this: 'situational couple violence', 'mutual violent control', 'violent resistance' and 'intimate terrorism'. 'Situational couple violence' is low in frequency and severity, and is more likely to be mutual as it arises out of specific arguments. It is not characterised by a desire to control by either partner. 'Mutual violent control' is another form of violence engaged in by both partners but in this case both want to control and both exert violence. 'Violent resistance', however, is perpetrated by women, but is done in self-defence in order to resist the violence of their partner. 'Intimate terrorism', though, is more likely to be severe, to escalate over time and be motivated by desire to control the person being abused. It is this type of violence that most directly challenges the idea of 'gender symmetry', as it is almost entirely perpetrated by males, is more systematic and results in more serious injuries (Hoyle, 2007).

In addition, evidence also suggests that female victims are more likely to suffer more serious injury and be hospitalised far more often than men (Harne and Radford, 2008). Twice as many women report being victims of domestic abuse since the age of 16 than men, and women are more likely to be repeat victims too (Walby and Allen, 2004). Also, CPS data for prosecutions of domestic violence cases in 2012–13 reveal that over nine out of ten defendants were men and eight out of ten victims were women (CPS, 2013: 19). Men are more likely to be repeat perpetrators, and to use physical violence, threats and harassment when they do so, than women (HMIC, 2014). The impacts of being targeted are also higher for women, who are more likely to experience heightened anxiety and fear, sleeplessness, eating disorders and depression (Hoyle, 2008). It is these sorts of impact issues (at both individual and group level) that have persuaded some scholars, such as Walters and Tumath (2014), that 'gender hostility' should be included within the UK's legislative hate crime framework.

In the contexts of discussions of hate crime, it is also interesting to note that some studies suggest that the risk of victimisation is heightened if the victim has a disability or is from a minority ethnic background (HMIC, 2014). The impact of this violence can also be higher, with black and Asian women more likely to attempt suicide (Maier and Bergen, 2012). In addition, victimisation within same-sex relationships is a hidden but significant issue (see Case Study 7.2). This may be a reflection of the way in which power structures constructed around issues such as class, 'race', sexual orientation and disability intertwine with patriarchy to create the kinds of prejudices that are reflected in patterns of domestic violence victimisation.

Case Study 7.2

Domestic violence in same-sex relationships

Domestic violence within same-sex relationships is an under-acknowledged issue, even though it may be at least as prevalent as that within heterosexual relationships. Figures from the British Crime Survey, for example, reveal that the percentage of gay or bisexual men who suffer partner abuse is nearly double that of heterosexual men, while the figure for victimisation rates for lesbian women is three times that of their heterosexual equivalents and far higher than for gay, bisexual or heterosexual men (Smith et al., 2010: 76). Other estimates put the rate of domestic violence victimisation within the LGBT communities at one in four (Donovan et al., 2006), with around half suffering emotional abuse, a fifth suffering physical abuse and around a half undergoing abusive sexual behaviour within the last twelve months (Donovan et al., 2014).

In many ways, the impact of domestic violence in same-sex partnerships is similar to that within heterosexual ones, ranging from the physical (bruises, cuts, broken bones) to the psychological (insomnia, eating disorders, anxiety, fear and depression (Lockhart et al., 1994)). The desire to control, and have power over, a partner may feature more strongly in relationships in which gay men, or heterosexual women, are victims (Hoyle, 2007). Gay victims can often struggle to come to terms with being targeted in this way, feeling confusion, embarrassment and shame as domestic violence was 'something that men do to women, it's not what gay people do' (victim cited in HMIC, 2014: 33).

These victims therefore face additional barriers to reporting the abuse they suffer to the police, as they have the same concerns about a homophobic police culture as gay victims of hate crime (see Chapter 4) and fear that they may not be received sympathetically. They may also be concerned about being 'outed' to friends, family and work colleagues by their partner who employs this threat as a control tactic to prevent them from reporting (Ristock, 2002). There is also a general lack of recognition of the issue of domestic violence by victims themselves and gay communities more generally. The problem, though, has received scant attention from feminist theorists who are inclined to frame the broader domestic violence debate around differentials in the power relationships between heterosexual men and women within patriarchal structures, with men seeking to dominate and control their partners by employing different forms of gendered violence. Structured action hate crime theorists may also struggle to accommodate intimate partner abuse within their own paradigms that are also reliant on notions of the powerful sections of society victimising the weaker.

Elder abuse

According to the 2011 census there are approximately 10,400,000 people over the age of 65 in the UK, equivalent to around 16% of the population (ONS, 2013: Table P01UK), with this figure set to rise to around 14.5 million, or a quarter of the population, by 2066 (Wolhuter et al., 2009: 115). The CPS identifies a crime against an older person occurring under the following circumstances: where there is a relationship and an expectation of trust; where the offence is targeted at an older person who is perceived to be vulnerable; where the offence is not initially related to the older person's age but becomes a factor during the commission of an offence; or when an offender targets an older person due to their hostility towards older people more generally (CPS, 2014: 37). Meanwhile, the widely used term of 'elder abuse' is defined by O'Keeffe et al. (2007: 13) as 'a single or repeated act or lack of appropriate action occurring within any relationship where there is an expectation of trust, which causes harm or distress to an older person' and which can include physical, sexual, psychological or financial abuse, neglect, and discriminatory treatment (Wolhuter et al., 2009: 108).[1,2]

As with disablist crimes though, there are particular difficulties in gaining accurate data about the extent of elder abuse as it tends to take place in 'hidden' environments, such as the home or institutional settings. O'Keeffe et al. (2007) estimate that around 227,000 people aged 66 and over in the UK were neglected or abused in the year leading up to their study, while the BCS estimated that there are around 143,000 incidents of age-motivated hate crime per year, with the youngest and oldest age groups the most likely to say they thought they had been victimised due to age (Smith et al., 2012: 25). Interestingly, the CPS (2014: 37) reports that the number of overall cases referred to them by the police was just 2,832. There is also some evidence that the abuse is most commonly perpetrated by partners and other family members, and to a lesser extent also by care workers or close friends (O'Keeffe et al., 2007: 59).

The fact that elder abuse is a hidden crime, and often perpetrated by those in a position of trust, may reveal some parallels with disablist hate crime (see Chapter 6). A reluctance to report incidents because they are perpetrated by carers, spouses or offspring, and the suggestion that older people may be viewed as 'easy' targets by offenders, may also link these two forms of victimisation. Similarly, older people, like disabled people, may be less likely to be believed when they do report victimisation. A further overlap between them is that around four out of ten older people have a disability, and thus may be subject to disablist *and* ageist harassment (Burnett, 2006).

Violence against sex workers

Of all of the groups on the borderlines of the hate crime debate perhaps the most socially stigmatised is that of sex workers.[3] Due to the 'hidden' nature of sex work accurate statistics regarding the numbers of those involved are hard to come by, but recent estimates place the number at around 30,000 in England and Wales, with over half being migrants (Westminster Sex Worker Task Group (WSWTG), 2013: 11). Yet this particular group is also one of the most vulnerable to abuse and assault, with Sanders and Campbell suggesting that street sex workers are particularly at risk from physical and sexual victimisation, being 12 times more likely to die from violence at work than women of their own age involved in 'conventional' employment (Sanders and Campbell, 2007: 2). In Canada, almost all of the street sex workers surveyed in one study reported being the subject of violence (O'Doherty, 2011: 944). Levels of rape and other sexual assaults are also worryingly high, with as many as 80% of sex workers experiencing this abuse in the course of their work (Campbell and Stoops, 2010: 9). As Sanders and Campbell state (2007: 3), much of the violence directed towards female sex workers is fuelled by a 'historical, cultural endurance of intolerance and hostility towards street workers fostered by a general culture of distaste and disrespect towards women who sell sex' (see also Kinnell, 2008). Furthermore, the rise in the numbers of sex workers in recent years in the UK has 'saturated' the market, forcing some sex workers to take on more 'high risk' clients, placing them in even greater danger of assault (WSWTG, 2013).

Within the broad category of 'sex workers' though, the level of vulnerability to assault varies. For instance, violence against female sex workers is estimated to be more prevalent than that directed at males, although reporting rates by the latter may be lower (WSWTG, 2013). Migrants are also thought to be especially at risk, with those that have been trafficked lacking the kind of support networks that could help them cope with being targeted (van Beelen and Rakhmetova, 2010).

Trans sex workers are thought to be amongst the most vulnerable of all. The comparatively high levels of trans women within the sex industry are a result of them suffering discrimination in the broader job market, meaning that sex work is often the only avenue of income open to them (Jacques, 2010). However, undertaking this kind of work places them at risk of the kinds of violence that are an 'inevitable consequence of widespread prejudice that frames transgenderism as unnatural, immoral or mentally disordered; [and] of legal frameworks that view transwomen as men, denying them respect, equality and dignity as women' (Slamah et al., 2010: 31). Globally, there is evidence of the abduction, rape and assault of trans women in places such as Mongolia, Bali, Vietnam and Turkey, and of them being humiliated and beaten by local police (2010: 30). This kind of violence, and of secondary victimisation by the police service, can lead to low self-esteem, depression and suicidal thoughts, highlighting the extremely difficult situation that many trans sex workers find themselves in.

Targeting of homeless people

Homelessness is a much broader phenomenon than just 'sleeping rough' on the streets at night as it covers a number of different situations in which people can be considered to lack permanent accommodation. The Department for Communities and Local Government (DCLG) provides statistics for two aspects of homelessness, noting that local authorities accepted nearly 82,400 households as homeless in England in 2013 (the 'statutory homeless' – Fitzpatrick et al., 2011), while counting 2,414 rough sleepers, the most visible form of homelessness (DCLG, 2014: Table 770; 2014b: 2).[4]

In many ways the homeless could be seen as being caught in a 'double-bind' situation: on the one hand they are among the most visible people in society, living their daily lives in public spaces and in full view of passers-by, while on the other they are also one of the most *invisible* populations, routinely ignored by the general public. Yet the homeless are at a high risk of harassment and abuse that can range from 'low level' anti-social behaviour through to extreme violence, with harassment an everyday occurrence for many. Newburn and Rock (2005: 12–13) found that just over half of the homeless people surveyed in various UK cities had been the subject of violence while around one in twelve had been sexually assaulted. A recent, and disturbing, new form of abuse is the staging and videoing of 'bum fights', which typically involve homeless males being plied with alcohol and drugs and then being 'goaded into performing ridiculous acts ... [and] fighting with each other and generally being humiliated' (Walshe, 2010). These videos are later posted online.

In the case of homeless women, the physical and verbal harassment directed toward them is frequently sexist, misogynistic and sexual, and made especially damaging by the fact that over a third of women who sleep rough do so in order to escape domestic violence in the home (Wachholz, 2009). Young gay and transgendered people are also more likely to be homeless due to the need felt by some to escape prejudiced attitudes among family and friends (Johnson et al., 2007). Equally significantly, the inherent vulnerability of being 'exposed' on the streets means that the homeless come into close contact with motivated offenders on a regular basis, but cannot 'retreat' into their own safe private space (Garland et al., 2010). The homeless often have to contend with other issues too, including drug or alcohol dependency and/or mental illness, which can reinforce their difficult life circumstances.

Conclusion

The chapter began by assessing recent developments in the theorising of hate crime, and how these may offer space within the hate debate that could be occupied by the types of victimisation that have previously sat on the 'borders' of such discussions. The key aspect of this notion of 'targeted victimisation' is that it challenges the idea that a hate crime victim group *must* be conceived of as a minority that has been historically marginalised and disadvantaged, and is targeted in order to maintain the privileged position of society's powerful groups. Instead, what is prioritised (within Mason's (2014a) 'politics of justice' framework) is the idea of the victim experience, and that being targeted because of one's identity *hurts* whatever that identity may be. This is not to belittle the historical struggles of the already recognised groups, but it does acknowledge that we *all* have the equal right to live our lives free from targeted harassment and violence.

Having said that, some of the issues discussed in this chapter have, at certain historical junctures, been regarded as hate crimes by practitioners and academics. Domestic violence is one of these, and the chapter sketched some of those theories that regard it as a product of a hierarchal, male dominated society. This standpoint is important within the context of this book as it suggests that, if domestic abuse is a form of *gendered* crime enacted to reinforce the position of the powerful, then there may be some parallels with the ideas of structured action hate crime of theorists like Perry or DeKeseredy. Indeed, DeKeseredy (2009) is persuaded that domestic violence *should* be viewed as a hate crime within this kind of framework. Importantly, domestic violence can also have a long-term impact on the mental health of the victim, just as the recognised hate crimes can – but so too, as we have seen in this chapter, can the targeting of the homeless, of sex workers, of the elderly and of alternative subcultures. Effects can include feelings of anxiety, fear, self-loathing and depression which leave the victim with a damaged sense of self-worth – something that undoubtedly links many of those that suffer targeted violence, whatever its hue.

As discussed in earlier chapters, Kelly's (1987) assertion that victims of sexual violence experience a 'continuum of violence', which has been so influential in the context of discussing racist harassment, for example, can also be adapted and applied to the types of 'borderline' victimisation highlighted here. As we saw, all of the groups of victim referred to in this chapter face the risk of potential victimisation on an everyday basis. And, like the recognised victim groups, the ones discussed in this chapter often present an easily identifiable, and perhaps 'soft', target, for those hostile towards them. Some of them – for example, sex workers and the homeless – regularly find themselves in very vulnerable situations, prone to assault and harassment. Indeed, the intersection of different aspects of identities evident within these groups on the 'margins' – androgynous goths or transgender sex workers, for example – makes them more susceptible to targeted harassment. The issue of intersectionality is a growing aspect of hate studies and deserves further exploration (Mason-Bish, 2013).

In summary, what we are suggesting is that the groups we have described in this chapter, and those in the 'recognised' hate victim chapters, have much in common. They are not necessarily targeted due to the perpetrator *hating* their actual or perceived identities, but rather due to feelings of enmity which are provoked by prejudice that is in itself interwoven with fear of or animosity towards difference. As we have argued elsewhere (Chakraborti and Garland, 2012), often what are commonly understood as 'hate crimes' are not actually motivated by hate, but by hostility that is the by-product of feelings of weakness, inadequacy or other, more complex emotional and psychological processes. It only takes a 'trigger' incident, and perhaps one fuelled by intoxication, jealousy or the heat of an argument, to bring such negative subconscious feelings to the surface – and all groups in vulnerable situations deserve protection from that.

Guide to further reading

Smyth's *Weirdo Mosher Freak* (2010) provides some excellent detail in relation to the Sophie Lancaster case while Armitage's *Black Roses* (2012) is a moving and beautifully written play concerning Lancaster's murder and its aftermath. For a detailed and informative introduction to issues relating to domestic violence see Harne and Radford's *Tackling Domestic Violence* (2008) while Maier and Bergen's 'Critical issues in intimate partner violence' (2012) is a useful summary of developing debates from a critical criminological perspective. Also worth referring to is Chakraborti and Garland's (eds) *Responding to Hate Crime* (2014), which includes a number of chapters covering under-explored forms of 'difference' and targeted hostility.

Links to online material

More detail on the work of the Sophie Lancaster Foundation can be found on its website at www.sophielancasterfoundation.com/ while the moving *Dark Angel* animation of Sophie Lancaster's murder can be viewed at www.youtube.com/watch?v=qW2ve6_BkRA. Useful background on issues of domestic violence in different contexts can be found via the Women's Aid domestic violence charity at www.womensaid.org.uk/ and Broken Rainbow UK: The LGBT Domestic Violence Charity at www.brokenrainbow.org.uk/.

Notes

1 The Equality Act 2010 makes it unlawful to directly or indirectly discriminate against someone, or harass or victimise them, when providing goods or services or when carrying out public functions, because of their age.
2 Interestingly, the Older People's Commissioner for Wales (2014: 5) rejects the term 'elder abuse', arguing that 'people should not be treated – or spoken about – differently because of their age ... this can result in discrimination. Offences against them

should be named for what they are – for example, theft, fraud, assault, coercive control and rape'.

3   'Sex work' refers to the exchange of sexual services for some form of payment (WSWTG, 2013: 10).

4   Fitzpatrick et al. (2011) list four types of homeless groups: rough sleepers; single people in temporary accommodation; those that are seeking housing assistance from local authorities (the 'statutory homeless'); and those homeless that are 'hidden' in 'shared' households.

8

PERPETRATORS OF HATE CRIME

Chapter summary

This chapter assesses the profile, motivations and activities of hate crime perpetrators. It debates evidence which suggests that those convicted of hate offences are typically male, from deprived backgrounds and with a history of criminal or violent behaviour, and argues that this portrait may only reveal some of the overall profile of a typical perpetrator of hate. It also examines whether hate acts are really 'stranger danger' crimes or whether the offender does, in many cases and at least to some extent, actually know their victim. The chapter also explores cultures of racism that develop in some communities and how these can be born out of frustration at perceptions that local minority ethnic groups are receiving preferential treatment.

The chapter then examines the success and influence of contemporary far-right groups. It suggests that while members of far-right political parties carry out only a small proportion of hate offences, these may be more severe and premeditated than 'everyday' hate crimes. The influence of some of the far right's ideas on immigration, multiculturalism and religion, and the potency of its symbolism, may also be more far-reaching than many would like to think.

Introduction

In the wake of the murder of Stephen Lawrence in 1993 much of the academic endeavour in the field of hate crime has focused upon the processes, forms and impact of victimisation, including how victims are treated by the police service and other statutory and voluntary agencies. This has been an important development as it has given victims of targeted hostility a voice and a profile that have not been evidenced previously. More broadly, these developments have coincided with a rise in the 'victims' agenda' within the criminal justice system, which has seen the range of support services for victims expand as interest in their experiences and expectations has grown.

Within the study of hate crime less attention has been paid, though, to the motivation and behaviour of perpetrators. While there have been various studies of far-right parties (mainly by political scientists) there has been comparatively little criminological examination of the causes and patterns of hate-related offending perpetrated by those who are not part of such groups. As we will see in this chapter, however, it is an 'uncomfortable truth' that it is 'ordinary' members of the public that are responsible for the vast majority of the types of 'everyday' targeted hostility that blight the lives of so many victims.

Profiling offenders

The influential work of McDevitt and partners provides a good starting point in our brief exploration of hate offender profiles (see McDevitt et al., 2002, 2010). Their typology of perpetrators, developed from an examination of 169 hate crime cases investigated by the Boston Police Department, suggests that the most common offender is a teenager or young adult who, acting in a group, commits a hate crime in order to satiate their desire for excitement (these account for around two-thirds of the cases assessed). In most of these cases the perpetrator(s) left their neighbourhood to search for someone to victimise, and this target was selected on the basis of animosity towards their perceived 'difference' (McDevitt et al., 2010).

The second group of offenders in the typology are those labelled 'defensive', whose profile is similar to those in the 'thrills' cases but commit a hate offence because they feel their neighbourhood needs 'protecting' from incomers (these cases made up around a quarter of the total). 'Retaliatory' hate offenders make up the third aspect of the typology (less than one in ten of the overall cases), and these typically travel to the victim's territory in order to retaliate against a previous incident that they perceive the victim, or victim's social group, have committed.

The last category identified is those offenders (only around 1% of the sample) who feel that they are on a 'mission' when perpetrating a hate crime; the fully committed 'haters' who commonly have far-right leanings (McDevitt et al., 2010). Their allegiance to a bias ideology is much stronger than that of offenders in the other three categories. Notwithstanding this, it is those other three categories that contain the vast majority of offenders, and that such a large proportion of incidents is apparently perpetrated for 'thrills' points to the fact that much of what we think of as 'hate crime' is relatively mundane and 'routine' (Iganski, 2008). This is not to say that these are motiveless crimes perpetrated by bored youths simply seeking 'thrills', as they reveal the existence of negative attitudes and stereotypes about marginalised outgroups that play a part in the selection of the target. However, these biases may be relatively marginal to the committing of the act, as Walters (2011: 324) suggests:

> There exists a crucial intersection here between the socio-structural influences affecting an individual's perception of 'difference' and his or her desire for instant gratification (the thrill). Hence, in acquiring the thrill, offenders use their prejudices, the result of constructions of difference, stereotyping and the perceived threats posed by certain minority individuals, as a means of justifying their partly hate motivated actions.

The work of Byers, Crider and Biggers (1999) provides some background to Walters' assertion. They studied the motivations of (mainly) groups of young men who targeted members of the Amish community in Fulham County, USA, and concluded that these men were dominated by the desire for thrills, with the markedly different 'other', the Amish, being the 'quarry' in this quest. Common to this and a number of similar studies is the finding that hate crime offenders typically act in groups, making them different from 'other aggressive [non-hate] offences' (Craig, 2002: 87).[1] The sense of group identification is strong, and the creation of 'enemy outgroups' important. As Michener (2010: 41) remarks, if any member of the enemy outgroup attacks the ingroup, then 'All the members of that [out]group are suspected of being inclined to repeat the same pernicious behaviour. At the level of emotion, they are considered already to have done it'.

Group dynamics may affect the nature of the incident too, with larger gangs of perpetrators committing more severe hate offences (Dunbar, 1997). Craig also asserts that individuals within this context may feel 'pressured to behave in unusual ways when encountering or interacting with either victims or members of the victim's social group' (Craig, 2002: 87). There may also be a diffusion of responsibility within groups coupled with a lack of recognition of normal social constraints, meaning that 'the outcome of their behaviours is especially likely to be extreme' (p. 88). As is the case with McDevitt et al.'s (2010) so-called 'fellow travellers' (who actively or hesitantly participate in the group offence) and 'unwilling participants' (who do not actively participate in the perpetration yet do nothing to stop it either), those acting in groups may lose their normal sense of perspective and get carried away in the moment, while others, to a greater or lesser extent, will go along with the violence anyway.

Socio-economic factors

Sibbitt's (1997) study of the perpetrators of racist violence on deprived south London housing estates found that cultures of racism, reinforced by successive generations of white residents, create environments that are hostile towards minority ethnic residents. Many of these white people feel bitterly let down by local authorities whom they blame for giving 'preferential treatment' to the 'undeserving' (minority ethnic groups) at the expense of the 'deserving' (themselves). This resentment manifests itself in racist harassment that can become violent. Hardy (2014) uncovered similar sentiments in her study of young white working class people living in deprived and marginalised white areas of a multi-cultural city. Within that study the apparent 'lived reality' of multiculturalism helped to foment the types of values that could manifest themselves as hate crimes committed by those with little or no commitment to the multicultural 'ideal'. Hardy (2014: 152) found that their prejudiced views were formed, and then given legitimacy, by:

> being surrounded by friends, family and a wider community who all believe and verbalize 'stereotypical', 'biased' views about minority ethnic and religious groups, which are then reinforced when seeing those individuals in positions of employment, living in better housing or being markedly more wealthy.

In parallel with the work of Ray, Smith and Wastell (2004) and Dunbar and Crevecoeur (2005), Sibbitt (1997) suggests that those who engage in hate crime often have a history of criminal behaviour and routinely invoke aggressive behaviour to resolve disputes. They are commonly part of families that have poor physical or mental health, coupled with a lack of formal education. Similarly, the perpetrators of racist offences that formed the basis of Gadd, Dixon and Jefferson's (2005) analysis (see also Gadd and Dixon, 2009; Roxell, 2011) typically have life stories characterised by deprivation, mental health problems, domestic violence, drug and alcohol issues, and patterns of criminal behaviour. Surprisingly, perhaps, Fisher and Salfati (2009) posit that much of the US research contradicts this evidence by revealing that perpetrators are commonly middle-class and with no criminal records.

For Perry (2001), hate offending is designed to maintain social hierarchies, which privilege white, heterosexual males and stigmatise those who do not conform to these hegemonic identities. If the position of the dominant group is threatened then this can lead to the enactment of hate crimes against those subordinate to them. The boundaries between 'in-' and 'outgroups' – 'essentialist, mutually exclusive categories of belonging' (Perry, 2001: 46 – see Chapter 1) – are thereby reinforced, with victims reminded of their 'lower' place within that hierarchy. In the cases of deprived neighbourhoods like those in the studies discussed here, it is the *relative* position of the dominant and subordinate groups that confers 'dominance, normativity, and privilege' on certain identities – of which whiteness is one – 'and subordination, marginality and disadvantage' on others, such as those of minority ethnic communities (Perry, 2001: 47). Walters develops Perry's ideas by arguing that among those who are experiencing actual or perceived strain, and who feel the need to 'defend' their own territories and sense of socio-economic security, will be those who possess low self-control and low tolerance thresholds who will 'be less able to control any feelings of animosity towards those who they deem as "different"' (Walters, 2011: 325).[2]

The victim–perpetrator relationship

Nascent hate crime scholarship commonly viewed hate offences as those in which the individual identity of the victim is *irrelevant* to the perpetrator, who targets them solely because they are an identifiable member of a despised minority group (Maxwell and Maxwell, 1995; Perry, 2001). It is their prejudice towards that group that drives their harassment of the victim rather than any personal animosity that may exist between the two individuals. Hate crimes, so it was suggested, are thus classic 'stranger danger' crimes that are designed to send an intimidating message not just to the individual victim but to other members of that group.

However, more recent work in the field has suggested that the relationship between offender and victim may be more complex than initially thought. Roxell's (2011) analysis of over 1,900 official offence reports for over 550 persons suspected of hate crimes in Sweden notes that in just over four out of ten cases the perpetrator is classified 'related or superficially acquainted to the victim' (Roxell, 2011: 207). The work of Moran (2007), Mason (2005a) and Jarman and Tennant (2003) also suggests that victim and assailant are often familiar with each other, at least to a degree. The location of hate incidents may have a bearing on this. Mason's (2005b) examination of homophobic and racist harassment cases reported to the police reveals that 90% occurred at or near the victim's home and 10% at work, which indicates that there is a strong likelihood of some pre-existing relationship between victim and perpetrator in both of these scenarios.

Ray, Smith and Wastell's (2004: 351) study of racist offenders would seem to support this premise as they conclude that 'virtually all offenders knew their victims, though not well'. This knowledge was usually gained as a result of commercial transactions with shopkeepers, taxi drivers, or those working in restaurants and takeaways, where many of the incidents took place. Mason argues that although both 'sides' involved in a hate incident are emotionally estranged from one another, their physical proximity means that it is 'virtually impossible for them to be strangers in terms of the interpersonal relations of everyday life' (Mason, 2005b: 587). Indeed, it may be the case that most perpetrators know just enough about their intended victim to realise that they offer a suitably 'soft' target.

Other research suggests that it may be possible to know how familiar the victim and perpetrator are with each other from the *type* of hate incident that has occurred, with strangers more likely to be involved in cases of physical assault. Sibbitt (1997), for example, found that common and indirect assaults were often carried out by groups of white youths or adult males against people they did not know, but for acts of 'lower-level' intimidation there was evidence of perpetrators routinely abusing those who lived near them and whom they must therefore have some knowledge of. Docking, Kielinger and Paterson's (2003) analysis of faith hate incidents also found that the extreme cases, such as GBH or murder, were more likely to have been committed by strangers than by someone the victim knew. For other, less extreme types of harassment the perpetrator was someone known to the victim, whether as neighbours, local schoolchildren or work colleagues.

Interestingly, Roxell (2011: 208) implies that the depth to which a perpetrator knows their victim may vary across different types of hate crime. In her analysis of three strands, the proportion of cases in which the perpetrator and victim knew each other was higher for 'xenophobic' hate crimes (44.3%) and homophobic (42.0%) than it was for Islamophobic (29.3%). The growing body of work on disablist hate crime (detailed in Chapter 6) suggests that victims of that type of offence may be very familiar with perpetrators, who are often their carer or 'friend'. Indeed, Quarmby (2011) notes that this is especially the case with extreme disablist hate crimes (such as murders) when the perpetrator is commonly someone that the victim knows and trusts very well. She therefore suggests that these types of disablist crimes differ markedly from their racist or homophobic equivalents where the victim and perpetrator *are* very often strangers.

However, Roxell suggests that much of the disparity with regard to some of the findings relating to the victim–perpetrator relationship may be down to definitional or methodological issues. This is evident in cases of repeat victimisation when the victim is often asked to describe the most *serious* incident they have experienced, which, as we have seen with racist of homophobic offences, will most probably be one in which neither party knows the other (Roxell, 2011). In addition, these debates often take place within the framework of more traditional understandings of the victim–perpetrator relationship, in which they occupy the same geographical space. Such accounts fail to acknowledge the relatively recent phenomenon of 'cyberbullying', which is now seen as a significant form of bias-related harassment (Henry, 2013). It occurs via social networking sites such as Facebook or Twitter, via text message or apps such as WhatsApp and Viber, where discussions are often unregulated and in which a perpetrator, under the guise of anonymity, can feel less constrained than they might in the 'real world' and thus more at liberty to abuse their target (Hinduja and Patchin, 2008). However, whether such anonymity means that the perpetrator and their target are necessarily strangers is a moot point, as it may be that such anonymity is embraced by the offender as a way of keeping their identity concealed from the victim through this online disguise.

Therefore, within the context of the hate debate perhaps the concept of the 'stranger' needs to be reconfigured into a more complicated figure that the victim can simultaneously *know* and yet be emotionally *distant* from: familiar and yet still remote. This may help us understand hate crimes as 'stranger danger' crimes even if they are, in fact, commonly perpetrated by people who are familiar with their target. As Stanko (2001: 323) suggests, it is how 'assailants turn *those known* to them into *strangers*' that is of crucial importance here, rather than simply whether the two parties know, or know of, each other, whether in the 'real' world or the virtual one. After all, if someone is capable of committing an act of targeted hostility towards another then it indicates that they cannot feel much empathy for the victim, and thus must inherently be *apart* from them – in other words, a stranger, at least to a degree.

The influence and impact of the far right

Before the chapter turns to an assessment of three significant far-right groupings in Britain (the British National Party (BNP), the English Defence League (EDL) and Combat 18), it is worth reflecting upon several pertinent definitional issues. Fascism, according to Copsey (2007: 64), is 'a revolutionary ultra-nationalist ideology, an attempt to create a new type of post-liberal national community – an alternative modernity – by a movement or regime that *aspires* to the total or "totalitarian" transformation of culture and society'. For Goodwin, extreme right parties are characterised by hostility towards liberal democratic processes, an uncompromising opposition to immigration and, in some instances, a link to neo-Nazism (Goodwin, 2011). He sees four types of such organisations: those that operate like conventional parties and attempt to gain power through the ballot box (the BNP, for instance); those that avoid such methods and position themselves as activist street movements (the EDL); those that are 'extra-parliamentary' and eschew attempting to gain popular support in favour of recruiting committed, elite cadres (Combat 18); and last, individual 'lone wolves' who act in isolation and who may act violently (2011: 5–6 – see case studies 8.2 and 10.1).

Judged by their name, 'hate crimes' would appear to be offences committed by these types of extremists, and indeed some of the most notorious perpetrators of violent hate-related acts, such as David Copeland in England and Anders Behring Breivik in Norway (see Case Study 10.2), conform to this idea. The overall picture, though, may be very different from this, as there is evidence, as we saw earlier, that extremists only perpetrate a low percentage of hate crimes (McDevitt et al., 2010). Similarly, Gadd et al. (2005: 9) found that perpetrators were not 'hardened race haters committed to attacking or harassing people from other ethnic groups'. However, they did note that organisations like the BNP appealed to those who felt that the main political parties had forgotten them by prioritising instead the needs of minority ethnic residents, migrants and asylum seekers (see Case Study 8.1 for an example of the way that the far right can play upon the fears of such 'forgotten' communities). This had created a strong sense of injustice amongst these white communities, and in this climate the BNP's vocal opposition to immigration and multiculturalism, together with its determination to stand up for 'British culture', gained it a significant amount of support. It is difficult to discern whether in this racialised and tense situation the BNP's popularity directly led to an increase in racist harassment, but of those 15 perpetrators of such incidents in Gadd et al.'s study, two were BNP activists, two had far-right associations and another had sympathies with extremist groups (2005: 2).

Case Study 8.1

Prejudice, the far-right and community tensions in a multicultural city

During 2012, a seemingly innocuous decision taken by the local authority in the multicultural East Midlands city of Leicester regarding the future use of one of its scout huts inadvertently created a situation that sparked community tensions, triggered the involvement of far-right activists and culminated in a religiously ag-gravated hate crime. Leicester City Council's initial decision to allow the As-Salaam Trust (a Muslim community group) sole use of the disused hut in the mainly white area of Thurnby Lodge sparked protests by local residents who felt that the facility should be available to all. In an attempt to reverse the policy, the Committee for the Forgotten Estates of Thurnby Lodge and Netherall was formed, a campaigning group that organised a series of demonstrations against the decision, and drew up a petition that contained 1,500 signatures (Porter and Jones, 2012).

However, soon allegations began to surface that these protests, which were being staged on an almost daily basis outside Thurnby Lodge Community Centre and often attended by hundreds of people, had been hijacked by far-right groups such as the English Defence League and the British National Party, keen to capitalise upon rising community tensions and inflame an already volatile situation.

On Christmas Eve 2012 a pig's head was left outside the Community Centre in an apparently deliberate attempt to insult, antagonise and intimidate the next users of the Centre, local Muslims, as the pig is an unclean animal for those of Islamic faith. Subsequently a local man was successfully prosecuted and given a suspended prison sentence at Leicester Magistrates' Court after admitting to a religiously aggravated public order offence. Recognising the impact of the incident, the presiding magistrate stated: 'It is easy to imagine the shock, distress and disgust [local Muslims] would have felt ... But the harm you caused goes further. Others in the local community and beyond would also have been affected when news of this incident spread, prompting profound alarm, fear and insecurity' (Healy, 2013). Although the Council eventually reached a compromise solution that satisfied both 'sides', by allowing the Forgotten Estates Committee to lease the scout hut while providing an alternative facility for As-Salaam, the case exposed just how fragile relations can be between different ethnic and religious communities, even in cities where multiculturalism has been embedded for decades.

There is some evidence that members of extremist groups commit a more preda-tory form of hate offending by going to greater lengths to seek out their targets

(Dunbar, 1997). Such offenders may commit more severe hate crimes that have a bigger impact upon victims than perpetrators who are not members of these groups (Dunbar and Crevecoeur, 2005). Therefore, although the numbers of such incidents are comparatively small, they are often more extreme and more harmful. Furthermore, the same research found that members of extremist groups who commit hate crimes had more extensive criminal and violent histories than other hate crime offenders and posed a greater risk of perpetrating ongoing aggressive acts, thereby reflecting 'the popular image of the violent hate crime offender as a highly dissocial and aggressive individual' (2005: 13).

Organised hatred: the British far right

Although the far right has historically achieved very little success at the ballot box in Britain, during the early part of the twenty-first century the British National Party attained a degree of electoral reward that saw it hailed as the 'most successful extreme right political party in British history' (Goodwin, 2011: 171). In this period the BNP gained dozens of council seats and entry into the European Parliament, before its fortunes waned in the early 2010s. As a party, it is still relatively young, only forming in 1982 after the collapse of the neo-fascist National Front (NF) after the 1979 general election. Initially the BNP adopted many of the NF's fascist and racist policies, opposing all immigration and supporting the repatriation of minority ethnic people (Copsey, 2007). However, the BNP's electoral success in the 1990s was minimal, precipitating a change in its leadership in 1999. Its new figurehead, Nick Griffin, was a 'moderniser' determined to rid the party of its old fascist image. The 'new' BNP's stance therefore focused on being tough on law and order, opposing the European Union, preserving sterling and promoting British farming and countryside 'traditions'.

However, the beliefs of the 'old' BNP were never far from the surface. In 2001 the BNP appeared deliberately to inflame tension between local white and Asian communities in Oldham that culminated in several days of rioting in May of that year (see below), while in 2004 Griffin was caught on camera by a BBC undercover reporter describing Islam as a 'wicked, vicious faith' at a BNP meeting (Collins, 2012: 123). Despite these potentially damaging associations with extremism, during the first decade of the twenty-first century – and playing upon public concerns over immigration, Islamic extremism and disillusion with the three main parties – the BNP had some success in local elections, gaining around fifty council seats mainly in Stoke, Burnley, and Barking and Dagenham (Goodwin, 2011). Most notably, the party also gained two seats in the European Parliament in the 2009 elections, with Griffin himself winning one of them, after the party polled nearly a million votes nationally.

However, just as it looked as though it might be on the verge of a serious electoral breakthrough, the BNP's fortunes plummeted. Suffering from a period of vicious in-fighting and financial turmoil, the party saw its council seats all but disappear in local elections in the early 2010s and lost both of its MEPs in the European elections in 2014.[3] It was also eclipsed by the eurosceptic United Kingdom Independence Party (UKIP), which provided 'a less disreputable home than the BNP for anti-immigration and anti-Muslim sentiment' (Gable, 2013: 6), and by a new, more energetic and more focused far-right grouping: the English Defence League.

Formed in Luton in 2009 the EDL was the brainchild of two cousins, Tommy Robinson[4] and Kevin Carroll. Both men had been infuriated by the abuse directed at a homecoming parade of Anglian troops in Luton in May of that year by a Muslim extremist group, Ahle Sunnah al Jamah, and formed the EDL directly as a consequence. Tapping into public concerns about Islamic extremism while harnessing broader Islamophobic sentiment, the EDL staged marches in a number of English towns and cities in the remainder of the year, often focusing upon places where community relations between different ethnic groups were troubled. Meanwhile the organisation distanced itself from racism and fascism, stating that it was simply opposed to what it called 'militant Islam'. Also, and unusually for such a grouping, the EDL was vocal in its opposition to homophobia, and encouraged the creation of gay divisions within its ranks (Goodwin, 2011).

Street-based activism was the EDL's main tactic for gaining support, as it did not stand in elections and offered no formal mechanism for joining. A year into its existence, this tactic appeared to be working. Numbers at its demonstrations grew rapidly and soon it was regularly attracting over a thousand people, drawn mainly from marginalised and disenfranchised white working-class communities (Garland and Treadwell, 2012). However, with close links to Casuals United (an umbrella organisation for a number of football hooligan 'firms'), the EDL's marches were seen by many as aggressive and intimidating, seemingly designed to provoke a violent reaction from local Muslim communities. A number of its demonstrations descended into chaos and disorder, with dozens of arrests in places such as Birmingham, Bolton and Leicester (Treadwell and Garland, 2011). While its leaders called for peaceful participation, it appeared as though the EDL's 'footsoldiers' were following a different agenda, turning up at rallies in order to engage in drink- and drug-fuelled fighting with Muslim youths, the police or anti-fascist activists (Treadwell, 2014).

However, after staging a 'homecoming' march in Luton in February 2011 that attracted over 4,000 supporters, the EDL's popularity began to wane as a lack of progress in achieving its (rather vague) aims, coupled with the very strict policing of its events (which reduced the opportunity for disorder), saw attendance on its marches fall. The horrific murder of soldier Lee Rigby in Woolwich by

Islamic extremists in May 2013 saw a brief resurgence in its popularity, with a march in Newcastle at the height of public outrage over the incident attracting over 7,000 people – easily the EDL's largest ever event (Garland, 2013). Again, though, the organisation failed to capitalise, with subsequent demonstrations only attended by hundreds rather than thousands. Later in 2013, apparently disillusioned with the violent nature of its core support and at the lack of prospects of further progress, the EDL's founders and leaders, Robinson and Carroll, left the organisation. Although members pledged to continue without them, after only five years in existence the EDL's 'moment' appeared to have gone.

Another contributory factor to the EDL leadership's decision to leave was its frustration at the presence at its marches of current and former members of Combat 18, a neo-Nazi grouping formed in the early 1990s by ex-members of the BNP who were frustrated at the party's desire to 'modernise' (Lowles, 2002). Taking the '1' in its name from the 'A' in Adolf (the first letter in the alphabet) and the '8' from the 'H' in Hitler (the eighth), Combat 18 (or C18) was open in its belief that the Aryan 'race' was being corrupted by immigration and multiculturalism. It also exuded a potent antisemitism exemplified by the conviction that the global economy was in the grip of a Jewish conspiratorial elite that could only be overthrown through revolution.

Case Study 8.2

Lone wolves

The last two decades have seen a rise in the number of far-right extremists acting on their own or with minimal help from others, who have plotted and/or engaged in violent acts designed to maim or kill their targets (Gable and Jackson, 2011). In 2011, for instance, the BBC estimated that there were 14 right-wing extremists in prison for terrorism offences, with the security services monitoring a further 70 (BBC, 2011). Simon (2013: 43-45) identifies five broad categories of these 'lone wolves': those who are inspired to act by political convictions; religion; single-issues (such as animal liberation); the desire for financial gain, or as a result of severe personality or psychological problems.[5]

In the United States and Europe most of the recent high-profile lone wolves can be grouped into the first and perhaps last of these categories (political and personality/psychological). In July 2011 in Norway, neo-Nazi Anders Behring Breivik embarked upon a killing spree that claimed the lives of 77 people (discussed in Case Study 10.1). Sixteen years earlier an American lone wolf detonated a bomb outside a government building in Oklahoma City, killing 168 people. The device was planted by Timothy McVeigh, a war veteran furious at the actions and policies of the US government (Gerstenfeld, 2013).

(Continued)

(Continued)

McVeigh had also drawn inspiration from the white supremacist novel *The Turner Diaries*, a book that also influenced David Copeland, whose nailbombing campaign in London in April 1999 resulted in the deaths of three people and the wounding of 129. Copeland deliberately targeted the capital's minority ethnic and gay communities and, under police interrogation, confessed to being racist, homophobic and a committed national socialist (McLagan and Lowles, 2000). More recently there has been a series of 'near misses' where police have caught a number of individuals before they had the chance to execute their plans. In 2009, for example, National Front member Neil Lewington was in the process of assembling a homemade arsenal of devices when his home was raided by police. He had been caught only by chance when police arrested him for causing a disturbance on a train in Suffolk, only to find the components for two firebombs in his holdall (Batty, 2009). A year later a former member of the BNP Terence Gavan was sentenced to eleven years for terrorism offences after police found a large number of guns and explosive devices at his house, while Ian Davison became the first person to be convicted for producing a prohibited substance under the 1996 Chemical Weapons Act (Feldman and Jackson, 2011: 56). However, in 2013 Pavlo Lapshyn initially avoided the attentions of the police as he undertook a short hate-fuelled campaign in the West Midlands. During this period Lapshyn murdered an elderly Muslim male and targeted three mosques with explosive devices, which detonated but failed to cause any casualties. When interviewed, Lapshyn informed police that he had 'a racial motivation and racial hatred' (Lumb and Casciani, 2013).

Made up of loosely affiliated cells united under the concept of 'leaderless resistance', C18 initially attracted a mixture of football hooligans, racist skinheads and disaffected Nazis, swelling its numbers in the mid-to-late 1990s to around 200 nationally but with many more occasionally becoming involved in its activities (Ryan, 2003: 17). Its fearsome reputation for violence was gained through attacks upon minority ethnic people, immigrants, left-wing radicals and anti-racist campaigners. The long-time presence of the Redwatch website, where personal details and pictures of anti-racist activists are publicised, coupled with the group's use of the Internet to sell white power music and organise meetings via Facebook, showed that it was adapting to utilising contemporary media (Feldman and Jackson, 2011).

During the 1990s in particular C18's links to football hooliganism were significant, and it has been alleged that these links played a pivotal role in the outbreak of racialised disorders in Oldham in May 2001. As noted above, in early 2001 the north-west town had been experiencing heightened tension between its local Asian and white communities. In an attempt to inflame this situation, Combat 18 attracted sympathisers from its national hooligan network to Oldham for the last match of the 2000/01 football season, ostensibly to engage in disorder in Westwood, an area with a large Asian population. Three weeks later, they recongregated in the town and engaged in a violent confrontation with local Asians, precipitating widespread rioting (Lowles, 2002)

However, in the early part of the twenty-first century it appears as though C18 has lost some of its potency. A number of factors have contributed to this, including the negative publicity surrounding David Copeland's murderous campaign (see Case Study 8.2 above), the imprisonment of several of its figureheads and the suspicion that C18 may have been infiltrated by the security services. Into its place, though, have stepped other white power groups, such as the Racial Volunteer Force, British Freedom Fighters and Combined Ex-Forces, which seem to offer new paramilitary vehicles for intimidation and violence.

Conclusion

This chapter set out to explore typologies of hate crime offenders, as well as their motivations and their relationships with their victims. It was noted that in the majority of instances hate crimes are enacted for the excitement and thrill involved. This is not to deny the bias element within those crimes, but to suggest that it is not perhaps the prime motivator behind them – and neither was the stronger emotion of 'hate'. The chapter then outlined the typical profile of hate offenders as young men, with criminal records, who acted in groups and who were used to routinely employing violence as a method of settling disputes. Their resentment of minority ethnic outgroups was fuelled by their suspicion that these communities were somehow stealing their jobs and other resources, and were also responsible for the deterioration of the local environment. For Walters (2011), though, these accounts fell short of explaining why it was that some people committed hate crimes while others did not, arguing that it is those whose low self-control combines with their intolerance of the 'other' and feelings of frustration and 'strain', that are more likely to become hate offenders.

It was also noted that there has been a widespread perception among perpetrators that the main political parties had neglected the needs of white British communities whilst prioritising those of minority ethnic populations, something that both the British National Party (at the ballot box) and the English Defence League (on the streets) have capitalised on. Importantly for the context of this book, a significant amount of research indicates that far-right extremists are only responsible for the perpetration of a small proportion of hate crimes, although when they do commit hate offences, perhaps in the form of 'lone wolf' activity, then these may be more extreme than those perpetrated by 'ordinary' members of the public.

Therefore, although it may well be the case that the far right is not responsible for significant amounts of hate crime, its symbolic importance, both in the damage that it can cause via its more 'spectacular' acts of hate offending or in the way that its more 'routine' activities can instil fear and anxiety in minority communities, should not be underestimated. The way that the ideas of far-right groups like the EDL can be absorbed by many within deprived and 'forgotten' white working-class estates should also not be disregarded, as these give credence to the prejudiced opinions that are already forming in the minds of some.

To a degree, though, these findings present something of a smokescreen in our endeavours to understand who it is who actually commits hate crime: given that these empirical studies were conducted in economically deprived areas with communities who generally lack social capital, invariably then a 'typical perpe-trator' is likely to possess these characteristics too. While this may give us a useful picture of hate crime in these areas it fails to reflect the broader picture of hate offending in other locations, such as more affluent places or isolated rural towns and villages. The work of Neal (2009) and our own earlier research (Chakraborti and Garland, 2004; Garland and Chakraborti, 2006) may be useful in providing another dimension to the debate. They suggest that hate offending is evident within more middle-class communities too, although this is com-monly left unacknowledged by many in those communities and also by the police and other service providers.

Guide to further reading

Walters' 'A General Theories of Hate Crime?' (2011) offers persuasive theories of the perpetration of hate crime. McDevitt et al.'s *Hate Crime Offenders* (2010) and Chapter 4 of Gerstenfeld's *Hate Crimes* (2013) provide an overview of US perspectives on hate crime perpetration. Those interested in far-right extremism should read Lowles, *White Riot* (2002), Collins, *Hate* (2012) or Trilling, *Bloody Nasty People* (2012).

Links to online material

A useful starting point for those interested in the contemporary fortunes of the BNP is the *Guardian's* resource at www.theguardian.com/politics/bnp, while the anti-fascist magazine *Searchlight* provides an extremely informative account of the far right's activities, both past and present, at www.searchlightmagazine. com/, as does the campaigning organisation Hope Not Hate at www.hopenothate. org.uk/. Those interested in examining the profiles of far-right extremists should read the bizarre and fascinating tale of neo-Nazi Nicky Crane at www.bbc.co.uk/news/magazine-25142557.

Notes

1 The exception to this is Roxell's Swedish research, which surprisingly suggests that it is 'uncommon for individuals to be registered as suspected co-offenders' (2011: 209).

2 The CPS (2014: 4) reports that the majority (83.3%) of defendants prosecuted for hate crime offences in 2012/13 across all hate crime strands were men, with 71.6% of defendants identified as belonging to the White British category: 57.7% of defendants were aged between 25-59 and 27.0% between 18-24.

3 After polling almost 950,000 votes in the 2009 European elections the BNP's vote collapsed at the 2014 equivalents, to under 200,000 (BBC, 2014).

4 Tommy Robinson is a pseudonym copied from that of a notorious Luton football hooligan. Robinson's real name is Stephen Yaxley Lennon.

5 Grunewald et al. (2013) suggest that two-fifths of the lone wolves in their study had previously been diagnosed with a mental illness.

9

RESPONDING TO HATE CRIME

Chapter summary

In the years following the Stephen Lawrence Inquiry, the police service has been required to address hate crime issues with more transparency and greater priority than ever before. Criminological research has consistently shown that the troubled relationship between the police and minority communities has had a profound impact upon police responses to hate crime and upon levels of confidence in the police amongst those groups most at risk of hate-related victimisation. Addressing these problems has formed a central feature of the post-Macpherson policing agenda.

This chapter examines some of the conceptual, cultural and operational difficulties that have plagued the policing of hate crime. Through its analysis of these difficulties, together with its assessment of the more positive developments that have taken place in recent times, the chapter highlights the need for caution when drawing definitive conclusions about police responses. The chapter then considers responses to hate crime more broadly, and gives particular attention to the scope and limitations of existing retributive responses and to the relevance of alternative models of justice and pathways of support.

Introduction

Responding to hate crime is an inherently complex task, not least in the context of policing. The police service is responsible for recording hate offences and for implementing related legislation, and through their policies and practices they can influence the way in which hate crime issues are thought of by the state and by the general public (Gerstenfeld, 2013). In addition, the police service will often be the initial source of contact for victims of hate crime and therefore police responses will need to be sufficiently sensitive to their requirements. However, this is by no means straightforward. Earlier chapters have provided insights into the profound physical and emotional impact of victimisation on individuals, families and wider communities, and have illustrated the importance of recognising this impact within the police response. At the same time, the types of groups who more often than not constitute the core victims of hate crime are not renowned for having especially high levels of trust and confidence in the police service. For reasons that will be explored shortly, these minority groups and the police have experienced an uneasy, and at times fractious relationship that has impacted upon the way in which hate crime is reported and prioritised.

These issues and their implications for the effectiveness of police responses to hate crime will be considered over the course of this chapter, as will other forms of assistance offered to victims. Previous chapters have described recent legislative developments with regard to various strands of hate crime, and we explore the capacity of these largely retributive modes of response to address the needs of hate crime victims alongside more restorative approaches that seek to repair the harms of hate.

The police response

Within the UK, hate crime has received increased levels of strategic prioritisation since events such as the murder of Stephen Lawrence and the actions of David Copeland pushed it to the forefront of policing agendas towards the end of the 1990s. Until recently, the most significant form of acknowledgement in policing terms came through the guidance issued by the Association of Chief Police Officers (ACPO). One of the three main police representative bodies (together with the Police Federation and the Superintendents' Association),[1] ACPO is seen as the most senior, and to all intents and purposes the most effective, police lobbying group in terms of its capacity to influence governmental thinking (Newburn, 2013). Consequently, the guidance document *Hate Crime: Delivering a Quality Service* (ACPO, 2005), commissioned jointly by ACPO's Race and Diversity Working Group and the Home Office Police Standards Unit, served as a key reference document for police officers and support staff in England, Wales and Northern Ireland.

The ACPO manual contained a number of features that had important implications for the policing of hate crime. One such feature relates to the distinction made between hate incidents and hate crimes. According to the guidance (2005: 9) all hate crimes are hate incidents, whereas some hate incidents may not actually constitute a criminal offence and therefore will not be recorded as a crime. This requirement for all incidents to be recorded by the police, even if they lack the requisite elements to be classified as a crime, widens the reach of the hate crime umbrella: any hate incident, whether a *prima facie* 'crime' or not, must be recorded if it meets the threshold originally laid down by the Macpherson definition of a racist incident – namely, if it is perceived by the victim or any other person as being motivated by prejudice or hate. By doing this, victims' experiences are prioritised at the expense of police officer discretion and a broader range of incidents is considered beyond what would typically be classed as crimes. At the same time though, ACPO's guidance – subsequently reinforced through the UK Government Action Plan (HM Government, 2012a) – sought to develop a common framework to encourage consistency in the recording and monitoring of hate crime by referring to five 'strands' or protected characteristics: namely disability; gender-identity; race; religion or faith; and sexual orientation (2012a: 6). Although contemporary hate crime policy, research and activism have tended to centre around these five strands, the Action Plan makes clear that local areas are free to include other strands in their responses to hate crime to reflect local concerns and priorities (see Case Study 9.1 for an example of localised practice in this context).

Since then, fresh guidance has been published by the College of Policing, the body responsible for setting standards in professional development across English and Welsh police forces. The 2014 Hate Crime Operational Guidance is an update of the ACPO 2005 manual, and provides a comprehensive overview of definitions, legislation and a range of issues directly relevant to the recording, investigation and supervision of hate offences. This revised guidance is discussed at greater length within Chapter 11. However, it is worth noting several points at this juncture. First, the new guidance follows a similar line to that taken in the ACPO manual by distinguishing between hate incidents and crimes; by identifying the perception of the victim or any other person (such as a witness, family member or carer) as the defining factor in establishing a hate incident or crime; and by referring to the five monitored strands of hate crime described above (College of Policing, 2014). Second, in addition to offering significantly more instruction to reflect developments in policing requirements, the College of Policing guidance states that the focus on monitored strands should not be used to deny the existence of other hate crimes and thereby re-affirms that agencies and partnerships are free to extend their policy responses to other strands beyond the monitored five (2014: 7).

Case Study 9.1

The Merseyside model

The Merseyside model refers to the decision made in 2006 by Merseyside Police to become the first police force in England and Wales to treat crimes against sex workers as hate crimes. This move came in the wake of concerns about the high levels of unreported violent crime against sex workers, including murder, rape, sexual and physical assault, and acknowledges their vulnerability to acts of violence and intimidation designed to 'put them in their place' (Campbell, 2014 – see Chapter 7).

The nature of this targeted violence and harassment – as expressions of prejudice and power towards some of the most socially marginalised, stigmatised and vulnerable members of society – has clear parallels with definitions of hate crime discussed in earlier chapters. As Campbell (2014: 58) observes, 'sex workers share the outgroup status of the "other" central to discrimination faced by other groups who experience hate crime. The interplay between "othering", marginalisation and criminalisation contributes to a lack of social and legal protections creating conditions in which sex worker hate victimisation can flourish.'

The approach in Merseyside has resulted in some very positive outcomes. Jacobs (2013) notes that in 2010 the overall conviction rate in Merseyside for crimes against sex workers was 84%, with the 67% conviction rate for rape standing in marked contrast to the national average of 6.5%. However, while the effectiveness of the Merseyside model has been recognised at a national level (ACPO 2011; College of Policing, 2014; CPS, 2012a; Home Office, 2011) Campbell (2014) highlights a number of challenges in sustaining this approach, including the uncertainty created through cuts to services and resources and the importance of maintaining 'buy-in' across all ranks of the police, and not just senior officers. As she suggests, ongoing initiatives are required to maintain levels of trust amongst street sex workers, to extend proactive community liaison work, to sustain quality victim support, and to embed sex workers in wider hate crime practices.

The National Ugly Mugs (NUM) scheme has also played an important role in supporting sex workers who have experienced violence or harassment and in preventing future offences. Initially funded by the Home Office, the scheme has enabled sex workers across the country to report experiences of victimisation without the need for direct contact with the police, and to receive warnings about suspicious or dangerous individuals posing as clients. Further details about the NUM scheme are available at https://uknswp.org/um/.

The emphasis given to the policing of hate crime in recent times is symptomatic of the sensitivity that surrounds relationships between the police and minority communities. Concerns over the discriminatory policing of minorities, and in particular ethnic minorities, have been raised by criminologists throughout the past thirty years or so, and while this body of criminological research – together with the momentum for reform that arose through high-profile cases, changes in public attitudes and the Stephen Lawrence Inquiry – has shaped a policing agenda that is more equipped to address the needs of a diverse society, some of these concerns still remain.

A variety of cultural explanations have been put forward over the years in order to account for the prejudice expressed towards minority groups by police officers. In general terms the notion of police culture has been used 'to explain and condemn a broad spectrum of policing practice' (Waddington, 1999: 287) and is commonly presented as one of the most significant barriers to police reform. In so doing, however, writers have, often unwittingly, conveyed the misleading assumption that police practice is informed by a culture that is singular, monolithic and unchanging, rather than the more contemporary criminological standpoint that recognises cultural variation within and between police forces (Chan, 1997; Foster, 2002; Newburn, 2013). Acknowledging the existence of police *cultures*, or *culture and subcultures*, facilitates a more nuanced understanding of cultural bias and its influence upon police–minority relations. Moreover, recognising that there is more than just one set of cultural values – or a singular belief system – that informs police behaviour can help us to appreciate why the prioritisation of hate crime at a managerial or corporate level may not always be matched by a similar standard of commitment at a 'street cop' level.

In his authoritative analysis of police culture, Reiner (2010: 113–38) refers to a collection of values, norms and perspectives that influence police officers' conduct and that constitute the core characteristics of street cop culture, including a sense of mission, suspicion, solidarity, conservatism, machismo, racial prejudice and pragmatism. While there are positive elements to some of these characteristics – including, for instance, a desire to catch 'the bad guys', collective responsibility, dedication, bravery – they also have more sinister implications in terms of their capacity to foster an inward-looking, cynical and prejudiced police service. Of particular relevance here is the cultural trait of racial prejudice and stereotyping within the police. For Reiner (2010) this prejudice derives to a large degree from societal racism that places ethnic minorities in the lower strata of society together with other marginal groups – the unemployed, alcoholics, deviant youth, sex workers – and which therefore legitimates their treatment as 'police property'.

The capacity for cultural bias to tarnish relations between the police and minority communities has of course received official acknowledgement through the Scarman Report of 1981 and the Macpherson Report of 1999. Both reports were described as watershed moments in the context of policing and race relations, and have resulted in extensive programmes of reform. However, questions remain over the extent to which problems of institutional prejudice have been resolved, especially in the years since the Macpherson Report. Studies suggest that progress has been mixed in a number of respects, not least in the context of the disproportionate use of stop and search (EHRC, 2009b); the effectiveness of police diversity training (Rowe and Garland, 2007); police officers' understanding of institutional racism (Holdaway and O'Neill, 2006); and the recruitment, retention and progression of minority ethnic officers (Bowling et al., 2008).

Research has also shown that these concerns have implications not just for relations between the police and minority ethnic communities, but for the policing of homophobic and transphobic hate (Dittman, 2003; Moran, 2007; Stonewall, 2014; Williams and Robinson, 2004), the policing of faith communities

(Awan, 2013a; Chakraborti, 2007; McGhee, 2005) and the policing of disability-related harassment (Deal, 2007; EHRC, 2011). The nature of these concerns will be discussed shortly.

Problems associated with the policing of hate crime

Eliciting the support and trust of the public is a priority for contemporary policing, but this has proved to be especially problematic in the context of hate crime where negative attitudes towards the police may have become entrenched through media reports, indirect knowledge and personal experience of discriminatory practice. Such attitudes are often rooted in the historical tensions and oppressive policing that have blighted police–minority relations over the past fifty years or so. The issue of over-policing and under-protection has been documented extensively, particularly with regard to the policing of black communities (Bowling, 1999; Hall et al., 1978; Hunte, 1966), and has resulted in the under-reporting of hate crime by minority groups. We have seen in earlier chapters the sizeable difference between official police records of hate crime and the consistently higher numbers identified through victim surveys, and this variation is reflective of victims' reluctance to report incidents to the police.

Crucially, the problem of under- or non-reporting is not confined exclusively to minority ethnic communities. For example, in their survey of more than 2,500 lesbian, gay and bisexual people across Britain, Stonewall (2014) found that more than three-quarters of those experiencing a hate offence did not report it to the police and two-thirds did not report to anyone. Equally, Herek, Cogan and Gillis's (2003) Californian-based research illustrated that victims of homophobic hate crime were considerably less likely to report incidents to the police than victims of 'ordinary' crimes, and Williams and Robinson (2004) have suggested that up to three-quarters of such victims fail to report to the police primarily because they perceive them to be 'anti-gay' and are fearful of secondary victimisation from officers. Similar concerns have been expressed over the policing of transphobic hate crime (Dittman, 2003), while the under-reporting of disablist hate crime may stem from victims not knowing who to report to; or from fear of either the consequences of reporting, of naming a carer, family member or 'friend' as the perpetrator, or of not being believed by the police or other authorities (EHRC, 2011; Sin, 2012; Thomas, 2011).

Chakraborti, Garland and Hardy (2014a) have identified a range of other factors relevant to the non-reporting of hate crime. Victims in their study commonly referred to the amount of time required to report a hate crime as being a problem that they felt was often under-appreciated by the police and other organisations. For those with work and childcare commitments or caring responsibilities, taking time off to report hate crimes was not a viable option, particularly as these experiences were commonplace for large numbers of victims. Equally, the level of courage, resilience and emotional stamina needed to share harrowing experiences with a stranger was something that many believed was commonly overlooked by practitioners, as were the cultural and linguistic barriers faced in particular by victims from new and emerging communities and those for whom English was not a first language.

The problem of under-reporting may also be related to the more conceptual problem of the process–incident contradiction. Earlier chapters have underlined the importance of viewing hate crime victimisation as an ongoing social process that should be considered in the context of a broader range of factors including historical patterns of prejudice; the lived experiences of the individuals, families and communities targeted; the dynamics of the local population; the attitudes and behaviour of offenders, their families and communities; and wider local, national and global discourses (Bowling, 1999). Conceiving of hate crime victimisation in this manner encourages recognition of the broader dimensions of such victimisation, and gives emphasis to 'low-level' or everyday experiences of prejudice which in themselves may not appear especially serious but which cumulatively, and when considered in their proper context, can have a lasting impact upon the victim, their family and the wider community.

However, the police, together with other criminal justice agencies, generally respond to incidents and not this ongoing social process. For Bowling (1999: 285–6) it is this contradiction that explains why hate crime victims may feel dissatisfied with police responses while officers on the other hand may believe that they have responded effectively:

> ... the process of law enforcement – policing and the administration of criminal justice – is constituted in the response to tightly-defined **incidents** [emphasis in original]. An incident is a one-dimensional, narrowly restricted time-slice within which only the actions of the immediate protagonists are of any relevance ... Incidents are describable and measurable but appear random and inexplicable. When context is drained from lived experience, it becomes impossible to understand the significance of the event to the individual or community targeted, or how and why the event occurred. As the incident is transformed from the world of the victims' experience into an object for policing it is placed in the new context of the police organisational and cultural milieu.

Reducing the process of victimisation to a series of disconnected, 'one-off' events may allow the policing of hate crime to become more measurable or quantifiable but can result in police officers failing to treat experiences with the gravity that they deserve, regardless of any procedural changes introduced at a strategic level. A related idea, developed by Bowling following the earlier work of Grimshaw and Jefferson (1987), offers further insights into the problems that arise in the policing of hate crime. The 'hierarchy of police relevance' refers to a hypothetical set of values that police officers use, sometimes subconsciously, other times knowingly, to inform their response to different types of incident. Depending on the nature of the incident and requirements of the law, officers may be required to exercise discretion in determining the relevance of the incident to the police, and this process of categorisation will invariably be informed by that officer's understanding of the 'natural agenda' of police work.

At the summit of this imaginary hierarchy is what Bowling refers to as 'good crime': unambiguous criminal offences with a 'good' victim (credible, high status, willing to testify), a 'good' perpetrator (an experienced or ideally a professional criminal) and cases that offer the prospect of a 'good' arrest being made (a high likelihood of securing a conviction). Lower down the hierarchy is 'rubbish' crime, so called because of the low social status of the victim, the low likelihood of detection and arrest and the possibility that the victim might withdraw their allegation at a later date. At the bottom end of the hierarchy are incidents described as 'disputes' or 'disturbances', which include those events regarded as highly irrelevant or legally ambiguous (Bowling, 1999: 246–51).

In his analysis of police officers' categorisation of racist incidents, Bowling (1999: 256) found that patterns of harassment were rarely recognised by officers, who instead tended to view racist incidents as spontaneous or random acts of yobbishness which by and large fell under the banner of 'rubbish crime'. Only the most serious racist incidents were regarded as 'crimes' and in only the most serious of these was prosecution initiated[2]; in all other cases incidents were mostly seen as having little or no practical relevance to the police. Even in the incidents typically classified as 'good crime' – robberies, assaults and thefts – Bowling observed that evidence of racial motivation was irrelevant to how officers went about their work aside from requiring the completion of an additional item of paperwork.

Clearly, in the years since Bowling's research there has been considerable change to the policing agenda as a result of the prioritisation of racist and other forms of hate crime. One could argue, therefore, that hate crime has now been afforded a much higher and more meaningful status within the hierarchy of police relevance as a result of these developments. At the same time though, one of Bowling's key findings – namely, that the 'top down' view of racist incidents as a force priority conflicted with the operational 'common-sense' attitudes held by rank and file officers – is significant as it suggests that some of the more negative aspects of police occupational culture can retain a stubborn influence on police practice irrespective of changes to police policy.

These concerns have again resurfaced through the crisis engulfing the Metropolitan Police following fresh revelations in the Ellison Review (2014) about the role of undercover policing in the Stephen Lawrence case, revelations that prompted Janet Hills, Chair of the Metropolitan Police's Black Police Association, to conclude that the force was still institutionally racist, with continued failings around disproportionate stop and search and the under-representation and lack of progression of ethnic minorities confirming to her that 'there has been no change, no progression' (Dodd and Evans, 2014). Campaigners have also highlighted continued failings in the policing of disability-related hate (Disability Hate Crime Network, 2014b; Pring, 2014), which suggest that only limited progress has been made following the flawed response to the Fiona Pilkington case (see Chapter 6).

These problems may be attributable to individual, institutional and cultural prejudice or ignorance. Hall (2013) offers several further pertinent observations in this context. The enforcement of hate crime laws in effect requires the police to reverse long-held stereotypes about minority groups in the sense that they are more likely to be victims than perpetrators, a reality which, as Hall notes, might not sit comfortably with some of the more enduring features of occupational culture. Equally, a reluctance to apply the hate crime label to a case may stem from officers' failing to recognise qualitative differences between a crime and a hate crime in terms of the impact on victims, and therefore deliberately choosing to bypass having to think about the 'hate' element because they can still secure a 'result' for the underlying offence. While elements of police discretion have in theory been removed through successive pieces of hate crime guidance – and in particular through the instruction to record incidents in line with the Macpherson definition of a racist incident – the attitudes and decision-making processes of individual officers still have the capacity to influence responses to hate crime and relationships between the police and hate crime victims.

Wider responses

The complex relationship between the police and minority communities has been – and will no doubt continue to be – one that requires careful monitoring. Although it is important not to lose sight of the strategic and practical progress that has been made in the years since the Stephen Lawrence Inquiry (see, *inter alia*, Chakraborti and Garland, 2009; Hall, 2013; Rowe, 2004, 2007), the concerns outlined above are illustrative of the ongoing problems that continue to beset the policing of hate crime. They are also illustrative of the need for a more holistic approach which recognises that responses to hate require more than just effective police intervention. This is particularly pertinent given that only 40% of hate crime incidents come to the attention of the police according to the findings of the combined 2011/12 and 2012/13 sweeps of the Crime Survey for England and Wales (Home Office et al., 2013). The relevance of a holistic approach was acknowledged in the 2012 UK government Action Plan (see Case Study 9.2) whose recommendations around preventing hate crime and increasing reporting and access to support give emphasis to the importance of locally administered responses involving all criminal justice agencies as well as other professionals, voluntary organisations and communities.

Case Study 9.2

The UK government response to hate crime

In March 2012 the UK government published an Action Plan entitled *Challenge It, Report It, Stop It: The Government's Plan to Tackle Hate Crime*. Its symbolic relevance as the first piece of hate crime guidance to be issued by the Conservative-led coalition is noted by Hall (2013: 144), who refers to the action plan as a sign, at least in principle, of the Coalition's commitment to maintaining the prioritisation of hate crime policy evident from the laws introduced by previous successive Labour administrations.

The Action Plan is rooted in what is described as 'a new approach to cutting crime, based on freeing professionals from top-down micro-management and performance targets, and making the police democratically accountable to the communities they serve' (2012a: 8). With reference to hate crime, this new approach is based on three core principles: preventing hate crime (by challenging the attitudes that underpin it and prioritising early intervention); increasing reporting and accessing support (by building victim confidence and supporting local partnerships); and improving operational responses (by better identifying and managing cases and dealing effectively with offenders) (2012a: 9).

A 23-point plan is outlined under the theme of preventing hate crime which sets out actions to be led by a range of government departments, criminal justice agencies and the government's Independent Advisory Group on Hate Crime in conjunction with local agencies and voluntary sector organisations. These action points include improving the evidence base on hate crime; reducing negative media stereotypes of particular victim groups; more work in schools and in other educational contexts to challenge bullying; developing a programme of work to tackle Internet-related hate; and continued support for cross-government working groups on antisemitic and anti-Muslim hatred.

In a similar vein, a 16-point plan is offered to increase reporting and access to support, including identifying areas for improved data collection and dissemination; more engagement with 'at risk' communities; continued support for True Vision and other alternative reporting schemes; and increased funding for individual organisations and projects to facilitate improved practice. Finally, 16 action points are identified for the third stream of improving operational responses, which include the publication of new guidance to follow on from the 2005 ACPO hate crime manual; updates to training for all police roles; a review of legislation and guidance around disability-related and transphobic hate; and assessing the scope of alternative disposals for less serious hate crimes.

The principles underpinning the Action Plan are laudable, and a follow-up report outlining ways in which its action points have been delivered was published in 2014 (see Chapter 11 for further discussion). Evaluating the long-term success and sustainability of those actions is an area that, we would argue, demands greater attention. However, the value of the 2012 Action Plan as an indicator of the current – and likely future – preference for a more rounded, localised and multi-layered response to hate crime is significant.

This has implications for members of the wider police family who support the work of sworn officers, such as community support officers, special constables, neighbourhood wardens and other forms of municipal policing and private security guards, as well as those who oversee their work such as Police and Crime Commissioners and members of the Independent Police Complaints Commission. Within this context, responding to hate crime is not simply the responsibility of the police service *per se* but that of a far wider range of actors (Chakraborti, 2009). This also includes other criminal justice agencies such as the Crown Prosecution Service (CPS) and the National Offender Management Service (NOMS), who all work to the same common definition of monitored hate crime in order to ensure consistent approaches to recording and monitoring (HM Government, 2012a).

On paper at least there are signs of progress with regard to their responses to hate crime. In the years between 2006/07 to 2011/12 the number of cases charged by the CPS rose from 8,390 (or 59% of all cases considered) to 10,845 (73%), with the number of successful prosecutions over the same period increasing from 9,621 to 11,843 (CPS, 2012b). The number of successful prosecutions for 2012/13 dropped to 10,794, as did the number of cases charged (8,891) although the charge rate in 2012/13 was broadly similar to the previous year's figure (72% of all cases considered compared with 73%) (CPS, 2014).

Other recent developments include a Criminal Justice Joint Inspection (CJJI) of CPS, police and probation trusts' responses to disability hate crime policy (CJJI, 2013); an audit of disability hate crime cases from initial report to prosecution outcome; and a review of the CPS Code of Practice for Victims of Crime (Home Office et al., 2013). In July 2013 the NOMS published its own Hate Crime Framework which applies to offender management in both the community and in custody and sets out expectations in relation to the identification, assessment, provision of interventions and management of convicted hate crime offenders (Home Office et al., 2013). Examples such as these are illustrative of a flurry of activity at a criminal justice policy level, although the extent to which this strategic prioritisation translates to 'real-life' improvement is difficult to gauge, as noted above in relation to policing.

Previous chapters have outlined the way in which acts and expressions of hate have been criminalised through the introduction of various legislative provisions. These chapters have also explored the symbolic and practical value of these provisions. Hate crime laws and their enforcement have the capacity to express our collective condemnation of prejudice and the value of diversity and equality; to send a declaratory message to offenders; to convey a message of support to victims and stigmatised communities; to build confidence in the criminal justice system within some of the more disaffected and vulnerable members of society; and to acknowledge the additional harm caused by hate offences (for further discussion see, *inter alia*, Iganski, 2008; ODIHR, 2009a; Walters, 2014a). Effective legislation and enforcement, therefore, are important both for individual freedoms and security and for cohesive communities.

At the same time, the needs of hate crime victims (and offenders, as discussed shortly) are not always addressed through the conventional punitive approach. Williams and Tregidga (2013) refer to a disjuncture between victim-centred reporting mechanisms and evidence-driven criminal justice prosecution processes that can leave victims – and in particular vulnerable victims of persistent 'low-level' hate incidents – frustrated and additionally traumatised by the absence of stringent evidential proof required for prosecution. Their analysis of victims' perceptions also highlights the relevance of education as an appropriate response to hate crime (see also Chakraborti et al., 2014a) and the importance of restorative approaches.

The benefits of restorative approaches to hate crime have become increasingly relevant as scholars have begun to highlight the shortcomings of exclusively punitive responses. As Hall (2013) notes, prisons have limited deterrent value, offer limited opportunity for rehabilitative programmes and can be 'hotbeds' for prejudice, intolerance and hate group activity and recruitment (see also Blazak, 2009; Gerstenfeld, 2013). Walters (2014b) too suggests that the punishment and labelling of offenders as 'hate offenders' do little to challenge hate-motivated behaviours and equally little to support the healing of hate victims – beyond perhaps appeasing a visceral desire for an offender to receive his 'just deserts'. On the other hand, the restorative approach offers a viable, more inclusive alternative by seeking to 'restore harm by including affected parties in a (direct or indirect) encounter and a process of understanding through voluntary and honest dialogue' (Gavrielides, 2007: 139). By actively bringing together victims and offenders, restorative interventions offer a form of dialogue which enables offenders to be confronted with the harms of their actions and which can help to break down the fears, stereotypes and prejudices that give rise to hate crimes.

Walters and Hoyle (2012) have shown how mediated interventions can be especially effective in the context of hate incidents that arise as a result of acrimonious disputes between people who know each other at some level – as neighbours or acquaintances for instance. Whereas conventional criminal justice involvement in such cases can often exacerbate conflicts and reinforce compartmentalised, de-contextualised pictures of hate offences, Walters and Hoyle's research illustrates that the process of facilitated mediation can reduce levels of anger, anxiety and fear and can prevent further incidents from recurring or escalating.

It is important to note that these kinds of restorative interventions will not be appropriate in all circumstances. There will inevitably be cases where offenders' prejudices are so deeply entrenched that restorative dialogue will only ever be of limited transformative effect (Walters, 2014b); equally, the approach is often contingent on the offender being caught and convicted, the victim being willing to meet them, and cooperation being established between the respective parties (Hall, 2013). Nonetheless, as an alternative to conventional law enforcement approaches and as a mechanism to challenge and change the behaviour of hate crime offenders, the restorative approach has much potential in appropriate contexts.

Conclusion

This chapter began by considering issues relating to the policing of hate crime. On the basis of what we have learnt in this chapter, there are three key points to take forward when evaluating policing in this area. First, and crucially, we must acknowledge the progress that has been made in the years since the Lawrence Inquiry. The strategic prioritisation of hate crime during the past fifteen years or so has required the police service to develop a more informed and inclusive stance towards hate crime, and a raft of policies, programmes and initiatives have been established which give greater recognition to the needs of hate crime victims. Second though, despite those positive developments some of the more problematic aspects of policing hate crime still present major challenges for the police service, whether in terms of raising levels of confidence in the police or encouraging victims of targeted hostility to report.

Third, there is evidence to suggest that the residual mistrust affecting the policing of hate crime has left its mark not just upon minority group perceptions of the police but also upon police perceptions of minority groups and other vulnerable targets of hate and prejudice. As noted in our first edition, it is difficult to say conclusively whether the strategic prioritisation of hate crime has fundamentally altered the way in which police officers relate to the process of victimisation or recognise the wider harms of hate crime. This is relevant more broadly to other statutory and third sector organisations. Hate crime leads and representatives within these organisations may have a sound understanding of key issues but problems of policy-drift, a lack of key-worker engagement and an over-reliance on designated hate crime 'specialists' may affect the quality of response (James and Simmonds, 2012), as may an organisational failure to translate policy into meaningful action and engage in preventative work (Chakraborti et al., 2011).

However, this chapter has highlighted that responses to hate crime require understanding and intervention at a range of other levels too. This and other chapters have referred to the importance of challenging prejudicial attitudes before they fully develop, and in this context education and early intervention within and beyond the classroom have an important role in raising awareness of the harms of hate. Equally, health and social care services can offer crucial support and treatment to victims, and their capacity to recognise and respond to hate crimes is pivotal given that such crimes often have severe consequences for physical and emotional health and well-being. Non-Governmental Organisations (NGOs) play a key role in a variety of ways, not least by monitoring and reporting incidents, acting as a voice for victims and campaigning for action and improvements to legislation (ODIHR, 2009b). Victim Support, the Samaritans and other charitable services can also be a significant source of help for those seeking emotional and practical guidance.

These are just some of the pathways of support which individually and collectively can play a valuable part in developing effective responses to hate crime victimisation. However, prioritising, monitoring and investing in these responses within a climate of austerity and public spending cuts is a further challenge which can undermine responses to hate crime. This context is often under-analysed within hate crime scholarship and is something readers should be mindful of.

Guide to further reading

There are a number of very useful texts that explore issues relating to the policing of hate crime, although for the most part these have centred on race and racist crime. Among them, Bowling and Phillips, *Racism, Crime and Justice* (2002) and Rowe, *Policing, Race and Racism* (2004) offer comprehensive accounts of the historical and contemporary relationship between the police and minority ethnic communities, whilst the progress made following the Lawrence Inquiry is assessed in Hall, Grieve and Savage (eds), *Policing and the Legacy of Lawrence* (2009) and Rowe (ed.), *Policing Beyond Macpherson: Issues in Policing, Race and Society* (2007).

Chakraborti and Garland (eds), *Responding to Hate Crime: The Case for Connecting Policy and Research* (2014) contains a series of contributions that identify ways of improving wider responses to hate crime, and several of the chapters in Hall, *Hate Crime* (2013) are especially relevant, particularly Chapters 7 and 8. Equally, Walters, *Hate Crime and Restorative Justice: Exploring Causes, Repairing Harms* (2014c) is an excellent starting point for readers interested in the effectiveness of restorative interventions.

Links to online material

The True Vision website offers information about hate crime, its various forms and sources of support, and provides a national online reporting facility as an alternative for those who prefer not to report directly to the police. The website can be accessed at http://report-it.org.uk/home.

In 2011 the Equality and Human Rights Commission initiated the first systematic investigation of what public authorities across England, Wales and Scotland are doing to eliminate targeted harassment and violence. The findings of this research are available at www.equalityhumanrights.com/uploaded_files/research/rr74_targeted_harassment.pdf.

Notes

1 By far the largest police representative body, the Police Federation represents 'rank and file' police officers, and is generally the most 'union-like' of the three bodies. The Superintendents' Association is a much smaller body representing the middle tier of the police service, which in some respects makes it less effective than the larger Police Federation and the more senior Association of Chief Police Officers (Newburn, 2013).

2 Bowling (1999: 278) notes that out of the 152 incidents recorded by the police in the 18 months between 1 July 1987 and 31 December 1988, the police conducted interviews with perpetrators in only ten cases and brought charges in two cases. This amounted to a prosecution rate of 1.3%.

10

INTERNATIONAL PERSPECTIVES
ON HATE CRIME

Chapter summary

The term 'hate crime' has been used since the 1960s when it was adopted by groups engaged in the civil rights movement in the United States as a way of underlining the commonalities of their struggles. However, while there has been growth in both the usage and currency of the hate crime concept since that era, there appears to be little in the way of a definitive international understanding of what hate crime actually is, how it manifests itself and how it can be challenged. In some countries its adoption has precipitated genuine attempts to combat the malign effects of targeted victimisation, while in others it has spawned initiatives that have appeared rather tokenistic and half-hearted.

Interestingly, though, much of the scholarship surrounding hate crime has focused upon developments in individual states, with comparatively little in the way of cross-national analysis. This chapter is a small step towards redressing this imbalance, although it should be acknowledged that a lack of space curtails any exploration of these complex themes in significant depth. What is contained here is nevertheless a timely examination of how understandings of hate crime have developed, primarily in Europe, the United States and Australia. It begins by considering how hate crime has 'translated' across national boundaries. Different legislative and other approaches designed to combat hate crime are assessed, and it is argued that while there have been some successes in combating hate crime in certain individual countries, in others much work still needs to be done in developing effective policies and practices that offer meaningful protection from targeted victimisation.

Introduction

In the United Kingdom the concept of hate crime is now well-established in both practitioner and academic circles. As highlighted in Chapter 1, the

Macpherson Report of 1999 ignited a debate in government, policy and scholarly circles that quickly broadened from the Report's narrow remit on the policing of race and ethnicity to a much wider discussion of how a range of minority groups related to, and were treated by, the criminal justice system as a whole. Much of this focused upon how the police, CPS and courts were dealing with the victims of targeted harassment and violence. Thus, gradually, the term 'hate crime' was adopted to describe the unique form of abuse and violence suffered by religious, gay, transgender and disabled communities, in addition to minority ethnic groups.

Interestingly though, the UK had been a little slow in grasping the utility of the notion of hate crime as it had been invoked in the United States since the 1960s as a conduit through which the shared experiences of those involved in the civil rights struggles could be affirmed. Since then its value as a means of encapsulating a particular form of targeted victimisation has generally been acknowledged across North America, although, as we shall see below, this process has not been without its own flaws and controversies.

Countries such as New Zealand, Canada and Australia have also developed their own approaches to developing hate crime initiatives over the last two decades, including the enactment of specific suites of legislation. However, it has only been within the last fifteen years or so that the idea of 'hate crime' has become current within the European Union. Indeed, the Office for Democratic Institutions and Human Rights (ODIHR) notes that the term 'hate crime' was only used officially for the first time by the Organization for Security and Co-operation in Europe (OSCE) in 2003, although some individual states had been employing it since the early 1990s (ODIHR, 2013). Since that time the concept has struggled to establish itself in many nation states that are part of the EU. In an era of austerity that has witnessed a concomitant rise in levels of hate crime and a flourishing far-right presence in some countries, there is a pressing need to persuade some governments of the moral obligation they have to protect their own minority communities from prejudice.

European understandings of hate crime

The intergovernmental organisation ODIHR has developed a definition of hate crime applicable to all of the 57 countries in the OSCE, including the 27 EU member states. ODIHR sees hate crimes as having two key aspects: first, they must constitute a criminal offence, and second, the victim of the offence must have been deliberately targeted 'because of [their] ethnicity, "race", religion or other status' (ODIHR, 2013: 6). ODIHR also uses the term 'bias' when defining the motivation behind hate crimes, rather than the more extreme emotion of hate, and suggests that 'bias' does not even have to be the primary motive for the offence: just being an element of it is enough for it to be considered a hate crime.

By way of contrast, in Germany an incident is deemed a hate crime if either hate or bias is identified as the *primary* motive for the offence, a narrower definition than that of ODIHR or those states, like the UK, where hate or bias only needs to be a *contributory* factor in the commissioning of the offence. In addition, the German situation is further complicated by the classification of the two main subcategories of hate crime (xenophobic and antisemitic) as 'politically motivated right-wing crimes', which means that hate crimes that do not conform to this notion (such as homophobic or minority on majority racist crimes, or those not committed by far-right extremists) are often misclassified as offences without a bias element (Glet, 2009). Meanwhile, in Sweden, for instance, where the concept of hate crime is comparatively new to criminal justice practitioners and academics (Roxell, 2011) the National Council for Crime Prevention's (Brå) definition of hate crimes is that they are 'motivated by fear of, or hostility or hate towards the victim based on skin colour, nationality or ethnic background, religious belief, sexual orientation or transgender identity or expression' (Brå, 2013: 6), thus acknowledging the varied but inclusive motivations of 'fear', 'hostility' and 'hate'.

As ODIHR acknowledges, collecting hate crime data from a diverse range of countries, each with their own understandings of the term as well as varying policy priorities, can be problematic (ODIHR, 2013). This is a longstanding issue within Europe, although in an effort to rectify the situation the EU adopted a Framework Decision (2008/913/JHA) on combating racism and xenophobia through criminal law in 2008, which was designed to 'harmonise' relevant legislation and create a common approach to tackling hate crime in those areas across the EU (Whine, 2014). As well as containing provisions on genocide, crimes against humanity and war crimes, the Decision required member states to criminalise incitement to hatred directed at people 'defined by reference to race, colour, religion, descent or national or ethnic origin' (FRA, 2012: 25). It also directed member states to ensure that 'racist and xenophobic motivation is considered an aggravating circumstance' which should be considered when sentencing in such cases is passed (2012: 25).

Furthermore, in late 2012 the EU adopted a Directive (2012/29/EU) which contained provisions that recognised the specific needs of victims of hate crime and the support they require. Among other things, the Directive instructed member states to make sure that employees throughout the criminal justice system were trained in recognising and dealing with hate crime cases. Article 22, meanwhile, obliged member states to identify, at the individual level, any measures that needed to be taken to 'protect' people from being victimised, based upon their 'personal characteristics' such as 'age, gender and gender identity or expression, ethnicity, race, religion, sexual orientation, health, disability, residence status, communication difficulties, relationship to or dependence on the offender and previous experience of crime' (ODIHR, 2013: 39).[1]

Despite these initiatives, a number of different approaches are still evident across the EU with regard to devising and then enforcing hate crime legislation. For example, some countries such as Belgium and the UK have introduced laws which state that the offender must have demonstrated some hatred, malice or hostility towards their victim in order to be convicted.[2] Some of these include separate 'racially aggravated' and 'religiously aggravated' offences,[3] although ODIHR (2009a) argues that this is relatively rare among EU states as most have laws that just offer courts the opportunity to enhance the penalty given to a perpetrator if the offence contains a bias element.[4] In contrast to these types of laws that require proof of motivation, in other states it is enough to secure a conviction if a causal link is apparent between the offender's actions and the victim's characteristics, regardless of any evidence of bias on the part of the perpetrator[5] (ODIHR, 2009a).

Compounding these differences in legislative approaches is the lack of consensus among academics and practitioners, noted in Chapter 1, regarding which groups are actually defined as hate crime victim groups and thus afforded protection under legislation. This debate extends not just to which *minority* groups are included but whether *majority* groups can also be incorporated (Chakraborti and Garland, 2012). These conundrums are reflected in the framing of laws within EU member states, with some protecting all groups and others just minorities. In the context of the UK, for instance, anyone from any background can potentially be the victim of a hate crime: thereby those belonging to minority *and* majority communities are protected by law against acts of targeted hostility. In Sweden, however, a member of a majority community cannot be deemed to be the victim of a hate crime if targeted by someone from a minority community, while similarly a minority community member cannot be treated as a hate crime victim if attacked by somebody from another minority background (Klingspor, 2008).

Lithuania and Slovakia provide notable examples of differing attitudes towards hate crime legislation. Both countries amended their criminal codes in relation to hate crime offences in 2009 but adopted contrasting approaches to doing so. The Slovakian modification made 'public incitement to violence or hatred' along the grounds of race, ethnicity, nationality or religion a criminal offence (ODIHR, 2010a). The Lithuanian amendment, however, was broader in scope, as it involved adding general aggravating circumstances provisions applicable to all crimes, which included (among others) such protected categories as language, social status, convictions and views – identity characteristics that are not evident in the legislation of many countries in the European Union and beyond.

However, as FRA (2012) acknowledges, the monitoring of hate crime and the collation of statistics are carried out in a far from uniform fashion across Europe. For example, a total of 25 EU states officially record data on racist/xenophobic crime, the most monitored type of hate crime among EU countries. Around half monitor antisemitic crime (12 states), a third homophobic (8), and just a quarter religiously motivated and Islamophobic crime (6 each). Only four monitor disablist or transphobic hate crime (FRA, 2012: 31), a worryingly low figure for these two types of hate crime that have often been marginalised from the broader 'hate debate'. The Charter of Fundamental Rights of the European Union obliges member states to combat racist, xenophobic, religiously motivated, disablist, homophobic and transphobic hate crimes, but it seems as though this obligation is not felt as keenly by as many states as it should be.

That some states do not demonstrate the expected commitment to tackling hate crime is of especial concern in the context of the recent EU-wide austerity climate, in which many minority groups across the EU, including Roma, Somalis, sub-Saharan Africans, Jewish, disabled, and lesbian, gay, bisexual and trans people, have been 'scapegoated' by some sections of the press and political classes, resulting in a rise in the number of hate incidents (FRA, 2013a; Sin, 2014). This has occurred against a backdrop of hostility towards immigration, evidenced by the electoral successes of parties that support such policies in a number of member states. This was perhaps most startlingly illustrated in Norway in 2013, where the country's general election saw the far-right, virulently anti-immigration Progress Party receive sufficient votes for it to be included as a junior partner in the nascent government. This occurred less than two years after Anders Behring Breivik's Islamophobia-fuelled killing spree had supposedly ushered in a mood of national 'soul-searching' by the Norwegian public regarding its attitudes to, among other things, multiculturalism. Instead, as Nilsen states, 'it seemed clear that [Breivik] had emerged from the fertile ground of a racism and an Islamophobia that had attained a degree of respectability in public debate in Norway' (Nilsen, 2013 – see Case Study 10.1).

Case Study 10.1

Lone wolf *in extremis*: Anders Behring Breivik

On 22 July 2011 Norway experienced the worst terrorist atrocities in its history. In mid-afternoon on that day, eight people died and over 200 were injured when a car bomb exploded without warning outside government buildings in the nation's capital, Oslo. Later that day, a further 69 people were killed and over 100 injured in a mass shooting on the island of Utoya, just off Norway's mainland, which had been hosting the Norwegian Labour Party's annual youth camp. While there was initial confusion as to which group or organisation was behind the acts, it quickly emerged that there was just one person responsible for both: 32-year-old

(Continued)

(Continued)

Norwegian Anders Behring Breivik, who openly confessed to the atrocities. He had picked his targets deliberately as he felt he had to act to save the country from its Labour government and supporters, who were, in his eyes, promoting 'an Islamic colonisation of Norway' (Fekete, 2012: 5). At his subsequent trial in 2012 an unrepentant Breivik was convicted of terrorist offences and given a prison sentence with a 'time frame' of 21 years, which included the possibility that it could be extended indefinitely if Breivik was still perceived to be a danger to Norwegian society.

In the period before his trial it became apparent that Breivik was a far-right extremist who had released his own 'manifesto' on the day of the massacres. Entitled *2083: A European Declaration of Independence*, the 1,500-page document had been sent via email to over a thousand addresses, and was awash with ultra-nationalism, neo-conservatism, racism and paganism. It called for a new monocultural Europe based on a form of Christian cultural conservatism, and was laced with vituperative Islamophobic sentiment (Institute of Race Relations, 2011). Breivik viewed himself as a 'Justiciar Knight Commander for Knights Templar Europe', a group he claimed to have co-founded with like-minded others (Stroud, 2013). He boasted of links to various far-right groupings including the English Defence League yet could provide scant concrete evidence to back up these claims.

However, what appears to be beyond doubt is that Breivik had spent years preparing for the events of July 2011. In that time he acquired firearms, protective armour, a police uniform, which he wore during his attack on Utoya, bought fertiliser and explosive primer for bomb-making, and supposedly honed his shooting skills while playing computer games (Pidd, 2012). On the day of his murderous spree, he described himself as 'Commander Anders Breivik of the Norwegian anti-communist resistance' to police (Fekete, 2012: 5), although there is no evidence of the involvement of anyone else in this 'organisation'. Indeed, while he participated in various far-right and neo-Nazi online forums and blogs, and attempted to network with others across Europe who shared his views, it seemed as though the idea for, and execution of, his mid-summer murdering rampage were all his own work.

Other international perspectives

Unsurprisingly, it is not just within Europe where there is a lack of consensus regarding the parameters of the concept of hate crime and which targeted groups should be classified as hate crime victim groups. Of the 57 member states of the Organization for Security and Cooperation in Europe (which in reality has more of a global reach than just Europe), 51 have reported to ODIHR that they collate hate crime data under a number of different bias categories (ODIHR, 2013). As Table 10.1 shows, the most widely used categories are those based around (broadly speaking) race, ethnicity and religion, which are utilised by two-thirds of OSCE states for data collection. Interestingly, statistics are compiled on gender and language in a significant minority of states, while 13 gather them for categories other than those in Table 10.1 – including right-wing extremism, wealth, health and political beliefs. Interestingly, FRA (2012) notes that there is a 'readiness' to include a wider range of protected characteristics in a significant number of countries, including Croatia, Finland, The Netherlands and Spain.

Table 10.1 Numbers of states collecting hate crime data by different identity characteristics

Identity characteristic	Number of states
Ethnicity/origin/minority	35
'Race'/colour	35
Religion	34
Sexual orientation	21
Gender	17
Citizenship	16
Disability	16
Language	14
Transgender	11
Other	13

Source: ODIHR, 2013: 18–19

The issue of which identity characteristics are included under the legislative hate crime 'umbrella' has been brought into sharp relief by two remarkable court cases that occurred in the 2000s in Australia, in which legal judgments ruled that paedophiles should receive official recognition as a hate crime victim group (McDonald, 2014 – see Case Study 10.2). However, international problems with hate crime are not just limited to issues of its definition, which group should be protected in law and how it should be monitored. As Table 10.2 shows, there is a vast disparity in the number of recorded hate crimes, and the number prosecuted, between differing nations. The figure for the United Kingdom, for example, of over 50,000 recorded hate crimes for 2011, is by far the highest number recorded by any nation in that year: the next highest is the United States, with 7,254. On the surface, this extraordinary statistic for the UK would appear to indicate that it has a problem with hate crime that dwarfs that of any other nation, and that it is far behind others in its attempts to tackle that problem. As earlier chapters have outlined however, the UK has in fact been proactive in combating the effects of hate crime and the prejudices that lie behind it (although it is acknowledged that some of its policies and practices have been flawed). The UK may, therefore, simply be the victim of its own 'success', as the very high number of officially recorded incidents may indicate that victims of hate crime are more aware of reporting procedures, and have more confidence in them (and in the police and wider criminal justice system), than similar victims in other countries that have seen less progress in this area (Garland and Chakraborti, 2012).

Table 10.2 Hate crime offences recorded and prosecuted by selected OCSE states, 2011

	Cases recorded by police	Cases prosecuted
Austria	57	38
Canada	1,322	_[1]
Czech Republic	238	246
Germany	4,020	_[2]
Poland	222	43
Sweden	5,493	347
Ukraine	5	2[3]
United Kingdom[4]	50,688	19,802
United States	7,254	_[5]

[1,2,5] No data available.

[3] Data for prosecutions are for 2012.

[4] Figures are for England and Wales, Northern Ireland, Scotland.

Source: OSCE, 2013: 26–30

Case Study 10.2

Should hate crime law protect the socially reviled? The Australian hate crime paedophile cases

As we have seen throughout this book, there are concerns that some groups are protected under hate crime legal provisions while other, apparently deserving, victim groups are not. Even within the 'select' band of those that are included there are some that appear to receive more comprehensive protection than others. This has sometimes caused a degree of consternation among certain groups, whilst generating a certain amount of rivalry between those who feel they are 'competing' for recognition (Mason-Bish, 2013).

There are a number of difficult conundrums regarding which groups within society should be recognised under hate crime legislation. For example, are some forms of 'difference' more socially acceptable than others, and should those that are less acceptable nevertheless still receive legislative protection from being targeted because of that 'difference'? As discussed in Chapter 7, those who have been campaigning to get alternative subcultures recognised as hate crime victim groups, for example, have encountered opposition from parties who feel they are somehow not 'deserving enough' as they do not have a history of suffering oppression or an established currency in human rights discourse (Garland and Hodkinson, 2014a). Recent scholarly interest in the intersection of identity characteristics and how this relates to victimisation has added another layer of complexity to these debates (Chakraborti et al., 2014a).

This whole issue was thrown into sharp relief by two trials under hate crime legislation in New South Wales, Australia, in the early part of the twenty-first century, and this case study is based upon an analysis of them by Gail Mason (see Mason, 2014a). In Australia, three states, including New South Wales, have penalty enhancement provisions that allow for judicial discretion in determining which victim characteristics these can be applied to. In New South Wales, section 21A(2)(h) of the Crimes (Sentencing Procedure) Act 1999 states that an aggravating factor at sentencing occurs if:

> the offence was motivated by hatred for or prejudice against a group of people to which the offender believed the victim belonged (such as people of a particular religion, racial or ethnic origin, language, sexual orientation or age, or having a particular disability). (Mason, 2014a: 167)

The wording of this section infers that the types of characteristics covered relate to those minority groups generally thought of as hate crime victim groups: those who have a history of experiencing discrimination, harassment and violence, and who are generally seen as 'deserving' of protection under related legislation (Schweppe, 2012). However, the words 'such as' in s21A(2)(h) facilitate the inclusion of groups other than those listed, and in two extraordinary court cases this applied to an extremely controversial, socially outcast group: 'paedophiles'.

What happened was as follows. The Supreme Court of New South Wales applied s21A(2)(h) in two cases, *R v Robinson* in 2004 and *Dunn v The Queen* in 2007, where the offender targeted the victim because of perceptions that the victim was a paedophile. In the first case, the victim, a prisoner, was murdered by fellow inmates after they had found out that he had been convicted of child sex offences. In the second, the victim (a Mr Arja) had suffered an arson attack due to one of his neighbours being under the misapprehension that he was a paedophile. The New South Wales Court of Criminal Appeal upheld the judge's verdict that paedophiles *could* be viewed as a victim group to which the aggravated provisions could apply:

(Continued)

(Continued)

> Applying s21A(2)(h) to those facts, it is clear that the offences come fairly and squarely within it. The offence was motivated by a hatred or prejudice against Mr Arja solely because the applicant believed him to be a member of a particular group, i.e. paedophiles. (*R v Dunn*: 32, cited in Mason 2014a: 168)

This ruling poses a number of questions for those involved in studying or working in the field of hate crime. Should hate crime law include provisions for groups who are socially reviled, or who hold views or have sexual preferences that the average person finds deplorable? Or are *all* groups deserving of protection, no matter what their background or beliefs? Alternatively, are hate crime laws deeply flawed if they protect social groups whose inclusion challenges the ethical basis of the original purpose of the legislation? Mason suggests that we need to frame the answer to these questions around the idea of a 'politics of justice', and argues persuasively that hate crime laws 'depend, for their very justification, upon labels of criminalization and principles of punishment that address the vulnerability that flows from undeserving and unjustified intolerance, inequality, disrespect or animosity towards forms of social differentiation between humans ... [embodying] ... the ideals of social cohesion, cultural diversity and justice' (Mason, 2014a: 176). Hate crime laws are therefore not the appropriate mechanism for dealing with attacks upon groups who contravene those ideals, like paedophiles.

Rather than being too preoccupied with the UK's high figures, perhaps attention should instead be directed towards the reasons behind the very low numbers of hate crime offences recorded in certain countries, such as the United States and Ukraine, noted in Table 10.2. In the United States, for example, the figure of 7,254 is the total number of hate crimes recorded for a population nearly six times that of the UK. Within this overall total, the state of California recorded the highest number of offences (at 1,204), while Mississippi recorded the lowest, a rather meagre 'one' for 'simple assault' (FBI, 2012).[6] By way of further contrast with the UK's figure of over 50,000 recorded hate crimes for 2011, Ukraine, with a population of around three-quarters of that of the UK, recorded just five offences, a statistic as troubling as it is remarkable. It simply cannot reflect the true levels of hate crime in that country.

As acknowledged above, though, the United States has been at the international forefront of developing hate crime legislation and policy, at both the federal and state levels. At the federal level, the first piece of hate crime legislation was the Civil Rights Act 1968, which contained provision for the prosecution of offences that target the victim's race, colour, religion or national origin under certain specific circumstances. The next piece of legislation, the Hate Crime Statistics Act 1990, required the collation of national hate crime statistics on the basis of bias against a person's race, ethnicity, religion, disability or sexual orientation.

Two further federal laws, the Hate Crimes Sentencing Enhancement Act 1994 (which contained provisions for penalty enhancement) and the Matthew Shepard and James Byrd Jr. Hate Crimes Prevention Act 2009 (which removed some of the legal anomalies thrown up by the earlier Act), followed. Meanwhile, the first piece of state legislation was enacted by California in 1978.

The overall range of protected characteristics under state laws is now impressively wide and yet markedly different from state to state. Almost all states include ethnicity/race/nationality/religion/colour (or something similar), reflecting the importance of the historical legacy of the period of slavery (Schweppe, 2012). Just over half include disability, sexual orientation and sex/gender, while thirteen states include gender identity and five, homelessness (Woods, 2014: 156). Within this framework, it is therefore surprising that the number of officially recorded offences is so low. The FBI's own figures for 2011, for example, show that of the 14,575 law enforcement agencies responsible for collecting hate crime data, 87% reported that no hate crimes occurred in their jurisdiction in 2011 (FBI, 2012), something that may be explained by a 'lack of participation, lax recording, and different hate crime practices' evident among them (Woods, 2014: 158).

The number of recorded hate crimes in 2011 for Canada, 1,322, is also surprisingly low, especially as Canada, like the United States, had developed some of the earliest policy and legal interventions in the field of hate crime. Sections 318–320 of the Canadian Criminal Code, for example, which cover 'hate propaganda' and incitement to hatred, were adopted by the Canadian Parliament as early as 1970. However, problems with how this legislation was framed – a police officer needs to obtain written consent from the Attorney General before s/he can proceed with charges for these offences, causing severe delays in many cases – may provide an explanation for this anomaly (Corb, 2014).[7] Meanwhile, outside of Russia there has been growing unease at the intensification of a climate of homophobia within the country over the last decade, something compounded by the fact that Russia returned no hate crime data at all to ODIHR for 2010–12 regarding the number of hate crimes recorded by police (ODIHR, 2013: 29).

Conclusion

This chapter has highlighted some of the key issues associated with the international development of hate crime, both as a useful conceptual tool and as a device around which meaningful interventions against targeted victimisation can occur. Some of the problems discussed have mirrored those more UK-specific issues raised in earlier chapters, such as the seemingly inherent difficulties with defining hate crime and the process of deciding which groups are included under its auspices, on what basis such decisions should be made (and how they should be actioned), and what the benefits are of doing so. Similarly, the apparent lack of appreciation at government level of the importance of tackling hate crime – or of putting resources into doing so – which is evident in some nations, has also been touched upon earlier in this book in other contexts.

That divergent understandings of hate crime exist across different nations is in some ways a problem, not least because they render any meaningful international comparisons problematic. Furthermore, individual nations' examples of best practice when combating hate crime could be shared to better effect if there was a more uniform understanding of the phenomenon itself. Islamophobia, for example, is a contemporary problem that may have different dynamics in different countries (and have diverse Islamic communities that suffer it), but which also has enough commonalities in its motivations and manifestations for initiatives that have successfully challenged it to be shared across borders. Yet it seems as though not all European countries even include religion or faith as protected characteristics (Portugal does not, for instance), while others, such as Finland, Germany and France, count incidents of certain forms of faith hate (such as antisemitism) separately. Others categorise religiously motivated hate crime under 'racist hate' (ODIHR, 2013).

However, in other ways the development of these various localised understandings of hate crime is not unduly problematic, as organisations such as ODIHR and FRA are providing pan-national commentaries on hate crime that are helpful for developing shared perspectives. Moreover, localised conceptions may simply reflect specific nation-based concerns that need to be addressed at that level (and as authors we are certainly not calling for identical laws and policies across nations). They will inevitably be a reflection of historical factors, with countries such as Austria, Germany and Italy understandably sensitive about far-right activity and manifestations of antisemitism. Similarly, it is to be hoped that countries such as Belgium, where the concept of hate crime has developed broadly and inclusively to include a significant number of identity characteristics and markers (such as wealth, health and political conviction), can provide some guidance and leadership regarding the pluses and minuses of adopting this sort of approach. As Case Study 10.2 highlighted, policy-makers in Australia may also have learned some valuable lessons from the way some hate crime laws have worked in practice that would be of benefit to other nations with similarly worded legislation.

However, marked differences in the way that states define hate crime, monitor incidents and recognise certain identity characteristics as 'protected' mean that it is very difficult to gauge the true extent, nature and impact of hate crime internationally. In an era in which homophobia is flourishing and apparently condoned by the governments of some countries (such as in Russia and a number of African nations including Uganda and Nigeria), and while racist and ethnic prejudice towards some groups (such as the Roma and Sinti in some central and eastern European countries) remains a serious problem, the lack of a common understanding is a worry. More than forty years after first being utilised, it is a shame that the concept of hate crime, rather than uniting countries in a common drive against manifestations of bigotry, in some respects merely highlights the differences in attitudes between them.

Guide to further reading

An excellent place to start for anyone seeking to explore global perspectives of hate crime is the work of ODIHR, whose annual report *Hate Crimes in the OSCE Region* provides clearly presented summaries of OSCE countries' different and sometimes complex understandings of the concept of hate crime. Garland and Chakraborti's (2012) 'Divided by a common concept?' article in the *European Journal of Criminology* focuses upon different European notions of hate and targeted hostility. Volume One of Perry's *Hate Crimes* (2009) offers a number of differing international perspectives on the hate debate, as does Hall et al.'s edited collection *The Routledge International Handbook on Hate Crime* (2014).

Links to online material

A number of very useful reports can be found at the FRA homepage at http://fra. europa.eu/en and at ODIHR's site at www.osce.org/odihr. US hate crime definitions and statistics can be found at the National Institute of Justice's site at www. nij.gov/topics/crime/hate-crime/pages/welcome.aspx and at the FBI's website at www.fbi.gov/about-us/investigate/civilrights/hate_crimes. The Australian Hate Crime Network (part of the University of Sydney's Institute for Criminology) has some extensive resources that are worth exploring at http://sydney.edu.au/law/ criminology//ahcn/index.shtml.

Notes

1 Other ODIHR initiatives include the Training Against Hate Crimes for Law Enforcement (TAHCLE) programme, which trains police officers in recognising, understanding and investigating hate crimes. There are also UN Conventions that space precludes discussion of, including those on the Prevention and Punishment of the Crime of Genocide

(1948), and on the Elimination of Racial Discrimination (1965). The Rabat Plan of Action (2012), which was born out of a series of workshops organised by the Office of the United Nations High Commissioner for Human Rights, contained provisions for combating hate speech.

2 In Belgium, for instance, this is Article 337 of the Penal Code, and in Scotland, Articles 1–2 of the Offences (Aggravated by Prejudice) (Scotland) Act 2009.

3 Sections 29–32 of the UK's Crime and Disorder Act 1998, for example, or Article 196(2) of the Czech Republic's Criminal Code.

4 Only seven EU countries (including the UK) chose the 'enhanced penalty' route, while fifteen chose the 'aggravating circumstance' method of punishment (FRA, 2012).

5 See Article 132-76(1) of the French Penal Code or Section 81 (vi) of Denmark's Criminal Code.

6 A further four states – Alaska (8), Louisiana (7), Vermont (9) and Wyoming (3) – recorded fewer than 10 hate crimes in 2011.

7 Section 718.2(a)(i) of the Canadian Criminal Code contains provisions for considering motivation based upon bias, prejudice or hatred towards the victim's 'race, national or ethnic origin, language, colour, religion, sex, age, mental or physical disability, sexual orientation, or any other similar factor' as aggravating factors when sentencing (Schweppe, 2012).

11

CONCLUSIONS AND FUTURE DIRECTIONS

Chapter summary

This final chapter presents us with an opportunity to reassess the concept of hate crime in light of the issues raised throughout the book. It begins by reviewing key points from previous chapters, and by taking stock of the various complexities that have been outlined thus far – such as the similarities and differences between the more recognised and more marginalised forms of hate crime, the nature of hate crime victimisation and perpetration, or the effectiveness of criminal justice responses – we can begin to recognise just how problematic a concept this can be.

   Drawing these ideas together, the chapter goes on to consider future directions for both theory and research and for policy and practice. We identify themes that have been un- or under-theorised and researched, and in doing so observe how scholars have started to move beyond rigid interpretations in order to broaden our understanding of the realities of hate crime victimisation and perpetration. This knowledge has filtered into recent policy responses to hate crime, and we outline a series of developments that have led to an improved recognition of new and emerging harms. Although important challenges remain, not least in ensuring that such developments have real and sustainable benefits for all victims of hate crime, there are significant signs of progress evident within contemporary frameworks and responses.

A brief recap

This book has identified the various forms that hate crime can take, the nature and impact of hate crime victimisation, factors that motivate hate crime perpetrators and challenges relating to criminal justice responses. In so doing, previous chapters have highlighted the complexity that surrounds this subject area: there is little that is straightforward or unproblematic about hate crime, whether one is approaching the subject through a theoretical or empirical lens or from a political or policy-making perspective. This means that making sense of the topic can be a difficult and at times bewildering process unless and until one accepts that hate crime is not a fixed entity but rather a more fluid social construct that can mean different things to different people. We shall return to this point in due course, but first it is worth briefly re-capping some of the main themes covered thus far.

We began in Chapter 1 by establishing the origins of hate crime and examining a variety of definitions that have shaped our understanding. This process confirmed that there might be more to the concept than meets the eye: rather than referring simply to crimes motivated by hatred, the hate crime label has been associated with a complex range of characteristics including notions of group identity, hostility and prejudice, and frameworks of power, hierarchy and oppression, all of which feature prominently in various interpretations. While hate crime scholars have engaged with some of the perceived intricacies associated with the term, frameworks used by criminal justice practitioners and legislators have tended to be simpler, though not without their own ambiguities. This process has resulted in a series of hate crime laws, which adhere to the principle that crimes motivated by hostility or prejudice towards particular features of the victim's identity should be treated differently to 'ordinary' crimes.

Subsequent chapters then went on to explore specific forms of hate crime. Racist hate crime was the focus of Chapter 2, and this chapter began by charting the development of the UK's 'race' agenda and the post-Macpherson surge of interest in the victimisation of ethnic minorities before discussing the scale and scope of racist hate crime. Noting that official accounts paint an incomplete picture of the extent and nature of this problem, Chapter 2 drew attention to the marginalisation of some groups' experiences as a result of the narrow frameworks used by researchers and policy-makers, and highlighted some of the problems associated with legislative provisions covering racist hate.

The next two chapters examined religiously motivated and homophobic hate crime respectively. Religiously motivated hate crime has been an issue of growing significance to academics and policy-makers, and Chapter 3 explored various factors that have resulted in increased levels of political and legal intervention, not to mention media interest, in issues of religious identity and intolerance. Chapter 4, meanwhile, drew out some of the distinctive issues surrounding homophobic hate crime, including the worrying normalisation of some forms of homophobic language in educational and workplace settings and the extreme forms of violence that are often evident when gay people are physically attacked. Despite the general improvement in relations between LGB communities and the police in the recent past, the historical mutual enmity between many gay men and the police service still clouds the policing of homophobia and contributes to the under-reporting of incidents.

Transphobic hate was the subject of Chapter 5, where the complexities of definitional issues surrounding sexuality, sex and gender were outlined. This chapter examined the nature and extent of hostility directed towards transgendered people, and it was suggested that whilst there are commonalities between hate crimes suffered by trans and by gay communities, there are also enough differences between the experiences of victims to cast doubt over the utility of grouping them together under the oft-used and all-embracing 'LGBT' term.

Chapter 6 outlined the forms, frequency and impact of a crime that has often been marginalised from the hate debate: disablist hate crime. While the profile of this form of targeted hostility has risen in recent years there is still evidence that the criminal justice system and other agencies responsible for safeguarding vulnerable adults can be slow in recognising disablist harassment and violence for what it is. This has led to a number of tragic cases when the abuse of disabled people has remained unchallenged by relevant authorities, allowing it to escalate into violence, torture and then murder. These cases highlight the fact that, even in the wake of some improvements in the services provided to victims of disablist hate following the 2007 Pilkington case, much more still needs to be done.

Chapter 7 moved on to explore those kinds of targeted harassment and violence, such as attacks upon members of alternative subcultures, domestic violence, elder abuse and assaults upon sex workers and the homeless, that appear to bear all of the hallmarks of the monitored 'five strands' of hate crime yet are rarely referred to or treated as such by the police or wider criminal justice system. The theoretical implications of including these forms of harassment under the hate crime 'umbrella' were outlined and it was suggested that structural conceptions of hate crime, which have been so influential within the field of hate studies, will need to be reassessed if these 'borderline' issues are to be included in mainstream discussions of hate crime in the future.

Chapter 8 examined theories of hate crime perpetration and the typologies of offenders that have been developed over the last two decades. It suggested that hate crime offenders are typically not members of far-right parties and nor are they solely from disadvantaged and marginalised white backgrounds. Hate crime, it was argued, is a complex phenomenon with a number of differing motivations, making the profile of a 'typical' hate offender difficult to compile.

Within Chapter 9 we examined conceptual, cultural and operational difficulties that have plagued the policing of hate crime, together with some of the more positive developments that have taken place in recent times. This chapter also considered wider responses to hate crime, and outlined the scope and limitations of existing retributive responses as well as the relevance of alternative models of justice and pathways of support for victims. Of course, the kinds of challenges confronting scholars, law-makers and enforcers and activists when shaping responses to hate crime are not unique to this country, and Chapter 10 offered an international perspective through its analysis of how the concept of hate crime has developed in contrasting ways across the globe. This chapter considered the impact that these differing understandings have had upon the development of hate crime laws in various nations, and suggested that much of what unites differing approaches to the problem of hate crime also divides these.

Moving forward

Theory and research

It should be fairly apparent by this stage that the process of theorising about and developing policy around hate crime can be divisive. It will be of little surprise that we, the authors, fully support the underlying principles of the hate crime movement, not least because we believe that everyone has a right to be free from persecution because of who they are or what they look like. But at the same time we would support, and indeed encourage, those more sceptical voices within the academic, professional and political worlds to engage in meaningful debate around hate crime theory and policy, as that process of debate is crucial to the construction of effective, legitimate and sustainable responses.

One of the most influential and oft-cited critiques of the hate crime concept comes from Jacobs and Potter (1998), whose concerns about its expansiveness are illustrated through use of the theoretical model displayed in Table 11.1 (1998: 22–8; see also Hall, 2013: 13–17 for further explanation). The horizontal axis denotes the level of the offender's prejudice (high prejudice or low prejudice) while the vertical axis marks the strength of the causal relationship between prejudice and the offending behaviour (high causation or low causation).

By looking at each cell individually one can begin to appreciate Jacobs and Potter's line of argument. In Cell I we can include offences that are carried out by highly prejudiced perpetrators whose prejudice has a strong causal bearing on their offending behaviour. These are what Jacobs and Potter (1998: 22) describe as 'clear-cut, unambiguous hate crimes' – crimes that one might immediately think of when conceiving of 'hate' in its literal sense, including organised extremist hatred (the activities of the Ku Klux Klan, for example) or acts of violence clearly motivated by hatred of a particular group identity (the murder of Stephen Lawrence or the actions of David Copeland). As Jacobs and Potter observe (1998: 23), there would be nothing ambiguous or controversial about hate crime were its scope restricted to cases like these, but equally the label would cover relatively few cases and would have little practical utility since such extreme crimes will already be punishable under the highest possible sentencing structure.

Table 11.1 Jacobs and Potter's model of hate crime causation and prejudice (1998: 23)

		High Degree of offender's prejudice	**Low** Degree of offender's prejudice
Strength of causal relationship	*High*	**I** High prejudice/high causation	**III** Low prejudice/high causation
	Low	**II** High prejudice/low causation	**IV** Low prejudice/low causation

It is the other three cells which are more contentious. Cell II contains offences that, again, are committed by highly prejudiced offenders but whose offending behaviour is not strongly or exclusively linked to their prejudice. This cell, therefore, would contain offenders whose prejudice bears little or no relation to the offence in question; as such, for Jacobs and Potter it would be wrong to assume that all offences committed by prejudiced offenders against minority groups are hate offences for their offences might well be motivated by other factors and not their prejudice. Conversely, Cell III includes offenders who are not especially prejudiced individuals but whose prejudice, perhaps subconsciously, bears a strong link to the offence. Within this cell one could expect to find offenders who, according to Jacobs and Potter (1998: 25), 'are not ideologues or obsessive haters' but who might be 'professional or at least active criminals with short fuses and confused psyches ... hostile and alienated juvenile delinquents ... [or] ignorant, but relatively law-abiding'. Cell IV, meanwhile, includes what they refer to as situational offences; offences that are neither the product of highly prejudiced beliefs nor are strongly linked to the offender's prejudice, but which instead arise from 'ad hoc disputes and flashing tempers' (1998: 26). Such offences are sometimes classed as hate crimes and sometimes not, depending on differing interpretations.

Ultimately, Jacobs and Potter's typology helps to confirm what we know already: namely, that hate crime is a social construct open to different interpretations. Arguably, it is this malleability – and the implications this has in terms of creating hierarchies of acceptable and unacceptable prejudices and potentially criminalising behaviour motivated only in part by prejudice – that leaves it so susceptible to criticism. While concerns over the criminalisation of prejudice are understandable, it is equally important not to become unduly alarmist about the implications of this conceptual ambiguity. As Hall (2013: 35–6) rightly asserts, it is not a crime to harbour prejudiced attitudes nor is it a crime to hate: that prejudice or hate needs to be manifested through some form of behaviour or action before criminal justice agents can decide whether it constitutes a hate crime and deserves to be dealt with in accordance with the laws in place to punish the perpetrators of such crimes.

Moreover, as Iganski (2001, 2008) and others have shown through their research, using the law to penalise such behaviour is justifiable because hate crimes cause greater harms than comparable non-hate offences. The multiple layers of damage caused by hate crimes are described by the Office for Democratic Institutions and Human Rights (ODIHR, 2009a) in terms of their violation of human rights and equality between members of society; the psychological injury and increased feelings of vulnerability inflicted on the individual victim; the sense of fear and intimidation transmitted to the wider community to whom the victim 'belongs'; and the security and public order problems that ensue from the escalation of social tensions. Within this context hate crime laws have played an important symbolic role in societies where the values and cultures of particular communities are under scrutiny. We have seen in earlier chapters how hate crimes have been described as 'message crimes' for their capacity to send a message from the perpetrator to the victim and their wider community that they 'don't belong'; likewise, the process of criminalising actions or expressions that violate a society's core values sends an equally powerful message of solidarity to victims of hate and marginalised communities (Chakraborti, 2012).

Nonetheless, there are other areas of concern within this field. As previous chapters have shown, the growth of academic interest in hate crime has led to the emergence of new knowledge, new ideas and new policies, and has facilitated a change in political and cultural attitudes towards the prejudice experienced by a range of minority groups. However, there are a number of themes that remain un- or under-explored. These have been referred to elsewhere (see, *inter alia*, Chakraborti, 2010a; Chakraborti and Garland, 2012; Hall, 2013; Perry, 2010;) and they highlight some of the limitations evident within our efforts to capture the lived realities of targeted violence and harassment experienced by those falling both outside and even within the strands of recognised hate crime victim groups.

Let us start by thinking of those 'on the outside' at it were. Chapter 7 highlighted the way in which research and policy frameworks can sideline acts of hate and prejudice directed towards certain groups of 'others' who are not associated with recognised hate crime victim groups. This ties in with the broader arguments of Bartkowiak-Théron and Asquith (2012), who use the terms 'vulnerable' and 'at risk' to describe people who are left out of the social development of the criminal justice system – young people, the elderly, the mentally ill, people with addictive behaviours to use some of their examples – because they are not invited to participate and/or not capable of participating. With reference to hate crime, this has reinforced the marginalisation of less visible victims who, as we have argued elsewhere (Chakraborti and Garland, 2012: 11), 'fall between the cracks of scholarship and policy frameworks [because they] lack the power of class or language, the privilege of advocacy groups and support networks or the bargaining clout of political, economic or social mobility'.

Such victims may not always 'belong' to a fixed identity group in the orthodox sense of hate crime victim identification, but may still be at heightened risk of victimisation because of their 'difference' or perceived vulnerability. Certainly if we think back to the definitions of hate crime introduced in Chapter 1, gaining recognition for the experiences of 'stigmatised and marginalised groups' (to use Perry's (2001) description) is precisely what the hate crime movement has set out to achieve. Acknowledging notions of 'difference', vulnerability and risk therefore allows us to move away from static constructions of group identity, and instead to foster more flexible and evolving criteria for hate crime victimisation (see also Mason, 2014b; Mason-Bish, 2013).

Those notions are also highly relevant to our understanding of the intersections and interactions at play *within* recognised hate crime strands. Although the identity-based approach to hate crime theorising and policy-formation outlined in previous chapters has done much to challenge those respective strands of hate, this approach can sometimes lead people to overlook the fact that we all have multiple identities. These identity characteristics – our sexuality, our race, our gender and so on – intersect with one another and with other situational factors and context. Ultimately it is this process of intersectionality that can increase our perceived 'difference', our perceived vulnerability and our chances of being victims of hate crime. Whereas a silo approach prompts us to think about hate crime victimisation narrowly and simplistically in discrete categories, a framework that recognises notions of 'difference', vulnerability and risk tells us more about the issues affecting those within and between discrete victim groups, and underlines the relevance of associated factors – our command of English, our area of residence, our socio-economic circumstances, our isolation, our physical size, to name just some examples – to the process of victim selection (Chakraborti and Garland, 2012; Hall, 2013).

The reality and context of 'everyday' hate and prejudice can also often be lost through narrow interpretations. Whilst the more violent, extreme cases tend to attract headlines and political attention, the more routine, cumulative, day-to-day experiences of harassment and abuse are often overlooked despite their profound, and sometimes tragic consequences for victims, their families and wider communities. Although these apparently minor incidents may not appear especially serious in themselves, they are often repeated to devastating effect over extended periods and can escalate into more serious acts of violence (Bowling, 1999; Garland and Chakraborti, 2006; Sibbitt, 1997; Walters and Hoyle, 2012).

This has implications not just for how we think about the nature and impact of hate crime victimisation but also for how we frame our responses to hate crime perpetrators. Walters and Hoyle (2012), for instance, have criticised the silo approach referred to above for compartmentalising 'offenders' and 'victims' into diametrically opposed roles, and thereby creating a de-contextualised picture that fails to account for the complex relationships evident within many 'everyday' hate incidents. Many of the hate crime cases they researched involved what they describe as 'messier, sometimes intractable disputes between people known to one another – neighbours, colleagues or other acquaintances – conflicts sometimes only partly motivated by prejudice' (2012: 7). This ties in with some of the concerns above raised by Jacobs and Potter and casts doubt over the capacity of conventional retributive penalties to adequately resolve conflicts and the harms suffered (see also Hardy, 2014). Instead, Walters and Hoyle advocate the use of community mediation as a means of addressing such harms and preventing further incidents from recurring or escalating. As we saw in Chapter 9, the use of restorative interventions can be extremely effective in reducing levels of anger, anxiety and fear and engendering more tolerant attitudes towards 'difference'.

Although there have been, and no doubt will continue to be, gaps in our understanding, the determination shown by academics and activists in seeking to plug those gaps offers much hope for the future. The preceding discussion has illustrated how hate crime research has begun to break the shackles of silo approaches by widening its lines of enquiry, and this is to be commended (see Case Study 11.1). As a result, we are starting to learn more about the realities of hate crime victimisation and those affected by it, and about ways to tackle hate crime perpetration. This knowledge has filtered into policy responses to hate crime, as discussed below.

Case Study 11.1

The Leicester Hate Crime Project

The Leicester Hate Crime Project provides an illustration of how contemporary research is developing a more complete picture of targeted violence and harassment based upon less rigid interpretations of the hate crime concept. This two-year project, which ran from September 2012 to 2014, was commissioned by the Economic and Social Research Council and was based within the city of Leicester – one of the UK's most diverse cities and home to a wide range of established and emerging minority communities.

In seeking to explore victims' experiences of hate crime and expectations of agency responses, the approach adopted within the Leicester Hate Crime Project is notable for a number of reasons. First, the project team used a deliberately broad definition of hate crime – 'acts of violence, hostility and intimidation directed towards people because of their identity or perceived "difference"' – in order to capture the broader forms and processes of victimisation so often overlooked by researchers, policy-makers and practitioners. Second, the sample of victims accessed by the research team (1,421) is among the very largest to have ever taken part in a single study of hate crime.

Just as importantly, this sample's profile was extremely diverse, and alongside the more familiar groups of victims referred to throughout this book it included sizeable numbers of participants from 'hidden', less familiar or emerging communities. This included, for example, people victimised because of their 'different' modes of dress, appearance or lifestyle; people with learning disabilities and/or mental ill-health; members of recently arrived migrant groups such as the Roma, Polish, Somalian, Congolese and Iranian communities; and homeless people.

The study is also notable for the strategies used to access victims and disseminate its findings. The project team used what they describe as a 'softer' approach when seeking to identify and engage with groups and communities who are typically vulnerable, politically disempowered and 'invisible' within wider society (Chakraborti et al., 2014a). Eschewing more formulaic approaches that commonly rely upon restricted pockets of interaction time or access through self-appointed community leaders, this 'softer' approach involved more creative modes of grassroots engagement in order to connect with and capture the voices of 'hard to reach' victims. In a similar vein, the project findings were shared with multiple community, practitioner and academic audiences and through a variety of formats – ranging from the more conventional (a full report, executive summary versions and an end-of-project conference) to the less familiar (a Victims' Manifesto; a series of practitioner briefing papers; a short film and a collection of audio podcasts) in order to shape attitudes and policy.

Among its many findings relating to the nature and impact of hate crime suffered by different groups and communities, the study revealed a disturbing lack of recognition amongst victims of the term 'hate crime' and associated awareness campaigns; a tendency to normalise distressing experiences of hate as a 'routine' feature of being 'different'; and a common reluctance to report experiences to the police and other agencies in a position to offer support. A full account of the project findings and recommendations, along with the range of other project outputs, can be found at www.le.ac.uk/centreforhatestudies (see also Chakraborti et al., 2014a).

Policy and practice

The complex, multi-layered problems posed by hate crime raise difficult questions for those working within the policy domain. Those problems will invariably be all the more challenging in the context of prevailing economic, political and social factors including the continued demonisation of 'marginal' communities, the dwindling opportunities for young people or the prevailing climate of austerity and public spending cuts. As we have noted elsewhere (Chakraborti and Garland, 2014), a collaborative response to the problems posed by hate from policy-makers, practitioners, academics and activists offers the best chance of success. Hall (2013: 197) also makes reference to the importance of political prioritisation within this context, noting that the 'political inclinations of the state (and its institutions) can have serious implications for shaping an environment in which hate can potentially flourish'.

These points seem to have been acknowledged through successive pieces of domestic policy guidance. Chapter 9 described the proposals within the UK government's Action Plan (2012) around the objectives of preventing hate crime, increasing reporting and access to support, and improving operational responses to hate crime, and noted the emphasis given the development of locally administered multi-agency responses based upon the needs and priorities of local victims and communities rather than those of national government. A follow-up report was published in 2014 outlining progress in addressing those three objectives and a series of case-study examples illustrating the delivery of work locally (HM Government, 2014). Much of this progress gives recognition to the complexities and lived realities referred to previously and to the value of collaborative working within and between domains.

Under the theme of preventing hate crime, for instance, the report calls for a focus on early intervention, and documents ongoing work with a range of criminal justice, community-based and academic partners that is helping to challenge various forms of hate (HM Government, 2014: 11–15). The second theme of increasing reporting and support for victims offers a similar breadth of examples of working practice, and makes specific reference to the isolation of particularly marginalised groups such as the Roma, Gypsy and Traveller communities and new migrants (2014: 16-20). Progress towards the third theme of improving the operational response to hate crime is described primarily in terms of changes to the law (including amendments to section 146 of the Criminal Justice Act 2003 to include transgender identity in the suite of aggravating factors, and to Schedule 21 of the same Act to increase the starting point for murders aggravated by disability or transgender identity from 15 to 30 years) and the publication of guidance for criminal justice practitioners (2014: 21–3).

In addition to these government reports, the ACPO guidance of 2005 has now been updated by new hate crime operational guidance issued by the College of Policing (2014). As noted in Chapter 9, this guidance follows the policy direction evident within those other reports, not least by reinforcing the message that the five strands of monitored hate crime are the minimum categories that police forces are expected to record because there are victims who are targeted because of other hate-related hostilities. Consequently – and as we have seen in earlier chapters with reference to the examples of attacks against members of alternative subcultures or against sex workers in particular police force areas – 'agencies and partnerships are free to extend their own policy response to include the hostilities that they believe are prevalent in their area or causing the greatest concern to a community (College of Policing, 2014: 7). Case Study 11.2 presents an overview of the new operational guidance and its implications.

Case Study 11.2

The College of Policing Hate Crime Operational Guidance 2014

This guidance document issued by the College of Policing in May 2014 is an update to the 2005 ACPO Hate Crime Manual. It reflects developments in policing practice and priorities with regard to hate crime, contains examples of innovative police work across the country and offers practical instruction on how service delivery to victims can be further improved. The guidance makes clear that forces can consider other forms of targeted hostility within their hate crime frameworks outside of the five monitored strands of disability, race, religion, sexual orientation and gender identity, and declares that 'hate crime policy should support a basic human right to be free from crime fuelled by hostility because of an individual's personal characteristics' (p. 2).

The guidance follows similar definitions of hate incidents and crimes to those used previously (pp. 3–4): namely 'any non-crime incident (or in the case of hate crimes, 'any criminal offence') which is perceived, by the victim or any other person, to be motivated by a hostility or prejudice based on a person's ...' (this last part then includes each respective strand: i.e. 'race or perceived race', 'religion or perceived religion', and so on). It offers advice on interpreting the term 'hostility', drawing from CPS guidance to suggest ordinary dictionary definitions such as 'ill-will, ill-feeling, spite, contempt, prejudice, unfriendliness, antagonism, resentment and dislike' (p. 5). A range of other practical issues is also covered, including advice on perception-based recording of hate crime (pp. 5–7), non-monitored hate crime (pp. 7–9), and recognising repeat and secondary victimisation (p. 10).

The guidance then outlines the domestic legislative framework governing hate crime and incitement (pp. 11–16) before moving on to discuss the monitored strands in more detail. This discussion acknowledges a number of important points which we have highlighted in this and previous chapters. For example, the guidance urges the police to take a more proactive response to recording and responding to low-level criminal acts in order to build confidence in policing services (p. 18) and includes a specific section on the under-reporting of hate crimes (pp. 48–53). It also makes direct reference to some of the less familiar victims of hate, such as Gypsy, Traveller and Roma communities (pp. 30–2) and asylum, refuges and migrant communities (pp. 32–5), and to some of the less familiar forms of hate such as anti-Sikh hate crime (pp. 38–9). Guidance is also provided on other significant areas that we have discussed in this book, including making a positive first impression in responses to victims from diverse backgrounds (p. 54); partnership working (pp. 64–6); minimum standards for response and investigation (pp. 67–92); community engagement (pp. 93–5); and Internet hate crime (pp. 115–22).

The 2014 Hate Crime Operational Guidance can be accessed through the College of Policing website at www.app.college.police.uk/app-content/major-investigation-and-public-protection/hate-crime/

The latest operational guidance from the College of Policing is a significant step forward, and shows a commendable recognition of new and emerging sets of harms; new and emerging groups of 'others'; and new and emerging ways of responding to victims. However, whilst there has been a marked (and welcome) increase in the level of regional, national and international activity to understand and challenge hate crime, the success of this activity is far harder to gauge. The limited amount of in-house and external evaluative work has been acknowledged both nationally (Chakraborti et al., 2011; HM Government, 2014) and internationally (Perry, 2014), and this makes it difficult to judge the extent to which improvements to policy and research frameworks translate into 'real-life' improvements for actual and potential victims. The paucity of rigorous evaluative work – allied to the dangers outlined by Chakraborti (2014: 3–4) of tokenistic 'tick-box' policy responses, talking shops or bandwagon jumping – illustrates that collectively we all have much to do in this regard. This should be obvious simply by reminding ourselves of the hundreds of thousands of people who continue to fall victim to hate crime every year in this country alone, many of whom still do not report their experiences to any third party.

These are very real concerns but at the same time they should not detract from the equally real signs of progress evident within contemporary hate crime scholarship, policy and activism. In line with the research and policy developments outlined above, Garland (2014a) draws from a host of ongoing initiatives to highlight that the field of hate crime *is* delivering tangible and worthwhile outcomes, which are underpinned by a sense of genuine commitment on the part of multiple actors across different domains. Such initiatives may well be successful because they are seeking solutions that transcend the conventional criminal justice response, whether this involves the delivery of restorative interventions (Iganski et al., 2014; Walters, 2014b); the development of educative resources (Perry and Dyck, 2014; Sophie Lancaster Foundation, 2011); or direct input from healthcare professionals, schools and other statutory, third sector and community-based organisations outside the sphere of criminal justice (Chakraborti et al., 2014a; Sin, 2014; Zempi, 2014). Equally, their success may be born from a recognition that there are no universal, one-size-fits-all solutions to hate crime, just as there are no universal, one-size-fits-all definitions of what hate crime is and whom it affects, as we learnt in Chapter 1.

We ended our first edition with both an observation and a plea: an observation that wading through hate crime's conceptual minefield had been a challenging yet fruitful journey; and a plea for readers not to allow these conceptual debates to overshadow the achievements and potential of the hate crime movement. Although much has changed since that time, those sentiments still hold true. The task of identifying the causes, impact and responses to hate crime remains inherently complex, and the search for answers is still likely to raise fresh and difficult questions. Nonetheless, however we conceive of the hate crime label across disciplines, across domains and across borders, our goals for hate crime scholarship and policy are ones that can be shared by everyone with an interest in this field: to tackle hate, prejudice and targeted hostility in all its guises, and to develop effective and sustainable ways of supporting those most affected. These common values form the basis of what we hope will be significant future progress.

Guide to further reading

A number of recent British texts offer much food for thought on the present and future direction of hate crime scholarship and policy. Hall, *Hate Crime* (2013) and Chakraborti (ed.), *Hate Crime: Concepts, Policy, Future Directions* (2010) cover numerous emerging areas of concern, while Walters, *Hate Crime and Restorative Justice: Exploring Causes, Repairing Harms* (2014c) draws from empirical research to show how restorative interventions can address the harms of hate. Hall et al's (eds) *The Routledge International Handbook on Hate Crime* (2014) examines key issues across different parts of the world and will undoubtedly be of interest to readers of this book.

Another text of relevance to themes within this chapter is Chakraborti and Garland (eds), *Responding to Hate Crime: The Case for Connecting Policy and Research* (2014), which considers an extensive range of challenges and solutions that have been under-explored. We would also direct readers to a special issue of the *International Journal of Victimology* published in 2012 (Volume 18, Number 1) which offers a series of thoughtful contributions on hate crime victimisation.

Links to online material

This chapter has underlined the value of collaboration between the domains of policy, scholarship and activism in the context of understanding and challenging hate crime. Formed in 2013, the International Network for Hate Studies facilitates the exchange of knowledge in those areas through its cross-jurisdictional and interdisciplinary membership and its work around information sharing and public policy engagement. Further information about the Network can be found at www.internationalhatestudies.com.

Within this and other chapters we have also highlighted the importance of using academic knowledge to inform policy and practice. An example of how this process can work in reality is provided through the Leicester Centre for Hate Studies. This Centre was established in 2014 and uses a variety of means, including training workshops, evaluation, research and educational resources, to bridge the gap between academic research and professional practice. Details about the Leicester Centre for Hate Studies and its programme of activities can be found at www2.le.ac.uk/departments/criminology/hate.

GLOSSARY

Ageism – prejudiced attitudes or discriminatory behaviour towards older people.

Aggravated offences – criminal acts that can attract longer sentences if it is proved they were motivated by, or contained acts of, hostility towards the victim's perceived minority status.

Alternative subcultures – those music- and style-based subcultures, such as punk, emo or goth, that are characterised by distinctive modes of dress and 'darker' musical styles which are separate from mainstream high street fashions and tastes.

Anti-Muslim hatred – hostility directed towards Muslim communities, and motivated by crude prejudices against Muslims rather than fear or hatred of Islam *per se*.

Antisemitism – prejudice against, or hatred of, Jewish people, culture and religion.

Association of Chief Police Officers (ACPO) – body representing senior police officers all of, or above, the rank of Assistant Chief Constable or their equivalent in the Metropolitan Police.

Asylum seeker – someone who has normally fled from persecution in their home country and is seeking permanent refugee status.

Biphobia – irrational fear, dislike or hatred of bisexual people.

Blood and Honour – neo-Nazi music network that mainly promotes white supremacist skinhead groups.

British Crime Survey (BCS) – former name of the Home Office's annual victim survey that examines experiences of crime and anti-social behaviour within England and Wales. Renamed the Crime Survey for England and Wales (CSEW) in 2012.

British National Party (BNP) – the most prominent far-right political party in the UK.

Burka (or Burqa) – the most concealing of outer garments worn by Muslim women, covering the face and body and leaving a veiled opening for the eyes.

Casuals United – an umbrella organisation for a number of football hooligan 'firms' affiliated to the English Defence League.

Cissexual – those whose gender identity matches the one they were biologically born with.

College of Policing – provides training and development of police officers and staff, and sets professional standards for the service in England and Wales.

Combat 18 (C18) – a violent neo-Nazi UK grouping formed in the mid-1990s.

Community Security Trust (CST) – organisation that monitors levels and forms of antisemitic activity in the UK.

Crime Survey for England and Wales (CSEW) – measures the extent of crime in England and Wales by asking people whether they have experienced any crime in the past year. Formerly the British Crime Survey until April 2012.

Crown Prosecution Service (CPS) – agency with responsibility for decisions relating to the prosecution (or otherwise) of cases passed on by the police in England and Wales, and the preparation of those cases that proceed.

Cuckooing – describes the situation when someone 'befriends' and then moves into the home of a disabled person (often those with learning difficulties) with an ulterior motive of stealing from or exploiting them, or using their home for criminal activities.

Cyberbullying – a form of bullying undertaken via communications and information technologies, such as mobile phones or the Internet.

Disabled – a physical or mental impairment that has a substantial and long-term adverse effect on someone's ability to carry out normal day-to-day activities.

Disablism – prejudiced attitudes or behaviour directed at disabled people based upon the belief that disabled people are inferior to others.

Domestic violence – acts of harassment, intimidation or violence perpetrated by someone intimately linked to the victim and often undertaken within a household setting.

Economic migrant – an immigrant whose main motive in moving to a new country is the hope of better economic prospects for themselves.

Elder abuse – action or inaction within a relationship based upon trust that causes harm to an older person.

English Defence League (EDL) – far-right street protest movement that campaigns against 'militant Islam'.

Ethnicity – the shared cultures (often including language, religion, music, dress, food etc.) of people who identify as coming from the same background.

'Faith-hate' – prejudice towards, or hatred of, someone because of their perceived religious identity.

Feminism – theories and activities centred around ideas of gender difference and inequality, and the championing of women's rights.

'Five strands' – colloquial name for the five categories of hate crime – race or ethnicity, faith, disability, sexual orientation and gender identity – monitored by criminal justice agencies and partner organisations in England and Wales.

Freedom of expression – the right to express any opinion without the threat of sanction.

FTM ('female-to-male') – a person who was female but has become male.

Gender – often described as socially constructed or expected patterns of behaviour based upon one's biologically determined sex.

Gender identity – refers to a person's own experience of gender, which may or may not correspond with the sex assigned to them at birth, and includes dress, speech and mannerisms.

Gender symmetry – theories that argue that men are as likely to be victims of domestic violence as women.

Gypsy – a Romany ethnic group whose members are often defined in terms of their nomadic lifestyle, cultural values and traditions as opposed to their race or origin.

Hate – extreme dislike or abhorrence.

Heterosexism – attitudes or behaviour that privilege heterosexuality within society.

Holocaust – the acts of genocide committed by Nazis in the Second World War which ultimately resulted in the deaths of an estimated six million Jewish people.

Homelessness – rough sleeping but also covers a number of other situations in which people can be considered to lack permanent accommodation.

Homophobia – irrational fear, dislike or hatred of lesbian, gay or bisexual people.

Incitement of hatred – acts or speech that are designed to 'stir up' hatred.

Institutional racism – the deliberate or unwitting enactment of policies or procedures that disadvantage minority ethnic people.

Islamophobia – prejudice towards, or hatred of, Islam or those of the Islamic faith.

July 7 attacks (7/7) – the four bombings by Muslim extremists that killed 52 people and injured 770 on London's transport network on 7 July 2005.

Ku Klux Klan – US white supremacist organisation notorious for being responsible for the murder of African Americans and Jews, particularly in the 1920s.

Law Commission – a statutory independent body created by the Law Commissions Act 1965 to keep the law under review and recommend revisions where needed to the UK government.

LGBT – the abbreviation commonly used to collectively represent lesbian, gay, bisexual or transgendered people (sometimes expressed as LGB and T, LGBTQ (where 'Q' is 'queer' or 'questioning'), or LGBTQI (where 'I' is 'intersex').

Lone wolf – far-right extremist, acting on their own, who plots and/or is engaged in violent acts designed to maim or kill their targets.

'Low-level' harassment – contested term used to differentiate non-violent hostile acts from so-called 'serious' criminal offences.

Masculinity – ideas, values, representations and practices associated with maleness which structure relations among men and between men and women.

Message crime – a hate crime designed to send a hostile or intimidating message to other members of the victim's identity group or community.

Migrant worker – a term used to describe a person engaged in a remunerated activity in a state of which he or she is not a national.

Mono-ethnic – term used to describe a population whose membership consists almost solely of one ethnic background.

MTF ('male-to-female') – a person who was male but has become female.

Multiculturalism – idea that encourages different ethnic groups to develop their own traditions and cultures whilst living alongside those from other ethnic backgrounds.

National Front (NF) – far-right anti-immigration political party especially prominent in the 1970s.

National Offender Management Service (NOMS) – an executive agency of the Ministry of Justice whose role is to commission and provide offender services in the community and in custody in England and Wales.

Neo-Nazi – contemporary extremists who adopt and adapt the ideologies of the German Nazi (National Socialist) Party of the 1930s.

New and Old Commonwealth migrants – immigrants to Britain from either the newly independent and decolonised developing nations of Asia, Africa and the Caribbean (the 'New' Commonwealth), or the predominantly white Commonwealth countries of Australia, New Zealand, South Africa or Canada (the 'Old' Commonwealth).

Non-Governmental Organisations (NGOs) – a term used to describe an organisation that is neither part of a government nor a conventional for-profit business and is formed to provide services or advocate specific policies.

Office for Democratic Institutions and Human Rights (ODIHR) – the human rights institution of the Organization for Security and Co-operation in Europe (OSCE), tasked with assisting OSCE member states in meeting their commitments in the field of human rights and democracy.

Organization for Security and Co-operation in Europe (OSCE) – an intergovernmental body working for stability, prosperity and democracy in its 57 participating states.

Politically correct – derogatory term used to denigrate notions of equal opportunities and their associated initiatives.

Prejudice – biased attitudes or feelings towards others based upon perceptions held about their social grouping.

Process–incident contradiction – the clash between the experience of hate crime victimisation as a series of connected events and the need by the police service to prioritise the investigation and prosecution of individual criminal acts.

Process of victimisation – victimisation experienced as a series of connected acts of harassment.

Queer theory – a radical theory of gender, sexuality and sexual identity that challenges society's accepted ideas of these concepts.

Qur'an (or Koran) – the holy book of Islam.

Race – the idea that biologically distinct groups of people exist and that these genetic differences manifest themselves not just in physical appearance but also in intelligence and ability. Now largely discredited as having any scientific basis.

Racism – prejudice towards, or hatred of, people on the basis of their perceived race or ethnic background.

Restorative justice – an approach that gives the victim a more active role in the process of justice, that encourages offenders to take responsibility for the harms of their actions, and provides an alternative to retributive modes of punishment.

Roma – historically itinerant and marginalised European community.

Samaritans – a registered charity available to offer emotional support to anyone in distress or struggling to cope in the UK and Ireland.

Secular – an absence of organised religion or religious belief.

September 11 attacks (9/11) – perpetrated by Muslim extremists on 11 September 2001 and involving the hijacking of four passenger aircraft which were subsequently crashed into the two towers of World Trade Center, the Pentagon and into a field in Somerset County, Pennsylvania. A total of 2,998 people lost their lives.

Sexual orientation – the general attraction felt towards people of one sex or another, or both.

Sex worker – someone who provides sexual services for some form of payment.

Sinti – traditionally itinerant Romany population of central Europe.

Stirring up of hatred – see incitement of hatred.

Stonewall – an organisation with offices in England, Scotland and Wales that campaigns in the interests of gay people.

'Stranger-danger' – the theory that the perpetrators and victims of hate crimes do not know each other and that the act was solely motivated by the perpetrator's prejudice against the victim's actual or perceived group identity.

Third-party reporting – the mechanism by which victims of hate incidents can report to other organisations rather than directly to the police service.

Transgender – someone who has adopted the lifestyle and behaviour of another gender without undergoing surgery. Can also be used as a broad term to cover both transgendered and transsexual people.

Transphobia – irrational fear or hatred of transgendered or transsexual people.

Transsexual – someone who has undergone hormone treatment and gender reassignment surgery in order to become a member of another sex.

Transvestite – someone who adopts the clothing of another gender as a lifestyle choice or for sexual pleasure but who does not view themselves as transgendered.

Traveller – communities of people with distinctive lifestyles, traditions and cultures that set them apart from the sedentary population. Often used as a collective term to describe a range of groups, including Irish, Scottish and New Travellers, Gypsies and Roma people.

United Kingdom Independence Party (UKIP) – Eurosceptic political party that campaigns for the withdrawal of the UK from the European Union.

Victim Support – an independent charity supporting victims and witnesses of crime in England and Wales.

Wolfenden Report (1957) – UK government-sponsored report that recommended the decriminalisation of sexual activity between males over 21 years of age.

Xenophobia – an irrational fear or hatred of those from another country.

Zionism – movement and philosophy of Israeli nationalism that offers support for the establishment of a Jewish homeland in Israel.

REFERENCES

ACPO (Association of Chief Police Officers) (2000) *ACPO Guide to Identifying and Combating Hate Crime*. London: ACPO.

ACPO (Association of Chief Police Officers) (2005) *Hate Crime: Delivering a Quality Service: Good Practice and Tactical Guidance*. London: ACPO.

ACPO (Association of Chief Police Officers) (2011) *ACPO Strategy and Supporting Operational Guidance for Policing Prostitution and Sexual Exploitation*. London: ACPO.

ACPOS (Association of Chief Police Officers in Scotland) (2010) *Hate Crime Guidance Manual 2010*. Glasgow: ACPOS.

Addley, E. (2012) 'Three Muslim men convicted over gay hate leaflets', *The Guardian*, www.theguardian.com/world/2012/jan/20/three-muslims-convicted-gay-hate-leaflets, 20 January (accessed 14 March 2014).

Ahmed, A. (2003) *Islam under Siege*. Cambridge: Polity Press.

Allen, C., Isakjee, A. and Young, O. (2013) *'Maybe We Are Hated'. The Experience and Impact of Anti-Muslim Hate on British Muslim Women*. Birmingham: University of Birmingham.

Antjoule, N. (2013) *The Hate Crime Report: Homophobia, Biphobia and Transphobia in London*. London: Galop.

Armitage, S. (2012) *Black Roses: The Killing of Sophie Lancaster*. Reading: Pomona Books.

Athwal, H. and Burnett, J. (2014) *Investigated or Ignored? An Analysis of Race-Related Deaths since the Macpherson Report*. London: Institute of Race Relations.

Awan, I. (2013a) *Let's Prevent Extremism by Engaging Communities, Not by Isolating Them, Public Spirit*. Bristol: University of Bristol.

Awan, I. (2013b) *Victims of Anti-Muslim Hate: Written Evidence Submitted to the All-Party Parliamentary Group on Islamophobia*. Birmingham: Birmingham City University.

Bardens, J. and Gay, O. (2014) *Domestic Violence*. Standard Note SN/HA/6337, London: House of Commons Library.

Bartkowiak-Théron, I. and Asquith, N. (2012) 'Vulnerability and diversity in policing', in I. Bartkowiak-Théron and N. Asquith (eds), *Policing Vulnerability*. Sydney: The Federation Press, pp. 3–19.

Bartlett, P. (2007) 'Killing Gay Men, 1976–2001', *British Journal of Criminology*, 47 (4): 573–595.

Batty, D. (2009) 'Neo-Nazi intent on bombing "non-British" convicted of terrorism', *The Guardian*, www.theguardian.com/uk/2009/jul/15/neo-nazi-bomber-guilty, 15 July (accessed 10 March 2014).

BBC (2011) *Newsnight*, BBC2, 14 July.

BBC News (2005) 'Hate crimes soar after bombings', BBC News Online, 3 August, at http://news.bbc.co.uk/1/hi/england/london/4740015.stm (accessed 8 March 2014).

BBC News (2008a) 'Phillips warns of race cold war', BBC News Online, 20 April, at http://news.bbc.co.uk/go/pr/fr/-/1/hi/uk/7356993.stm (accessed 8 March 2014).

BBC News (2008b) 'Boys sentenced over goth murder', BBC News, 28 April, at http://news.bbc.co.uk/go/pr/fr/-/1/hi/england/lancashire/7370637.stm (accessed 12 May 2014).

BBC News (2011a) 'Pair jailed for Trafalgar Square homophobic killing', BBC News, 26 January, at www.bbc.co.uk/news/uk-england-london-12283937 (accessed 14 April 2014).

BBC News (2011b) 'Destiny Lauren murder: Leon Fyle jailed after retrial', BBC News, 23 September, at www.bbc.co.uk/news/uk-england-london-15040106 (accessed 14 April 2014).

BBC News (2012) 'Winterbourne View: care workers jailed for abuse', BBC News, 28 October, at www.bbc.co.uk/news/uk-england-bristol-20092894 (accessed 8 March 2014).

BBC News (2013a) 'Murder victim Bijan Ebrahimi endured abuse and threats', BBC News, 28 November, at www.bbc.co.uk/news/uk-england-25017802 (accessed 27 May 2014).

BBC News (2013b) 'Bijan Ebrahimi murder: sentences appeal-bid dismissed', BBC News, 20 December, at www.bbc.co.uk/news/uk-england-bristol-25471346 (accessed 27 May 2014).

BBC News (2014) 'UK European election results', BBC News, 26 May, www.bbc.co.uk/news/events/vote2014/eu-uk-results (accessed 27 May 2014).

Beasley, C. (2005) *Gender and Sexuality: Critical Theories, Critical Thinkers*. London: Sage.

Bettcher, T.M. (2007) 'Evil deceivers and make-believers: on transphobic violence and the politics of illusion', *Hypatia*, 22 (3): 43–65.

Bhavani, R., Mirza, H. and Meetoo, V. (2006) *Tackling the Roots of Racism: Lessons for Success*. Bristol: The Policy Press.

Blazak, R. (2009) 'The prison hate machine', *Criminology and Public Policy*, 8 (3): 633–40.

Bornstein, K. (2006) 'Gender terror, gender rage', in S. Stryker and S. Whittle (eds), *The Transgender Studies Reader*. New York: Routledge, pp. 236–43.

Botcherby, S., Glen, F., Iganski, P., Jochelson, K. and Lagou, S. (2011) *Equality Groups' Perceptions and Experience of Crime: Analysis of the British Crime Survey 2007–08, 2008–09 and 2009–10*. London: Equality and Human Rights Commission.

Bourne, J. (2001) 'The life and times of institutional racism', *Race and Class*, 43 (2): 7–22.

Bowling, B. (1993) 'Racial harassment and the process of victimisation', *British Journal of Criminology*, 33 (2): 231–50.

Bowling, B. (1999) *Violent Racism: Victimisation, Policing and Social Context*. Oxford: Oxford University Press.

Bowling, B. (2003) 'Racial harassment and the process of victimisation: conceptual and methodological implications for the local crime survey', in B. Perry (ed.), *Hate and Bias Crime: A Reader*. London: Routledge, pp. 61–76.

Bowling, B. and Phillips, C. (2002) *Racism, Crime and Justice*. Harlow: Pearson.

Bowling, B., Parmar, A. and Phillips, C. (2008) 'Policing minority ethnic communities', in T. Newburn (ed.), *Handbook of Policing*, 2nd edn. Cullompton: Willan, pp. 611–41.

Brå (2013) *Hate Crime*. A Summary of Report No. 2013:16. Stockholm: Brå.

Bridges, L. (2001) 'Race, law and the state', *Race and Class*, 43 (2): 61–76.

Bristol Post (2013) 'Bijan Ebrahimi Bristol murder: judge's sentencing comments to Lee James and Stephen Norley', *Bristol Post*, November 28, at www.bristolpost.co.uk/Bijan-Ebrahimi-Bristol-murder-judge-s-sentencing/story-20237111–detail/story.html (accessed 27 May 2014).

Brookes, S. (2013) 'A case for engagement: the role of the UK Disability Hate Crime Network', in A. Roulstone and H. Mason-Bish (eds), *Disability, Hate Crime and Violence*. London: Routledge, pp. 126–34.

Burnett, A. (2006) 'Reassuring older people in relation to fear of crime', in A. Wahidin and M. Cain (eds), *Ageing, Crime and Society*. Cullompton: Willan, pp. 124–38.

Burnett, J. (2013) 'Britain: racial violence and the politics of hate', *Race and Class*, 54 (4): 5–21.

Burney, E. (2002) 'The uses and limits of prosecuting racially aggravated offences', in P. Iganski (ed.), *The Hate Debate: Should Hate Be Punished as a Crime?* London: Institute for Jewish Policy Research, pp. 103–13.

Burney, E. and Rose, G. (2002) *Racist Offences: How Is the Law Working?* London: Home Office Research Study 244.

Butler, J. (1990) *Gender Trouble: Feminism and the Subversion of Identity*. London: Routledge.

Byers, B., Crider, B.W. and Biggers, G.K. (1999) 'Neutralization techniques used against the Amish bias crime motivation: a study of hate crime and offender', *Journal of Contemporary Criminal Justice*, 15 (1): 78–96.

Campbell, R. (2014) 'Not getting away with it: linking sex work and hate crime in Merseyside', in N. Chakraborti and J. Garland (eds), *Responding to Hate Crime: The Case for Connecting Policy and Research*. Bristol: The Policy Press, pp. 55–70.

Campbell, R. and Stoops, S. (2010) 'Taking sex workers seriously: treating violence as hate crime in Liverpool', *Research for Sex Workers*, 12: 9–11.

Chahal, K. and Julienne, L. (1999) *'We can't all be White!' Racist Victimisation in the UK*. York: Joseph Rowntree Foundation.

Chakraborti, N. (2007) 'Policing Muslim communities', in M. Rowe (ed.), *Policing Beyond Macpherson: Issues in Policing, Race and Society*. Cullompton: Willan, pp. 107–27.

Chakraborti, N. (2009) 'A glass half full? Assessing progress in the policing of hate crime', *Policing: A Journal of Policy and Practice*, 3 (2): 121–8.

Chakraborti, N. (ed.) (2010) *Hate Crime: Concepts, Policy, Future Directions*. London: Routledge.

Chakraborti, N. (2010a) 'Crimes against the "other": conceptual, operational and empirical challenges for hate studies', *Journal of Hate Studies*, 8 (1): 9–28.

Chakraborti, N. (2010b) 'Beyond 'passive apartheid?' Developing policy and research agendas on rural racism', *Journal of Ethnic and Migration Studies*, 36 (3): 501–17.

Chakraborti, N. (2012) 'Introduction: hate crime victimization', *International Review of Victimology*, 18 (1): 3–6.

Chakraborti, N. (2014) 'Introduction and overview', in N. Chakraborti and J. Garland (eds), *Responding to Hate Crime: The Case for Connecting Policy and Research*. Bristol: The Policy Press, pp. 1–9.

Chakraborti, N. and Garland, J. (eds) (2004) *Rural Racism*. Cullompton: Willan.

Chakraborti, N. and Garland, J. (2012) 'Reconceptualising hate crime victimization through the lens of vulnerability and 'difference', *Theoretical Criminology*, 16 (4): 499–514.

Chakraborti, N. and Garland, J. (eds) (2014) *Responding to Hate Crime: The Case for Connecting Policy and Research*. Bristol: The Policy Press.

Chakraborti, N. and Zempi, I. (2013) 'Criminalising oppression or reinforcing oppression? The implications of veil ban laws for muslim women in the West', *Northern Ireland Legal Quarterly*, 64 (1): 63–74.

Chakraborti, N., Gadd, D., Gray, P., Wright, S. and Duggan, M. (2011) 'Public authority commitment and action to eliminate targeted harassment and violence', Equality and Human Rights Commission Research Report 74. Manchester: Equality and Human Rights Commission.

Chakraborti, N., Garland, J. and Hardy, S. (2014a) *The Leicester Hate Crime Project: Findings and Conclusions*. Leicester: University of Leicester.

Chakraborti, N., Garland, J. and Hardy, S. (2014b) *Leicester Hate Crime Project Briefing Paper 1: Disablist Hate Crime: Victims' Perspectives*. Leicester: University of Leicester.

Chan, J. (1997) *Changing Police Culture: Policing in a Multicultural Society*. Cambridge: Cambridge University Press.

Choudhury, T. and Fenwick, H. (2011) *The Impact of Counter-Terrorism Measures on Muslim Communities*. Equality and Human Rights Commission Research Report 72. Manchester: The Equality and Human Rights Commission.

CJJI (Criminal Justice Joint Inspection) (2013) *Living in a Different World: Joint Review of Disability Hate Crime*. London: CJJI.

Coleman, N., Sykes, W. and Walker, A. (2013) *Crime and Disabled People: Baseline Statistical Analysis of Measures from the Formal Legal Inquiry into Disability-related Harassment*. London: Equality and Human Rights Commission.

College of Policing (2014) *Hate Crime Operational Guidance*. Coventry: College of Policing.

Collins, M. (2012) *Hate: My Life in the British Far Right*. London: Biteback.

ComRes (2011) *Scope NDPP Survey February–March 2011*. London: ComRes.

Conrad, T. (2014) 'Sun executives to meet transgender group after Kate Stone furore', www.theguardian.com/media/2014/may/21/sun-executives-transgender-group-kate-stone, 21 May (accessed 21 May 2014).

Copsey, N. (2007) 'Changing course or changing clothes? Reflections on the ideological evolution of the British National Party, 1999–2006', *Patterns of Prejudice*, 41 (1): 61–82.

Copsey, N., Dack, J., Littler, M. and Feldman, M. (2013) *Anti-Muslim Hate Crime and the Far Right*. Teesside: Centre for Fascist, Anti-Fascist and Post-Fascist Studies.

Corb, A. (2014) 'Hate and hate crime in Canada', in N. Hall, A. Corb, P. Giannasi and J. Grieve (eds), *The Routledge International Handbook of Hate Crime*. London: Routledge, pp. 163–73.

CPS (Crown Prosecution Service) (2007a) *Guidance on Prosecuting Cases of Homophobic and Transphobic Crime*. London: Crown Prosecution Service.

CPS (Crown Prosecution Service) (2007b) *Guidance on Prosecuting Cases of Disability Hate Crime*. London: Crown Prosecution Service Equality & Diversity Unit and the Policy Directorate.

CPS (Crown Prosecution Service) (2010) *Disability Hate Crime – Guidance on the Distinction between Vulnerability and Hostility in the Context of Crimes Committed Against Disabled People*. London: CPS.

CPS (Crown Prosecution Service) (2012a) *Violence against Women and Girls: Crime Report 2011–2012*. London: Crown Prosecution Service.

CPS (Crown Prosecution Service) (2012b) *Hate Crime and Crimes against Older People: Report 2011–2012*. London: Crown Prosecution Service.

CPS (Crown Prosecution Service) (2013) *Violence Against Women and Girls: Crime Report 2012–2013*. London: CPS.

CPS (Crown Prosecution Service) (2014) *Hate Crimes and Crimes against Older People*. London: CPS.

Craig, K. (2002) 'Examining hate-motivated aggression: a review of the social psychological literature on hate crime as a distinct form of aggression', *Aggression and Violent Behaviour*, 7 (1): 85–101.

CST (Community Security Trust) (2013) *Annual Review: Antisemitism and Jewish Communal Security in Britain in 2012*. London: The Community Security Trust.

CST (Community Security Trust) (2014) *Antisemitic Incidents Report 2013*. London: The Community Security Trust.

Creese, B. and Lader, D. (2014) 'Hate Crimes England and Wales, 2013/14', *Home Office Statistical Bulletin 02/14*. London: Home Office.

Deal, M. (2007) 'Aversive disablism: subtle prejudice toward disabled people', *Disability and Society*, 22 (1): 93–107.

DeKeseredy, W.S. (2009) 'Male violence against women in North America as hate crime', in B. Perry (ed.), *Hate Crimes, Volume 3: The Victims of Hate Crime*. Westport, CT: Praeger Publishers, pp. 151–72.

DeKeseredy, W.S., Schwartz, M.D., Fagan, D. and Hall, M. (2006) 'Separation/divorce sexual assault: the contribution of male peer support', *Feminist Criminology*, 1: 228–50.

DCLG (Department for Communities and Local Government) (2014) *Statutory Homelessness: October to December Quarter 2013 England*. London: DCLG.

Dick, S. (2009) *Homophobic Hate Crimes and Hate Incidents*. London: Equality and Human Rights Commission.

Disability Hate Crime Network (2014a) *A Response to the Law Commission Report 'Hate Crime: Should the Current Offences Be Extended?'* London: Disability Hate Crime Network.

Disability Hate Crime Network (2014b) 'Attorney General's letter to disability Hate Crime Network re Bijan Ebrahimi case', available at http://dhcn.info/dhcn/category/blogs-and-stories/ (accessed 25 May 2014).

Disability Living Foundation (2012) Key Facts, at www.dlf.org.uk/content/key-facts, (accessed 23 June 2014).

Dittman, R. (2003) 'Policing hate crime. from victim to challenger: a transgendered perspective', *Probation Journal*, 50 (3): 282–8.

Dixon, B. and Gadd, D. (2006) 'Getting the message? "New" Labour and the criminalisation of "hate"', *Criminology and Criminal Justice*, 6 (3): 309–28.

Docking, M., Kielinger, V. and Paterson, S. (2003) *Policing Racist Incidents in the Metropolitan Police Service*. London: Metropolitan Police Service.

Dodd, V. (2005) 'Two-thirds of Muslims consider leaving UK', *The Guardian*, 26 July, p. 5.

Dodd, V. and Evans, R. (2014) 'Lawrence revelations: admit institutional racism, Met chief told', *The Guardian*, 7 March.

Donovan, C., Barnes, R. and Nixon, C. (2014) *The Coral Project Newsletter*, Spring 2014. Sunderland: University of Sunderland.

Donovan, C., Hester, M., Homes, J. and McCarry, M. (2006) *Comparing Domestic Abuse in Same Sex and Heterosexual Relationships*. Sunderland and Bristol: University of Sunderland/University of Bristol.

Doward, J. (2010) 'Vulnerable tenants targeted by drug gang "Cuckoos"', *Guardian*, 3 October, at www.theguardian.com/society/2010/oct/03/homeless-gangs-cuckoo (accessed 25 May 2014).

Duggan, M. (2014) 'Working with lesbian, gay, bisexual and transgender communities to shape hate crime policy', in N. Chakraborti and J. Garland (eds), *Responding to Hate Crime: The Case for Connecting Policy and Research*. Bristol: The Policy Press, pp. 87–98.

Dunbar, E. (1997) 'The relationship of DSM diagnostic criteria and Gough's prejudice scale: exploring the clinical manifestations of the prejudiced personality', *Cultural Diversity and Mental Health*, 3: 247–57.

Dunbar, E. and Crevecoeur, D. (2005) 'Assessment of hate crime offenders: the role of bias intent in examining violence risk', *Journal of Forensic Psychology Practice*, 5 (1): 1–19.

Dunn, P. (2012) 'Men as victims: "victim" identities, gay identities, and masculinities', *Journal of Interpersonal Violence*, 27 (17): 3442–67.

EHRC (Equality and Human Rights Commission) (2009a) *Beyond Tolerance: Making Sexual Orientation a Public Matter*. London: EHRC.

EHRC (Equality and Human Rights Commission) (2009b) *Police and Racism: What Has Been Achieved 10 Years after the Stephen Lawrence Inquiry Report?* Manchester: EHRC.

EHRC (Equality and Human Rights Commission) (2011) *Hidden in Plain Sight: Inquiry into Disability-Related Harassment*. London: Equality and Human Rights Commission.

EHRC (Equality and Human Rights Commission) (2013) *Crime and Disabled People*. London: Equality and Human Rights Commission.

Ekins, R. and King, D. (2006) *The Transgender Phenomenon*. London: Sage.

Elliot, P. (2010) *Debates in Transgender, Queer, and Feminist Theory: Contested Sites*. Surrey: Ashgate Publishing.

Ellison, M. (2014) *The Stephen Lawrence Independent Review: Possible Corruption and the Role of Undercover Policing in the Stephen Lawrence Case. Summary of Findings*. London: Home Office.

FBI (Federal Bureau of Investigation) (2012) 2011 Hate Crime Statistics, at www.fbi.gov/about-us/cjis/ucr/hate-crime/2011/hate-crime (accessed 2 August 2014).

Fekete, L. (2004) 'Anti-Muslim racism and the European Security State', *Race and Class*, 46 (1): 3–29.

Fekete, L. (2012) *Pedlars of Hate: The Violent Impact of the European Far Right*. London: Institute of Race Relations.

Feldman, M. and Jackson, P. (2011) 'The Aryan Strike Force: Britain's extreme right-wing and new media', in P. Jackson and G. Gable (eds), *Far-Right.Com: Nationalist Extremism on the Internet*. London: Searchlight. pp. 47–57.

Felson, R.B. and Pare, P.P. (2005) 'The reporting of domestic violence and sexual assault by non-strangers to the police', *Journal of Marriage and Family*, 67 (3): 597–610.

Fisher, C. and Salfati, C.G. (2009) 'Behavior or motivation: typologies of hate-motivated offenders', in R. Blazak (ed.), *Hate Crimes, Volume 4: Hate Crime Offenders*. pp. 103–136.

Fitzpatrick, S., Pawson, H., Bramley, G. and Wilcox, S. (2011) *The Homeless Monitor: Tracking the Impacts of Policy and Economic Change in England 2011–2013*. Edinburgh: Heriot–Watt University, University of York and Crisis.

Formby, E. (2012) *Connected Lesbian, Gay, Bisexual and Trans Communities? A Scoping Study to Explore Understandings and Experiences of 'Community' Among LGBT People*. Swindon: Arts and Humanities Research Council.

Foster, J. (2002) 'Police cultures', in T. Newburn (ed.), *Handbook of Policing*. Cullompton: Willan, pp. 196–227.

FRA (European Union Agency for Fundamental Rights) (2012) *Making Hate Crime Visible in the European Union: Acknowledging Victims' Rights*. Vienna: FRA.

FRA (European Union Agency for Fundamental Rights) (2013a) *FRA Brief: Crimes Motivated by Hatred and Prejudice in the EU*. Vienna: FRA.

FRA (European Union Agency for Fundamental Rights) (2013b) *Discrimination and Hate Crime against Jews in EU Member States: Experiences and Perceptions of Antisemitism*. Luxembourg: Publications Office of the European Union.

Furbey, R., Dinham, A., Farnell, R., Finneron, D. and Wilkinson, G. (2006) *Faith as Social Capital: Connecting or Dividing?* Bristol: The Policy Press.

Gable, G. and Jackson, P. (2011) *Lone Wolves: Myth or Reality?* London: Searchlight.

Gable, S. (2013) 'Shifting sands', *Searchlight*, 450: 5–8.

Gadd, D. (2006) 'The role of recognition in the desistance process: a case analysis of a former far-right activist', *Theoretical Criminology*, 10 (2): 179–202.

Gadd, D. (2009) 'Aggravating racism and elusive motivation', *British Journal of Criminology*, 49 (6): 755–71.

Gadd, D. and Dixon, B. (2009) 'Posing the "why" question: understanding the perpetration of racially motivated violence and harassment', in J. Levin (ed.), *Hate Crimes, Volume 1: Understanding and Defining Hate Crime*. pp. 77–94.

Gadd, D., Dixon, B. and Jefferson, T. (2005) *Why Do They Do It? Racial Harassment in North Staffordshire: Key Findings*. Keele: University of Keele Centre for Criminological Research.

Garland, J. (2010) 'It's a Mosher just been banged for no reason': assessing the victimisation of goths and the boundaries of hate crime', *International Review of Victimology*, 17 (2): 159–77.

Garland, J. (2012) 'Difficulties in defining hate crime victimisation', *International Review of Victimology*, 18 (1): 25–37.

Garland, J. (2013) 'Tragedy, prejudice and opportunism: how the murder of a soldier revitalised the English Defence League', International Network for Hate Studies Blog at www.internationalhatestudies.com/tragedy-prejudice-and-opportunism-how-the-murder-of-a-soldier-revitalised-the-english-defence-league-2/ (accessed 3 March 2014).

Garland, J. (2014a) 'Conclusions', in N. Chakraborti and J. Garland (eds), *Responding to Hate Crime: The Case for Connecting Policy and Research*. Bristol: The Policy Press. pp. 259–67.

Garland, J. (2014b) 'Reshaping hate crime policy and practice: lessons from a grassroots campaign – an interview with Sylvia Lancaster, founder of the Sophie Lancaster Foundation', in N. Chakraborti and J. Garland (eds), *Responding to Hate Crime: The Case For Connecting Policy and Research*. Bristol: Policy Press. pp. 39–53.

Garland, J. and Chakraborti, N. (2004) 'Racist victimisation, community safety and the rural: issues and challenges', *British Journal of Community Justice*, 2 (3): 21–32.

Garland, J. and Chakraborti, N. (2006) 'Race, space and place: examining identity and cultures of exclusion in rural England', *Ethnicities*, 6 (2): 159–77.

Garland, J. and Chakraborti, N. (2012) 'Divided by a common concept? Assessing the implications of different conceptualisations of hate crime in the European Union', *European Journal of Criminology*, 9 (1): 38–52.

Garland, J. and Hodkinson, P. (2014a) '"F**king freak! What the hell do you think you look like?" Experiences of targeted victimisation among goths and developing notions of hate crime', *British Journal of Criminology*, 54 (4): 613–31.

Garland, J. and Hodkinson, P. (2014b) 'Alternative subcultures and hate crime', in N. Hall, A. Corb, P. Giannasi and J. Grieve (eds), *The Routledge International Handbook of Hate Crime*. London: Routledge, pp. 226–36.

Garland, J. and Treadwell, J. (2012) 'The new politics of hate? An assessment of the appeal of the English Defence League amongst disadvantaged white working class communities in England', *Journal of Hate Studies*, 10 (1): 123–41.

Garland, J., Chakraborti, N. and Hardy, S.J. (2015) '"It felt like a little war": reflections on violence against alternative subcultures', *Sociology*, forthcoming.

Garland, J., Spalek, B. and Chakraborti, N. (2006) 'Hearing lost voices: issues in researching "hidden" minority ethnic communities', *British Journal of Criminology*, 46 (3): 423–37.

Garland, T.S., Richards, T. and Cooney, M. (2010) 'Victims hidden in plain sight: the reality of victimization among the homeless', *Criminal Justice Studies*, 23 (4): 285–301.

Gavrielidis, T. (2007) *Restorative Justice Theory and Practice: Addressing the Discrepancy.* Helsinki: HEUNI.

Gerstenfeld, P.B. (2013) *Hate Crimes: Causes, Controls and Controversies*, 3rd edn. London: Sage.

GIRES (2011) *The Number of Gender Variant People in the UK – Update 2011.* Ashtead: GIRES.

Githens-Mazer, J. and Lambert, R. (2010) *Islamophobia and Anti-Muslim Hate Crime: A London Case Study.* Exeter: European Muslim Research Centre.

Glet, A. (2009) 'The German hate crime concept: an account of the classification and registration of bias-motivated offences and the implementation of the hate crime model into Germany's law enforcement system', *Internet Journal of Criminology*, 1–20.

Goodall, K. (2007) 'Incitement to religious hatred: all talk and no substance?', *Modern Law Review*, 70 (1): 89–113.

Goodey, J. (2005) *Victims and Victimology: Research, Policy and Practice.* Harlow: Pearson.

Goodwin, M.J. (2011) *New British Fascism: Rise of the British National Party.* Oxford: Routledge.

Government Equalities Office (2011) *Headline Findings from our Transgender E-Surveys.* London: HM Government.

Grimshaw, R. and Jefferson, T. (1987) *Interpreting Policework: Policy and Practice in Forms of Beat Policing.* London: Allen and Unwin.

Grunewald, J., Chermak, S. and Freilich, J.D. (2013) 'Distinguishing "loner attacks" from other domestic extremist violence', *Criminology & Public Policy*, 12 (1): 65–91.

Guasp, A. (2012) *The School Report: The Experiences of Gay Young People in Britain's Schools in 2012.* London: Stonewall.

Guasp, A., Gammon, A. and Ellison, G. (2013) *Homophobic Hate Crime: The Gay British Crime Survey 2013.* London: Stonewall.

Gunaratnam, Y. (2003) *Researching 'Race' and Ethnicity: Methods, Knowledge and Power.* London: Sage.

Haas, A.P. et al. (2010) 'Suicide and suicide risk in lesbian, gay, bisexual, and transgender populations: review and recommendations', *Journal of Homosexuality*, 58 (1): 10–51.

Hall, N. (2005) *Hate Crime.* Cullompton: Willan.

Hall, N. (2013) *Hate Crime*, 2nd edn. London: Routledge.

Hall, N., Corb, A., Giannasi, P. and Grieve, J. (eds) (2014) *The Routledge International Handbook on Hate Crime.* London: Routledge.

Hall, N., Grieve, J. and Savage, S. (eds) (2009) *Policing and the Legacy of Lawrence.* London: Routledge.

Hall, S., Critcher, C., Jefferson, T., Clarke, J. and Roberts, B. (1978) *Policing the Crisis: Mugging, the State and Law and Order.* London: Macmillan.

Hardy, S. (2014) 'Developing themes on young people, everyday multiculturalism and hate crime', in N. Chakraborti and J. Garland (eds), *Responding to Hate Crime: The Case for Connecting Policy and Research.* Bristol: The Policy Press, pp. 141–54.

Harne, L. and Radford, J. (2008) *Tackling Domestic Violence: Theories, Policies and Practice*. Maidenhead: Open University Press.

Healy, T. (2013) 'Leicester man who placed pig's head outside Thurnby Lodge community centre used by Muslims spared jail', *Leicester Mercury* at www.leicestermercury.co.uk/Leicester-man-placed-pig-s-head-outside-Thurnby/story-18190674–detail/story.html, 20 February (accessed 15 March 2014).

Henry, J. (2013) 'Bias-based cyberbullying: the next hate crime frontier?', *Criminal Law Bulletin*, 49 (3): 481–503.

Herek, G.M. (2009) 'Hate crimes and stigma-related experiences among sexual minority adults in the United States: prevalence estimates from a national probability sample', *Journal of Interpersonal Violence*, 24 (1): 54–74.

Herek, G.M., Cogan, J.C. and Roy Gillis, J. (2003) 'Victim experiences in hate crimes based on sexual orientation', in B. Perry (ed.), *Hate and Bias Crimes: A Reader*. London: Routledge, pp. 243–59.

Hill, D.B. and Willoughby, B.L.B. (2005) 'The development and validation of the Genderism and Transphobia Scale', *Sex Roles*, 53: (7/8): 531–44.

Hinduja, S. and Patchin, J.W. (2008) 'Cyberbullying: an exploratory analysis of factors related to offending and victimization', *Deviant Behavior*, 29 (2): 129–56.

Hines, S. (2007) *TransForming Gender: Transgender Practices of Identity, Intimacy and Care*. Bristol: Policy Press.

Hiro, D. (1992) *Black British, White British: A History of Race Relations in Britain*, 3rd edn. London: Paladin.

HM Government (2011) *Working for Lesbian, Gay, Bisexual and Transgender Equality: Moving Forward*. London: HM Government.

HM Government (2012a) *Challenge It, Report It, Stop It: The Government's Plan to Tackle Hate Crime*. London: HM Government.

HM Government (2012b) Criminal Justice Act 2003 at http://www.legislation.gov.uk/ukpga/2003/44/section/146 (accessed 14 April 2014).

HM Government (2013) *Government's Progress on the Recommendations from the Equality and Human Rights Commission Inquiry into Disability-Related Harassment*. London: HM Government.

HM Government (2014) *Challenge It, Report It, Stop It: Delivering the Government's Hate Crime Action Plan*. London: HM Government.

HMCPSI (HM Crown Prosecution Service Inspectorate), HMIC (Her Majesty's Inspectorate of Constabulary) and HMI Probation (2013) *Living in a Different World: Joint Review of Disability Hate Crime*. London: HMCPSI, HMIC and HMI Probation.

HMIC (Her Majesty's Inspectorate of Constabulary) (2014) *Everyone's Business: Improving the Police Response to Domestic Abuse*. London: HMIC.

Hobson, A. (2012) 'The political (mis)management of (homo)sexuality and (in)securities', *Criminal Justice Matters*, 88 (1): 4–6.

Holdaway, S. and O'Neill, M. (2006) 'Institutional racism after Macpherson: an analysis of police views', *Policing and Society*, 16 (4): 349–69.

Home Office (2011) *A Review of Effective Practice in Responding to Prostitution*. Available at www.homeoffice.gov.uk/publications/crime/responding-to-prostitution (accessed 10 September 2011).

Home Office and Scottish Home Department (HOSHD) (1957) *Report of the Committee on Homosexual Offences and Prostitution*. London: HMSO.

Home Office, ONS and Ministry of Justice (2013) *An Overview of Hate Crime in England and Wales*. London: Home Office, Office for National Statistics and Ministry of Justice.

House of Lords Hansard (2008) at www.publications.parliament.uk/pa/ld200708/ldhansrd/text/80507–0007.htm, column 600: 8 May (accessed 10 September 2014).

Hoyle, C. (2007) 'Feminism, victimology and domestic violence', in S. Walklate (ed.), *Handbook of Victims and Victimology*. Cullompton: Willan, pp. 146–74.

Hoyle, C. (2008) 'Will she be safe? A critical analysis of risk assessment in domestic violence cases', *Children and Youth Services Review*, 30 (3): 323–37.

Hunt, R. and Jensen, J. (2007) *The School Report: the Experiences of Young Gay People in Britain's Schools*. London: Stonewall.

Hunt, S. (2005) *Religion and Everyday Life*. London: Routledge.

Hunte, J. (1966) *Nigger Hunting in England?* London: West Indian Standing Conference.

Iganski, P. (1999) 'Legislating against hate: outlawing racism and antisemitism in Britain', *Critical Social Policy*, 19 (1): 129–41.

Iganski, P. (2001) 'Hate crimes hurt more', *American Behavioural Scientist*, 45 (4): 626–38.

Iganski, P. (2008) *'Hate Crime' and the City*. Bristol: The Policy Press.

Iganski, P. (2011) *Racist Violence in Europe*. Brussels: ENAR and the Open Society Foundation.

Iganski, P., Kielinger, V. and Paterson, S. (2005) *Hate Crimes Against London's Jews: An Analysis of Incidents Recorded by the Metropolitan Police Service 2001–2004*. London: Institute for Jewish Policy Research.

Iganski, P., with Ainsworth, K., Geraghty, L., Lagou, S. and Patel, N. (2014) 'Understanding how 'hate' hurts: a case study of working with offenders and potential offenders', in N. Chakraborti and J. Garland (eds), *Responding to Hate Crime: The Case for Connecting Policy and Research*. Bristol: The Policy Press. pp. 231–42.

Institute of Race Relations (IRR) (2011) *Breivik, the Conspiracy Theory and the Oslo Massacre*, Briefing Paper No. 5. London: Institute of Race Relations.

IPCC (Independent Police Complaints Commission) (2011) *IPCC Report into the Contact between Fiona Pilkington and Leicestershire Constabulary 2004–2007*. London: IPCC.

Jacobs, J. and Potter, K. (1998) *Hate Crimes: Criminal Law and Identity Politics*. Oxford: Oxford University Press.

Jacobs, R. (2013) 'Why crimes against sex workers should be treated as hate crimes', *The F Word: Contemporary UK Feminism*, 19 August.

Jacques, J. (2010) 'No wonder many transsexual people end up in sex work', *The Guardian* at www.theguardian.com/lifeandstyle/2010/aug/25/transsexual-people-sex-work (accessed 4 June 2014).

James, Z. (2014) 'Hate crimes against Gypsies, Travellers and Roma in Europe', in N. Hall (ed.), *International Handbook on Hate Crime*. London: Routledge.

James, Z. and Simmonds, L. (2012) *Exploring Prejudice: Mapping Hate Crime in the South West*. Plymouth: Department for Communities and Local Government.

Jarman, N. and Tennant, A. (2003) *An Acceptable Prejudice? Homophobic Violence and Harassment in Northern Ireland*. Belfast: Institute for Conflict Research.

Jenkins, R. (2008) 'Youth aged 15 "kicked woman to death because she was a goth"' *The Times*, 13 March, p. 24.

Jenness, V. (2002) 'Contours of hate crime politics and law in the United States', in P. Iganski (ed.), *The Hate Debate: Should Hate be Punished as a Crime*. London: Profile Books. pp. 15–35.

Jinman, R. (2005) 'Anti-semitic attacks rise to a record level', *The Guardian*, 11 February, p. 9.

Johnson, K., Faulkner, P., Jones, H. and Welsh, E. (2007) *Understanding Suicide and Promoting Survival in LGBT Communities*. Brighton: University of Brighton.

Johnson, M.P. (2006) 'Conflict and control: gender symmetry and asymmetry in domestic violence', *Violence Against Women*, 12 (11): 1003–18.

Jones, M. and Williams, M.L. (2013) 'Twenty years on: lesbian, gay and bisexual police officers' experiences of workplace discrimination in England and Wales', *Policing and Society*, DOI: 10.1080/10439463.2013.817998.

Juang, R.M. (2006) 'Transgendering the politics of recognition', in S. Stryker and S. Whittle (eds), *The Transgender Studies Reader*. New York: Routledge, pp. 706–19.

Judiciary of England and Wales (2012) R v Ihjaz Ali, Razwan Javed and Kabir Ahmed: Sentencing Remarks of HHJ Burgess, 10 February 2012, Derby Crown Court. London: Judiciary of England and Wales.

Katz-Wise, S.L. and Hyde, J.S. (2012) 'Victimization experiences of lesbian, gay, and bisexual individuals: a meta-analysis', *Journal of Sex Research*, 49 (2–3): 142–67.

Kelly, L. (1987) 'The continuum of sexual violence', in J. Hanmer and M. Maynard (eds), *Women, Violence and Social Control*. London: Macmillan, pp. 46–60.

Kennedy, D. (2006) 'Killers of gay barman jailed for 28 years under new laws', *The Times*, 17 June, p. 4.

Keogh, P., Reid, D. and Weatherburn, P. (2006) *Lambeth LGBT Matters: The Needs and Experiences of Lesbians, Gay Men, Bisexual and Trans Men and Women in Lambeth*. Lambeth: Sigma Research.

Kidd, J. and Witten, T. (2008) 'Transgender and transsexual identities: the next strange fruit – hate crimes, violence and genocide against the global trans-communities', *Journal of Hate Studies*, 6 (1): 31–63.

Kinnell, H. (2008) *Violence and Sex Work in Britain*. Cullompton: Willan.

Klingspor, K. (2008) 'The challenges of collecting statistical data in the field of hate crime: the case of Sweden', in J. Goodey and K. Aromaa (eds), *Hate Crime: Papers from the 2006 and 2007 Stockholm Criminology Symposiums*. Helsinki: European Institute for Crime Prevention and Control, pp. 40–55.

Koenig, S. 'Dragon Fly' (2003) 'Walk like a man', *Journal of Homosexuality*, 43 (3–4): 145–59.

Kundnani, A. (2001) 'In a foreign land: the new popular racism', *Race and Class*, 43 (2): 41–60.

Kundnani, A. (2002) 'An unholy alliance? Racism, religion and communalism', *Race and Class*, 44 (2): 71–80.

Lane, F.J., Shaw, L.R. and Kim, M. (2009) 'Hate crimes committed against persons with disabilities', in B. Perry (ed.), *Hate Crimes Volume 3: The Victims of Hate Crime*, pp. 173–98.

Law Commission (2013) 'Hate crime: the case for extending the existing offences. Summary for non-specialists', Law Commission Consultation Paper No. 213. London: The Law Commission.

Law Commission (2014) 'Hate crime: should the current offences be extended? Summary for non-specialists', Law Commission Consultation Report No. 348. London: The Law Commission.

Leblanc, L. (2008) *Pretty in Punk: Girls' Gender Resistance in a Boys' Subculture*. New Brunswick, NJ: Rutgers University Press.

Levin, B. (2004) 'History as a weapon: how extremists deny the holocaust in North America', in P. Gerstenfeld and D. Grant (eds), *Crimes of Hate: Selected Readings*. London: Sage. pp. 186–207.

Levin, J. and McDevitt, J. (2002) *Hate Crimes Revisited: America's War on Those Who Are Different*. Boulder, CO: Westview Press.

Lockhart L.L., White, B.W., Causby V. and Isaac, A. (1994) 'Letting out the secret: violence in lesbian relationships', *Journal of Interpersonal Violence*, 9 (4): 469–92.

Lombardi, E. (2009) 'Varieties of transgender/transsexual lives and their relationship with transphobia', *Journal of Homosexuality*, 56 (8): 977–92.

Lombardi, E., Wilchins, R.A., Priesing, D. and Malouf, D. (2002) 'Gender violence: transgender experiences with violence and discrimination', *Journal of Homosexuality*, 42 (1): 89–101.

Lowles, N. (2002) *White Riot: The Violent Story of Combat 18*. London: Searchlight.

Lumb, D. and Casciani, D. (2013) 'Pavlo Lapshyn's 90 days of terror', www.bbc.co.uk/news/uk-england-birmingham-24586050, 21 October (accessed 7 March 2014).

Macpherson, Sir W. (1999) *The Stephen Lawrence Inquiry: Report of an Inquiry by Sir William Macpherson of Cluny*. London: TSO.

Maier, S.L. and Bergen, R. (2012) 'Critical issues in intimate partner violence', in W.S. DeKeseredy and M. Dragiewicz (eds), *Routledge Handbook of Critical Criminology*. Oxford: Routledge. pp. 328–39.

Mason, G. (2005a) 'Hate crime and the image of the stranger', *British Journal of Criminology*, (45) 6: 837–59.

Mason, G. (2005b) 'Being hated: stranger or familiar?', *Social and Legal Studies*, (14) 4: 585–605.

Mason, G. (2009) 'Body maps: envisaging homophobic, violence, and safety', in P. Iganski (ed.), *Hate Crimes Volume 2: Understanding and Defining Hate Crime*, pp. 49–72.

Mason, G. (2012) 'Naming the 'R' word in racial victimization: violence against Indian students in Australia', *International Review of Victimology*, 18 (1): 39–56.

Mason, G. (2014a) 'Victim attributes in hate crime law: difference and the politics of justice', *British Journal of Criminology*, 54 (2): 161–79.

Mason, G. (2014b) 'The symbolic purpose of hate crime law: ideal victims and emotion', *Theoretical Criminology*, 18 (1): 75–92.

Mason-Bish, H. (2013) 'Examining the boundaries of hate crime policy: considering age and gender', *Criminal Justice Policy Review*, 24 (3): 297–316.

Maxwell, C. and Maxwell, S. (1995) *Youth Participation in Hate-motivated Crimes: Research and Policy Implications*, Bolder: University of Colorado.

McCormack, M. and Anderson, E. (2010) 'It's just not acceptable any more': the erosion of homophobia and the softening of masculinity at an English Sixth Form', *Sociology*, 44 (5): 843–59.

McDevitt, J. (2014) 'New figures reveal dramatic increase in hate crimes against Polish people', *The Guardian*, 11 June.

McDevitt, J., Levin, J. and Bennett, S. (2002) 'Hate crime offenders: an expanded typology', *Journal of Social Issues*, 58 (2): 303–317.

McDevitt, J., Levin, J., Nolan, J. and Bennett, S. (2010) 'Hate crime offenders', in N. Chakraborti (ed.), *Hate Crime: Concepts, Policy, Future Directions*. Cullompton: Willan. pp. 124–48.

McDonald, D. (2014) 'The politics of hate crime: neoliberal vigilance, vigilantism and the question of paedophilia', *International Journal for Crime, Justice and Social Democracy*, 3 (1): 68–80.

McGhee, D. (2005) *Intolerant Britain: Hate, Citizenship and Difference*. Maidenhead: Open University Press.

McLagan, G. and Lowles, N. (2000) *Mr. Bad: The Secret Life of Racist Bomber and Killer David Copeland*. London: John Blake Publishing.

McLaughlin, E. (2002) 'Rocks and hard places: the politics of hate crime', *Theoretical Criminology* 6 (4): 493–498.

METRO Youth Chances (2014) *Summary of First Findings: The Experiences of LGBTQ Young People in England*. London: METRO.

Michener, W. (2012) 'The individual psychology of group hate', *Journal of Hate Studies*, 10: 15–48.

Ministry of Justice (2010) *Circular 2010/05: Offences of Stirring Up Hatred on the Grounds of Sexual Orientation*. London: Ministry of Justice.

Ministry of Justice (2013) *Statistics on Race and the Criminal Justice System 2012*. London: Ministry of Justice.

Moran, L. (2007) '"Invisible minorities": challenging community and neighbourhood models of policing', *Criminology and Criminal Justice*, 7 (4): 417–41.

Moran, L.J. and Sharpe, A.N. (2004) 'Violence, identity and policing: the case of violence against transgender people', *Criminal Justice*, 4 (4): 395–417.

Morris, T. (2013) 'Bristol police ignored murder victim Bijan Ebrahimi's pleas for protection', *Bristol Post* at www.bristolpost.co.uk/Bristol-police-ignored-murder-victim-Bijan/story-20239616–detail/story.html, 29 November (accessed 27 May 2014).

Morris, U.M. (2014) *Alternative Subculture Hate Crime: Reporting and Support*. London: Stop Hate UK.

Morrison, E.G. (2010) 'Transgender as ingroup or outgroup? Lesbian, gay, and bisexual viewers respond to a transgender character in daytime television', *Journal of Homosexuality*, 57 (5): 650–65.

Morton, J. (2008) *Transgender Experiences in Scotland: Research Summary*. Edinburgh: Scottish Transgender Alliance.

Muir, H. (2012) 'Hideously diverse Britain: what makes a Sikh join the far right?', *The Guardian*, 15 June.

Muir, H. (2013) 'Metropolitan police still institutionally racist, say black and Asian officers', *The Guardian*, 21 April.

Namaste, V.K. (2006) 'Genderbashing: sexuality, gender, and the regulation of public space', in S. Stryker and S. Whittle (eds), *The Transgender Studies Reader*. New York: Routledge. pp. 584–98.

Neal, S. (2002) 'Rural landscapes, representations and racism: examining multicultural citizenship and policy making in the English countryside', *Ethnic and Racial Studies*, 25 (3): 442–61.

Neal, S. (2009) *Rural Identities: Ethnicity and Community in the Contemporary English Countryside*. Farnham: Ashgate.

Newburn, T. (2013) *Criminology*, 2nd edn. London: Routledge.

Newburn, T. and Rock, P. (2005) *Living in Fear: Violence and Victimisation in the Lives of Single Homeless People*. London: Crisis.

Nilsen, A.G. (2013) 'Norway's disturbing lurch to the right', *The Guardian* at www.theguardian.com/commentisfree/2013/sep/10/norway-lurch-to-right, 10 September (accessed 30 July 2014).

Norton, A. and Herek, G. (2012) 'Heterosexuals' attitudes toward transgender people: findings from a national probability sample of U.S. Adults', *Sex Roles*, 1–16.

NSPCC (2014) 'Cyberbullying', www.nspcc.org.uk/help-and-advice/for-parents/online-safety/cyberbullying/cyberbullying_wda99645.html (accessed 4 April 2014).

ODIHR (Office for Democratic Institutions and Human Rights) (2009a) *Hate Crime Laws: A Practical Guide*. Warsaw: OSCE Office for Democratic Institutions and Human Rights.

ODIHR (Office for Democratic Institutions and Human Rights) (2009b) *Preventing and Responding to Hate Crimes: A Resource Guide for NGOs in the OSCE Region*. Warsaw: The OSCE Office for Democratic Institutions and Human Rights.

ODIHR (Office for Democratic Institutions and Human Rights) (2010a) *Hate Crimes in the OSCE Region: Incidents and Responses – Annual Report for 2009*. Warsaw: OSCE Office for Democratic Institutions and Human Rights.

ODIHR (Office for Democratic Institutions and Human Rights) (2010b) *Police and Roma and Sinti: Good Practices in Building Trust and Understanding*. Warsaw: The OSCE Office for Democratic Institutions and Human Rights.

ODIHR (Office for Democratic Institutions and Human Rights) (2013) *Hate Crimes in the OSCE Region: Incidents and Responses – Annual Report for 2012*. Warsaw: OSCE Office for Democratic Institutions and Human Rights.

O'Doherty, T. (2011) 'Victimization in off-street sex industry work', *Violence Against Women*, 17 (7): 944–63.

Office for Disability Issues (2011) *Life Opportunities Survey, Wave One Results 2009/11*. London: HM Government.

Office of Public Sector Information (2008) 'Schedule 16 Hatred on the Grounds of Sexual Orientation' at www.opsi.gov.uk/acts/acts2008/ukpga_20080004_en_33#sch16 (accessed 10 September 2014).

O'Keeffe, M., Hills, A., Doyle, M., McCreadie, C., Scholes, S., Constantine, R., Tinker, A., Manthorpe, J., Biggs, S. and Erens, B. (2007) *UK Study of Abuse and Neglect of Older People Prevalence Survey Report*. London: National Centre for Social Research.

Older People's Commissioner for Wales (2014) *Abuse of, and Crimes Against, Older People*. Cardiff: Older People's Commissioner for Wales.

ONS (Office for National Statistics) (2006) *Focus on Ethnicity and Religion 2006 Edition*. Basingstoke: Palgrave Macmillan.

ONS (Office for National Statistics) (2012) *Religion in England and Wales 2011*. London: Office for National Statistics.

ONS (Office for National Statistics) (2013) *Table P01UK: 2011 Census: Usual Resident Population by Five-year Age Group, Local Authorities in the United Kingdom*, London: Office for National Statistics.

ONS (Office for National Statistics) (2014) *Chapter 4 – Intimate Personal Violence and Partner Abuse*. London: ONS.

Oxford English Dictionary (2014) 'Homophobia', at www.oed.com/view/ (accessed 14 April 2014).

Pantazis, C. and Pemberton, S. (2009) 'From the "old" to the "new" suspect community: examining the impacts of recent UK counter-terrorist legislation', *British Journal of Criminology*, 49 (5): 646–66.

Parekh, B. (2000) *The Future of Multi-Ethnic Britain*. London: Profile Books.

Perry, B. (2001) *In the Name of Hate: Understanding Hate Crimes*. London: Routledge.

Perry, B. (2003a) 'Anti-Muslim retaliatory violence following the 9/11 terrorist attacks', in B. Perry (ed.), *Hate and Bias Crime: A Reader*. London: Routledge, pp. 183–202.

Perry, B. (2003b) 'Defenders of the faith: hate groups and ideologies of power', in B. Perry (ed.), *Hate and Bias Crime: A Reader*. London: Routledge, pp. 301–18.

Perry, B (ed.) (2009) *Hate Crimes Volume 1: Understanding and Defining Hate Crime.* Westport, CT: Praeger Publishers.

Perry, B. (2010) 'The more things change ... post 9/11 trends in hate crime scholarship', in N. Chakraborti (ed.), *Hate Crime: Concepts, Policy, Future Directions.* London: Routledge. pp. 17–40.

Perry, B. and Dyck, D.R. (2014) 'Courage in the face of hate: a curricular resource for confronting anti-LGBTQ violence', in N. Chakraborti and J. Garland (eds), *Responding to Hate Crime: The Case for Connecting Policy and Research.* Bristol: The Policy Press. pp. 185–97.

Perry, J. (2004) 'Is justice taking a beating?', *Community Care*, 1 April: 44–5.

Perry, J. (2014) 'Evidencing the case for hate crime', in N. Chakraborti and J. Garland (eds), *Responding to Hate Crime: The Case for Connecting Policy and Research.* Bristol: The Policy Press, pp. 71–83.

Petrosino, C. (2003) 'Connecting the past to the future: hate crime in America', in B. Perry (ed.), *Hate and Bias Crime: A Reader.* London: Routledge, pp. 9–26.

Phillips, C. and Bowling, B. (2002) 'Racism, ethnicity, crime and criminal justice', in M. Maguire, R. Morgan and R. Reiner (eds), *The Oxford Handbook of Criminology*, 3rd edn. Oxford: Oxford University Press, pp. 579–619.

Philo, G., Briant, E. and Donald, P. (2013) 'The role of the press in the war on asylum', *Race and Class*, 55 (2): 28–41.

Pidd, H. (2012) 'Anders Breivik 'trained' for shooting attacks by playing Call of Duty', *The Guardian*, 19 April, available at www.theguardian.com/world/2012/apr/19/anders-breivik-call-of-duty (accessed 24 February 2014).

Porter, D. and Jones, O. (2012) Thurnby Lodge Forgotten Estates at www.hopeno-thate.org.uk/news/article/2558/thurnby-lodge-forgotten-estates, 25 November (accessed 14 Match 2014).

Poynting, S., Noble, G., Tabar, P. and Collins, J. (2004) *Bin Laden in the Suburbs: Criminalising the Arab Other.* Sydney: Sydney Institute of Criminology.

Press Association (2013) 'Transgender woman's murderer jailed for life', *The Guardian*, www.theguardian.com/uk-news/2013/oct/18/chrissie-azzopardi-murder-life-sentence, 18 October (accessed 14 April 2014.)

Pring, J. (2014) 'Faruk Ali: public anger after force refuses to suspend officers over "assault"', *Disability New Service*, available at http://disabilitynewsservice.com/2014/03/faruk-ali-public-anger-after-force-refuses-to-suspend-officers-over-assault/ (accessed 8 January 2014).

Quarmby, K. (2011) *Scapegoat: Why We Are Failing Disabled People.* London: Portobello Books.

Ramesh, R. (2012) '"Scrounger" stigma puts poor people off applying for essential benefits', *The Guardian* at www.guardian.co.uk/society/2012/nov/20/scrounger-stigma-poor-people-benefits/print, 20 November (accessed 23 June 2014).

Ray, L. and Smith, D. (2001) 'Racist offenders and the politics of "hate crime"', *Law and Critique*, 12 (3): 203–21.

Ray, L. and Smith, D. (2002) 'Hate crime, violence and cultures of racism', in P. Iganski (ed.), *The Hate Debate: Should Hate be Punished as a Crime?* London: Profile Books, pp. 88–102.

Ray, L., Smith, D. and Wastell, L. (2004) 'Shame, rage and racist violence', *British Journal of Criminology*, 44 (3): 350–68.

Raymond, J. (1979) *The Transsexual Empire: The Making of the She-Male.* London: The Women's Press.

Reiner, R. (2010) *The Politics of the Police*, 4th edn. Oxford: Oxford University Press.

Richardson, D. and Monro, S. (2012) *Sexuality, Equality and Diversity*, Basingstoke: Palgrave.

Ristock, J. (2002) *No More Secrets: Violence in Lesbian Relationships*. London: Routledge.

Roulstone, A. and Mason-Bish, H. (eds) (2013) *Disability, Hate Crime and Violence*. London: Routledge.

Roulstone, A. and Sadique, K. (2013) 'Vulnerable to misinterpretation: disabled people, "vulnerability", hate crime and the fight for legal recognition', in A. Roulstone and H. Mason-Bish (eds), *Disability, Hate Crime and Violence*. London: Routledge, pp. 25–39.

Rowe, M. (2004) *Policing, Race and Racism*. Cullompton: Willan.

Rowe, M. (2007) 'Introduction: policing and racism in the limelight – the politics and context of the Lawrence Report', in M. Rowe (ed.), *Policing Beyond Macpherson: Issues in Policing, Race and Society*. Cullompton: Willan, pp. xi–xxiv.

Rowe, M. (2012) *Race and Crime*. London: Sage.

Rowe, M. (2014) *Introduction to Policing*, 2nd edn. London: Sage.

Rowe, M. (ed.) (2007) *Policing beyond Macpherson: Issues in Policing, Race and Society*. London: Routledge.

Rowe, M. and Garland, J. (2007) 'Police diversity training: a silver bullet tarnished?', in M. Rowe (ed.), *Policing Beyond Macpherson: Issues in Policing, Race and Society*. Cullompton: Willan. pp. 43–65.

Roxell, L. (2011) 'Hate, threats, and violence. a register study of persons suspected of hate crime', *Journal of Scandinavian Studies in Criminology and Crime Prevention*, 12 (2): 198–215.

Runnymede Trust (1997) *Islamophobia: A Challenge for Us All*. London: The Runnymede Trust.

Ryan, N. (2003) *Homeland: Into a World of Hate*. Edinburgh: Mainstream Publishing.

Said, E. (1978) *Orientalism*. New York: Pantheon.

Said, E. (1997) *Covering Islam: How the Media and the Experts Determine How We See the Rest of the World*, 2nd edn. New York: Vintage Books.

Sales, R. (2007) *Understanding Immigration and Refugee Policy: Contradictions and Continuities*. Bristol: The Policy Press.

Sandbrook, D. (2007) *White Heat: A History of Britain in the Swinging Sixties*. London: Abacus.

Sanders, T. and Campbell, R. (2007) 'Designing out vulnerability, building in respect: violence, safety and sex work policy', *British Journal of Sociology*, 58 (1): 1–19.

Schweppe, J. (2012) 'Defining characteristics and politicising victims: a legal perspective', *Journal of Hate Studies*, 10 (1): 173–98.

Sentencing Council (2011) *Assault: Definitive Guideline*. London: Sentencing Council.

Sheffield, C. (1995) 'Hate violence', in P. Rothenberg (ed.), *Race, Class and Gender in the United States*. New York: St Martin's Press, pp. 432–41.

Sheikh, S., Pralat, R., Reed, C. and Sin, C.H. (2010) *Don't Stand By: Hate Crime Research Report*. London: Mencap.

Sherry, M. (2010) *Disability Hate Crimes: Does Anyone Really Hate Disabled People?* Farnham: Ashgate.

Sibbitt, R. (1997) *The Perpetrators of Racial Harassment and Racial Violence, Home Office Research Study No. 176*. London: Home Office.

Simon, J.D. (2013) *Lone Wolf Terrorism: Understanding the Growing Threat*. New York: Prometheus Books.

Sin, C.H. (2012) 'Making disablist hate crime visible: addressing the challenges of improving reporting', in A. Roulstone and H. Mason- Bish (eds), *Disability, Hate Crime and Violence*. London: Routledge. pp. 147–65.

Sin, C.H. (2014) 'Using a "layers of influence" model to understand the interaction of research, policy and practice in relation to disablist hate crime', in N. Chakraborti and J. Garland (eds), *Responding to Hate Crime: The Case for Connecting Policy and Research*. Bristol: Policy Press. pp. 99–112.

Sin, C.H., Hedges, A., Cook, C., Mguni, N. and Comber, N. (2009) *Disabled People's Experiences of Targeted Violence and Hostility*. London: OPM for EHRC.

Slamah, K., Winter, S. and Ordek, K. (2010) 'Violence against trans sex workers: stigma, exclusion, poverty and death', *Research for Sex Workers*, 12: 30–1.

Smith, D. and Gray, J. (1983) *The Police in Action*. London: Policy Studies Institute. Police and People in London Vol. 4.

Smith, K. (ed.), Flatley, J. (ed.), Coleman, K., Osborne, S., Kaiza, P. and Roe, S. (2010) *Homicides, Firearm Offences and Intimate Violence 2008/09*. London: Home Office.

Smith, K. (ed.), Lader, D., Hoare, J. and Lau, I. (2012) *Hate Crime, Cyber Security and the Experience of Crime Amongst Children: Findings from the 2010/11 British Crime Survey*. London: Home Office.

Smyth, C. (2010) *Weirdo. Mosher. Freak: The Murder of Sophie Lancaster*. Reading: Pomona Books.

Solomos, J. (1993) *Race and Racism in Contemporary Britain*. London: Macmillan.

Somerville, W. (2007) *Immigration under New Labour*. Bristol: The Policy Press.

Sophie Lancaster Foundation (2011) The Sophie Lancaster Foundation Educational Game for Schools, Youth Groups and Other Young People's Organisations, available at www.sophielancasterfoundation.com/index.php?option=com_content&view=article&id=73&Itemid=16 (accessed 10 September 2014).

Spalek, B. (2002) 'Muslim women's safety talk and their experiences of victimisation: a study exploring specificity and difference', in B. Spalek (ed.), *Islam, Crime and Criminal Justice*. Cullompton: Willan, pp. 50–75.

Spalek, B. (2006) *Crime Victims: Theory, Policy and Practice*. Basingstoke: Palgrave Macmillan.

Spalek, B. (2008) *Communities, Identities and Crime*. Bristol: The Policy Press.

Stanko, E.A. (2001) 'Re-conceptualising the policing of hatred: confessions and worrying dilemmas of a consultant', *Law and Critique*, 12 (3): 309–29.

Stenson, K. and Waddington, P.A.J. (2007) 'Macpherson, police stops and institutionalised racism', in M. Rowe (ed.) *Policing Beyond Macpherson: Issues in Policing, Race and Society*. Cullompton: Willan, pp. 128–47.

Stewart, M. (ed.) (2012) *The Gypsy 'Menace': Populism and the New Anti-Gypsy Politics*. London: Hurst and Company.

Stone, A.L. (2009) 'More than adding a T: American lesbian and gay activists' attitudes towards transgender inclusion', *Sexualities*, 12 (3): 334–54.

Stonewall (2013) *Gay in Britain: Lesbian, Gay and Bisexual People's Experiences and Expectations of Discrimination*. London: Stonewall.

Stonewall (2014) *Homophobic Hate Crime: The Gay British Crime Survey*. London: Stonewall.

Stratton, A. (2011) 'Tory MP Philip Davies: Disabled people could work for less pay', *Guardian*, 17 June 2011, available at www.guardian.co.uk/society/2011/jun/17/tory-philip-daviesdisabled- people-work (accessed on 9 November 2012).

Stroud, J. (2013) 'The importance of music to Anders Behring Breivik', *Journal of Terrorism Research*, 4 (1), at http://ojs.st-andrews.ac.uk/index.php/jtr/article/view/620/537 (accessed 10 September 2014).

Thomas, P. (2011) '"Mate crime": ridicule, hostility and targeted attacks against disabled people', *Disability & Society*, 28 (1): 107–11.

Tomsen, S. (2002) *Hatred, Murder and Male Honour: Anti-Homosexual Murders in New South Wales, 1980–2000*. Research and Public Policy Series No. 43. Canberra: Australian Institute of Criminology.

Tomsen, S. and Mason, G. (2001) 'Engendering homophobia: violence, sexuality and gender conformity', *Journal of Sociology*, 37 (3): 257–73.

Transgender Europe (2013) *Transgender Europe*. TDOR Press Release November 13 2013. Berlin: Transgender Europe.

Transgender Europe (2014) IDAHOT 2014 (International Day Against Homophobia and Transphobia) at www.transrespect-transphobia.org/en_US/tvt-project/tmm-results/idahot-2014.htm, 1 May (accessed 2 May 2014).

Treadwell, J. (2014) 'Controlling the new far right on the streets: policing the English Defence League', in N. Chakraborti and J. Garland (eds), *Responding to Hate Crime*. Bristol: Policy Press. pp. 127–40.

Treadwell, J. and Garland, J. (2011) 'Masculinity, marginalisation and violence: a case study of the English Defence League', *British Journal of Criminology*, 51 (4): 621–34.

Trilling, D. (2012) *Bloody Nasty People: The Rise of Britain's Far Right*. London: Verso.

Trotter, J. (2006) 'Violent crimes? Young people's experiences of homophobia and misogyny in secondary schools', *Practice*, 18 (4): 291–302.

Turner, L., Whittle, S. and Combs, R. (2009) *Transphobic Hate Crime in the European Union*. London: Press for Change.

Van Beelen, N. and Rakhmetova, A. (2010) 'Addressing violence against sex workers', *Research for Sex Workers*, 12: 1.

Vasagar, J. (2007) 'Anti-semitic attacks hit record high following Lebanon War', *Guardian*, 2 February, p. 8.

Wachholz, S. (2009) 'Pathways through hate: exploring the victimization of the homeless', in B. Perry (ed.), *Hate Crimes: The Victims of Hate Crime*. Westport, CT: Praeger, pp. 199–222.

Waddington, P.A.J. (1994) *Liberty and Order: Public Order Policing in a Capital City*. London: UCL Press.

Waddington, P.A.J. (1999) 'Police (canteen) sub-culture: an appreciation', *British Journal of Criminology*, 39 (2): 286–309.

Walby, S. (1990) *Theorizing Patriarchy*. Oxford: Blackwell.

Walby, S. and Allen, J. (2004) *Domestic Violence, Sexual Assault and Stalking: Findings from the British Crime Survey*. London: Home Office Research Study 276.

Walklate, S. (1989) *Victimology*. London: Unwin Hyman.

Walklate, S. (2011) 'Reframing criminal victimization: finding a place for vulnerability and resilience', *Theoretical Criminology*, 15 (2): 179–94.

Walshe, S. (2010) 'Hate crimes against the homeless', *Guardian*, www.guardian.co.uk/commentisfree/cifamerica/2010/aug/20/homeless-bum-fight-hatecrime/ (accessed 21 June 2014).

Walters, M.A. (2011) 'A general theories of hate crime? Strain, doing difference and self control', *Critical Criminology*, 19 (4): 313–30.

Walters, M.A. (2013) 'Why the Rochdale Gang should have been sentenced as 'hate crime' offenders', *Criminal Law Review*, 2: 131–44.

Walters, M. (2014a) 'Conceptualizing 'hostility' for hate crime law: minding 'the minutiae' when interpreting *section* 28(1)(a) of the Crime and Disorder Act 1998', *Oxford Journal of Legal Studies*, 34 (1): 47–74.

Walters, M. (2014b) 'Restorative approaches to working with hate crime offenders', in N. Chakraborti and J. Garland (eds), *Responding to Hate Crime: The Case for Connecting Policy and Research*. Bristol: The Policy Press, pp. 243–58.

Walters, M. (2014c) *Hate Crime and Restorative Justice: Exploring Causes, Repairing Harms.* Oxford: Oxford University Press.

Walters, M. and Hoyle, C. (2012) 'Exploring the everyday world of hate victimization through community mediation', *International Review of Victimology*, 18 (1): 7–24.

Walters, M.A. and Tumath, J. (2014) 'Gender "hostility", rape, and the hate crime paradigm', *The Modern Law Review*, 77 (4): 563–96.

Webster, C. (2007) *Understanding Race and Crime.* Maidenhead: Open University Press.

Weiss, J.T. (2003) 'GL vs. BT', *Journal of Bisexuality*, 3 (2): 25–55.

Werbner, P. (2004) 'The predicament of diaspora and millennial Islam: reflections on September 11 2001', *Ethnicities*, 4 (4): 451–76.

Whine, M. (2014) 'Hate crime in Europe', in N. Hall, A. Corb, P. Giannasi and J. Grieve (eds), *The Routledge International Handbook of Hate Crime.* London: Routledge, pp. 95–104.

Whittle, S. (2002) *Respect and Equality: Transsexual and Transgender Rights.* London: Cavendish, ch. 1.

Whittle, S., Turner, L. and Al-Alami, M. (2007) *Engendered Penalties: Transgender and Transsexual People's Experiences of Inequality and Discrimination.* London: The Equalities Review.

Williams, M. and Robinson, A. (2004) 'Problems and prospects with policing the lesbian, gay and bisexual community in Wales', *Policing and Society*, 14 (3): 213–32.

Williams, M. and Tregidga, J. (2013) *All Wales Hate Crime Research Project: Research Overview and Executive Summary.* Cardiff: Race Equality First.

Willoughby, B.L.B., Hill, D.B., Gonzalez, C.A., Lacorazza, A., Macapagal, R.A., Barton, M.E. and Doty, N.D. (2010) 'Who hates gender outlaws? A multisite and multinational evaluation of the genderism and transphobia scale', *Journal of Homosexuality*, 12 (4): 254–71.

Wolfenden Report (1957) *Report of the Committee on Homosexual Offences and Prostitution.* London: HMSO. [Reprinted 1963 as *The Wolfenden Report: Report of the Committee on Homosexual Offences and Prostitution.* New York: Stein and Day.]

Wolhuter, L., Olley, N. and Denham, D. (2009) *Victimology: Victimisation and Victims' Rights.* Abingdon: Routledge–Cavendish.

Woods, J.B. (2014) 'Hate crime in the United States', in N. Hall, A. Corb, P. Giannasi and J. Grieve (eds), *The Routledge International Handbook of Hate Crime.* London: Routledge. pp. 153–62.

Wright, O. (2014) 'Race hate: a crime that the police will not solve', *Independent*, 13 January.

WSWTG (Westminster Sex Worker Task Group) (2013) *Violence Faced by Sex Workers in Westminster: Recommendations Report.* London: Westminster Sex Worker Task Group.

Zedner, L. (2002) 'Victims', in M. Maguire, R. Morgan and R. Reiner (eds), *The Oxford Handbook of Criminology*, 3rd edn. Oxford: Oxford University Press, pp. 419–56.

Zempi, I. (2014) 'Responding to the needs of victims of Islamophobia', in N. Chakraborti and J. Garland (eds), *Responding to Hate Crime: The Case for Connecting Policy and Research.* Bristol: The Policy Press, pp. 113–25.

Zempi, I. and Chakraborti, N. (2014) *Islamophobia, Victimisation and the Veil.* Basingstoke: Palgrave Macmillan.

INDEX